When Play Was Play

When Play Was Play

Why Pick-Up Games Matter

RONALD BISHOP

State University of New York Press
Albany, New York

Published by
State University of New York Press, Albany

Cover photo by Duncan Searl. Brooklyn 1972.

Printed in the United States of America

Excelsior Editions is an imprint of State University of New York Press

For information, address State University of New York Press, Albany, NY
www.sunypress.edu

Production by Kelli W. LeRoux
Marketing by Fran Keneston

Library of Congress Cataloging-in-Publication Data

Bishop, Ronald, 1961-
When play was play : why pick-up games matter / Ronald Bishop.
p. cm.
Includes bibliographical references and index.
ISBN 978-1-4384-2603-7 (hardcover : alk. paper)
ISBN 978-1-4384-2604-4 (pbk. : alk. paper) 1. Play—Social aspects—United States. 2. Child development—United States. 3. Children—United States. 4. Leisure—United States. I. Title.
HQ782.B57 2009
305.2310973—dc22

2008042347

10 9 8 7 6 5 4 3 2 1

Contents

ACKNOWLEDGMENTS

My heartfelt thanks to the more than 150 people who kindly shared their pick-up game experiences with me, either during one-on-one interviews, via written narratives, or through the online survey. Thanks to Samantha Swanson and to the many friends and former students (now friends) who circulated the pick-up games flyer. Thanks to the Center for History and New Media and George Mason University for the space to post my survey on the Center Web site. For those readers who want to share their pick-up game experiences, the survey will remain up on the site at http://chnm.gmu.edu/tools/surveys/form/343. I hope to someday create a Web site or blog where the significance of these experiences can be shared and discussed.

Special thanks to Bill McNelis, my brother-in-law and good friend, for his unerring transcriptions of the in-person interviews, and to the anonymous reviewers enlisted by the kind, patient folks at SUNY Press—in particular the reviewer who painstakingly edited the entire manuscript. I'm grateful—and a little ashamed of my sloppiness.

Thanks to Joel DiBartolomeo, the sixth grade principal at Haverford Middle School in Havertown, Pennsylvania, for his hospitality and his willingness to allow me, sight unseen, to visit his fine school to talk to his bright, friendly students—thanks also to Elizabeth, Bobby, Chelsea, and to Khrystoffer, who made me promise to spell his name correctly. Albert DiBartolomeo, Joel's uncle, was instrumental in putting me in contact with Joel; Albert is a valued Drexel colleague and good friend who puts up with my rambling attempts at writing fiction.

Thanks to Andrew Damiter and his students at Washington Middle School in Long Valley, New Jersey, and to his son, Andrew, my former student and current research colleague, for putting me in touch with his dad, who then graciously agreed to administer my survey to his enthusiastic charges. I am grateful to my Drexel colleague, Frank Linnehan of the LeBow College of Business, for his many words of encouragement and willingness to so freely share his own pick-up game memories, accumulated on the courts and baseball fields of Long Island. Thanks to Drexel history professor Dick Rosen and Donna Murasko, Dean of Drexel's College of Arts and Sciences, for their kind words about the project. I am fortunate to work in an environment where I can pursue such a wide range of research projects.

To Ernie Hakanen of Drexel's Department of Culture and Communication, long overdue thanks for getting me my first job at Drexel, and for being my mentor, advocate, and most important, my friend. Overdue thanks to Ray Brebach, the full measure of a modern-day department head, and one hell of a flutist. Long after Ernie and I and a few colleagues moved on to become part of the Department of Culture and Communication, Ray still fields my sometimes naïve questions about navigating the tricky political terrain of academia. I'm grateful for his help. Thanks to my Drexel colleague, Rachel Reynolds, and what seems like her entire family, for contributing their stories to this endeavor.

To Joe Kuhl, Chris Young, and the Taylor brothers, Chris and Steve: thanks for the seemingly endless afternoons and evenings on Kensington Terrace spent playing running bases, SWAT, baseball, street hockey, paddle tennis, and just sitting on my porch doing nothing. Thanks for the help building the hockey net. I miss you all and think of you often. Thanks, too, to Bob Zipse for being such a patient teacher, and for your willingness to share so much of your valuable adolescent time with the kids on Kensington Terrace.

I also want to recognize my grandmother, Virginia Pierson Bishop, who died in 1989, but whom I think about frequently. I'm not sure I ever thanked her for letting me drag her out to the parking lot behind her apartment building in South Orange, New Jersey, so that we could play catch every Sunday in the spring and summer. Every so often I picture her, standing in the lot in her polished shoes, matching purse, and elegant coat, throwing the ball to me, and then sending words of encouragement my way when I chose to just throw a tennis ball against one of the lot's retaining walls.

And to my mom and dad, Emmie and Ron Bishop: sorry for all of the broken windows and the chopped up porch steps. Thanks for giving me the space to allow my imagination to flower. I love you both.

Finally, to the love of my life, my wife Sheila: thanks for listening to me ramble about this project for the last five years. To quote the Carpenters: "You are the crowd that sits quiet, listening to me, and all the mad sense that I make." I love you with all my heart.

And to my son, Neil: it doesn't matter where, or how, we play catch. Your smile and bubbly laugh say it all. I'll always keep the mitts handy for you. I love you.

PERMISSIONS

Introduction

It seemed like a good idea at the time.

My friends and I had grown tired of using our sneakers, stones, and pieces of brick to simulate the width of a net for our pick-up hockey games, which usually took place somewhere on the street outside my house in northern New Jersey. The curbs were not high enough to stop even a low shot, and the fact that our street had a hump in it to promote drainage added to our problem; when we became skilled enough to get some real power behind our shots, the humped street acted like a golf tee, which posed a grave danger to nearby windows and the people behind them.

The "hump" also added a few degrees of difficulty to stick handling and passing the ball. Passes had to be fast and straight, or the curb would pull them astray. Stick handling moves had to be short and crisp, and they had to be made at the top of the hump—roughly a foot of space—or gravity would take its toll and pull the ball toward the curb.

I had discovered hockey in the winter of 1975. I was a newly minted Buffalo Sabres fan, thank to the exploits of the famed "French Connection" line. I tried to replicate the play of Gilbert Perrault, Rick Martin, and Rene Robert. Soon, my friends—perhaps because of my interest, or perhaps because hockey involved controlled violence meted out with sticks—took up the game. With only five or six players, we would rotate on offense or defense—two forwards against one defenseman and one "steady" goalie—"steady" because it was a real pain in the neck to take off our makeshift goalie equipment, which included my old catcher's shin guards and chest protector, to get in some time at another position.

The lack of a decent net frustrated my friends and me—now teammates on the so-called Maplewood Lightning—for some time. Several store-bought nets collapsed, thanks to the frightening speed and intermittent accuracy of our shots—or our rough and sometimes clumsy play (it all depends on who is telling the story). Finally, one winter in the mid-1970s, my friends and I appropriated enough wood, mainly from my family's rather dilapidated garage (my dad, a pipe organ tuner with a marked inability to separate work and family, was always receiving parts deliveries in large wooden crates), to fashion a fairly sturdy frame. It was roughly the same size as a regulation NHL net—with the emphasis on roughly. Because we didn't know how to fashion sound wood joints, it wobbled quite a bit. We ended up creating a play where one of our offensive players would sneak behind the net and pull or push one of its corners. The goalie usually could not cover the added space.

Creating the actual net was a larger challenge. We first nailed old bed sheets and later a plastic tarp to the frame, but we tore them both easily with our shots—a boost to our egos, but ultimately quite frustrating. We eventually found what we thought was the perfect material: two pieces of sheet metal, each about three by nine. Using a pair of tin snips lifted from the toolbox of our goalie's dad, we trimmed the excess length, and figured we could overlap the pieces on the frame. We never really knew where the metal came from, although the sexy, macho-wannabe narrative that emerged within our group revolved around a late-night theft from our high school's metal shop.

The metal gave the net needed stability, and made it impervious to our hardest shots—even those taken by Russell, our best player. The sound made by the hockey ball or puck hitting metal was a short clap of thunder. We liked that—the louder, the better. What we didn't like was our discovery that the net we were so proud of now weighed in the neighborhood of one hundred pounds. This was great when we were blasting shots at our steady goalie, or shoving each other into the net (the crashes resonated beautifully through the neighborhood), but it became a bit of an issue when neighbors chased us from in front of their homes (an exodus whose timing corresponded to how tired my dad was of fixing windows), or when we went "on the road" to the tennis courts at a nearby park. There were two courts, and we would play on one side of their nets, with our net usually set up against a bulging, creaky green chain-link fence. We soon learned that our game was best suited for our narrow, humped street. One of us would "bring the puck up" unchallenged until we reached the second court. This is probably why I never learned to stickhandle through or around the opposition; the defenseman would simply wait, and then check you. Still, 387 goals in a roughly sixty-five-game season is nothing to sneeze at.

OF SCHEDULES AND SPREADSHEETS

I revisited the exploits of the Maplewood Lightning, and my other pick-up game experiences, after I met my wife in 1994, and started getting to know her friends and family. Her older sister, Rose, and her husband Bill have two children: a boy, Brian, and a girl, Colleen, who were then six and four, respectively. They are talented, smart, funny, loving, wonderful kids (now young adults) whose daily schedules would test the mettle (and probably inspire the envy) of a *Fortune* 500 CEO. During a visit back in 1995, I had the chance to look at their schedules—closer to spreadsheets, actually—and wondered if they ever had any time to get a bunch of friends together to organize a game of something. Later, I would conclude that I had experienced an example of what Rosenfeld, Wise, and Coles (2001) call "hyper-parenting," where parents plan nearly every activity in their children's lives, from school to sports. Some experts fear that this approach to parenting—which includes doing time as "helicopter parents" once a child heads off to college—leaves young people unable (and sometimes unwilling) to master necessary life skills and deal with life's many curveballs.

Too much is going on in their lives, I thought, although in no way is my research an attack on the choices they or their parents make. I also noticed that they live quite a distance from many of their closest friends. They seemed to barely know the other kids their age who lived in this affluent suburb of Philadelphia. I realized how lucky I was that we could grab the net, which was stored in my garage, and play—without any parental involvement whatsoever (until our goalie's parents bellowed for him to come home). I also realized that I was lucky to have lived fairly close to most of my closest friends.

I also wondered if they had the energy or the inclination to play pick-up games. I had played basketball, hockey, and baseball with them during family parties, but did these unstructured games continue? I wondered if they might just be tired of the games they play all the time. This is not a rare set of circumstances for children from middle-class or affluent families, those that can afford to expose their children to a variety of activities. The key word there, though, is *variety*. Having our children do so many things in an organized fashion seems to take the fun, or at least the catalyst, out of unorganized play—just getting friends together to play around. In pick-up games, there is often no goal, no outcome, no achievement to be had, nothing to add to your resume that will get you into Penn or Harvard. It's just playing around for no reason, other than to play.

But while my research explores some of these issues, it is *not* an indictment of busy parents, or overachieving, overscheduled children, overcompensating parents, or suburban sprawl. I don't want my research to cause Baby Boomer parents to bore their children with endless "You kids are so lucky; you have no idea how rough I had it when I was a kid" stories. Instead, I will explore the cultural importance of pick-up games in order to develop a sense of what made them such valuable experiences and to perhaps encourage our kids to take some lessons from these experiences and apply them to their lives. Pick-up games have been pushed aside by our achievement-obsessed culture, but they have not disappeared. Still, *how* pick-up games are conducted, and the meaning they have in the lives of those who played them, has changed significantly. This change can teach us about slowing down and about the value of imagination.

Before we embark on our journey, a brief discussion of an irony that may (or may not) color much of what we will discuss: many of the "hyper-parents" who push their children came of age in the supposedly hedonistic "if it feels good, do it" 1960s and 1970s—the age, if you believe the ads thematically anchored in these decades, when nothing happened except Woodstock, hippies whirling frantically in the mud, smoking pot in VW vans (or doing lines of cocaine at Studio 54), and listening to "Going Up the Country," "Gimme Some Lovin'," or the soundtrack to *Saturday Night Fever*—*only* those songs.

While I certainly qualify as a romantic for that era, I wonder if these Baby Boomer parents aren't overcompensating just a little—demanding that their children not repeat what they now believe to be, thanks at least in part to the rise to prominence—and endless bellicosity—of conservative pundits such as Ann Coulter and Bill O'Reilly, their dalliance with aimless relativism. Our parents yelled at us to find something to do, but they more often than not let us do the finding. My friends and I used to receive only mild rebukes from our folks for "hanging out." Eventually, we'd do something—maybe not something structured or productive, but something. Not all of our activities provided opportunities for learning. But today, it seems as though kids won't choose to have an experience unless they can wring every drop of information or preparation (for the next task) out of it. There simply isn't any time for just "hanging out."

How did this happen, fellow Boomers?

EXPLORING THE JUNKYARD

A professor with whom I studied at Fordham University in the mid-1980s once told me that the study of communication is like exploring a junkyard or an antique store: you go in with a rough idea of what you're looking for, but you truly never know what kind of treasures you will find during your visit. Call it the "Forrest Gump" approach to research. Since my aim was not to generalize about individuals who played pick-up games, or make sweeping assertions about the impact of pick-up games, I decided to base the book on stories told by individuals about their pick-up game experiences.

To be sure, the stories I explore and which appear at the end of the book are sentimental, possibly inaccurate, and often overly romanticized. But even these characteristics help us to understand the shape and depth of the meaning that these games have had, and continue to have, for us.

The stories were gathered in unsystematic fashion beginning in the spring of 2003. In developing my approach, I followed the lead of noted media researcher Ien Ang (1985), who studied the experience of watching the popular 1980s television show *Dallas* by soliciting letters from avid viewers, and of Elizabeth Bird (1992), whose excellent study of why people read tabloid newspapers is built on responses garnered from an ad placed in a newspaper. My aim was to analyze the discourse about the pick-up game experiences that emerged from these stories—or, to use Bird's phrase, "to understand experience from the point of view of those involved" (111).

I developed a flyer that invited individuals to share in detail their pick-up game experiences. The flyer went through several revisions; the most recent revision appears in Appendix A. I asked participants to describe the games they played; their neighborhood and physical surroundings; the friends with whom they typically played pick-up games; and the equipment used (in some cases, made) during these games. Finally, I asked participants to comment on what they had learned from these experiences.

I limited my initial distribution of the flyer to several of my classes and my colleagues at Drexel, to my local library, and to several bookstores in New Castle County, Delaware. More recent versions of the flyer offered participants the option of visiting an online survey I created using Survey Builder software and posted on the Web site of the Center for the History of New Media at George Mason University's Web site. You can complete the survey and share your own pick-up game stories by visiting chnm.gmu.edu/tools/surveys/form/343.

More successful were my posts in the summer and fall of 2004 on various H-Net discussion boards and the recruitment efforts of my teaching assistant in 2003–04, Samantha Swanson. In all cases, I have encouraged all participants to pass my invitation along to friends and family members in the hope that they would share their experiences. This strategy, like the others, has thus far produced mixed results. Entire families have participated in some cases, only one or two family members in others. My efforts have to date produced nearly 150 responses. I continue to collect stories from individuals across the country; if you are willing to share your experiences, please send them to me through one of the means explained in the flyer (see Appendix A). My hope is to make the stories accessible to fellow pick-up games players, interested parties, and researchers, on a Web site dedicated to the sharing of pick-up game experiences.

In addition to the stories sent in response to the flyer, Samantha Swanson and I will, by the time this book is published, have conducted lengthy in-person interviews with nearly a dozen individuals (contacted through the first few rounds of flyer distribution) willing to discuss their pick-up game experiences in more detail. These interviews were transcribed with the help of my talented brother-in-law, William McNelis, a librarian at a New Jersey university. I read through the stories several times, looking for recurring themes. Here, I borrowed from the tenets of textual analysis. Leo Masterman (1995, 127) argues that "breaking through" a text or, in this case, a number of texts, enables the researcher to probe "the rhetorical techniques through which meanings are produced."

Noted scholar Jack Lule (1995) contends that textual analysis is a particularly effective tool for the researcher who wants to explore "*how* stereotypical depictions are invoked through the language and conventions of the press" (177). Analysis is based on the idea that we give meaning to our lives through language. A researcher seeks to understand what Lule calls "the world of the text," which is made up of "the references, assumptions, or beliefs on which a story is based (1989, 616). Stuart Hall (1975) explains that this kind of analysis is "more useful" than content analysis "in penetrating the latent meanings of a text," and that it preserves "something of the complexity of language and connotation which has to be sacrificed in content analysis in order to achieve high validation."

Textual analysis typically begins with what Hall (1975, 15) calls "a long preliminary soak" in the texts being reviewed, followed by several additional readings by the researcher to develop and refine themes uncovered in earlier stages of the analysis. According to Roy (1996), the researcher should "work back through the narrative elements of form, rhetoric, and style to uncover the underlying social and historical processes" and "the metalanguage that guided its production." Particularly significant are the "visual, verbal, rhetorical, and presentational codes that media (in this case, journalists) employ to make a story eventful" (318).

Analysis of messages is just a stepping stone to exploring the social processes suggested by the content. Johnson (1986/1987, 62) contends that a text "is only a means of cultural study." A text is the "raw material from which certain forms . . . may be extracted." The most significant part of textual analysis is "the social life of subjective forms at each moment of their circulation, including their textual embodiments." The most compelling aspects of a text, then, are "the subjective or cultural forms that it realizes and makes available" (62). Certain perspectives on the world are highlighted, while others are marginalized.

THE SIGNIFICANCE OF NARRATIVE

Some readers may wonder: Why stories?

Walter Fisher (1987) defines narratives as "symbolic actions—words or deeds—that have meaning for those who live, create, or interpret them." We are all storytellers; "enacted dramatic narrative is the basic and essential genre for the characterization of human actions," Fisher contends (58). We move from place to place, experience to experience, and use stories to keep others (and ourselves) posted about our progress. Fisher goes so far as to argue that "the world as we know it is a set of stories that must be chosen among in order for us to live life in a process of continual re-creation" (58). Sonja Foss (1997, 399) contends that we use narrative to "help us impose order on the flow of experience so that we can make sense of events and actions in our lives." Narrative's most salient quality is that it "provides clues to the subjectivity of individuals and to the values and meanings that characterize a culture" (Foss, 401).

Fisher rejects the claim that narrative is without rationality. "[N]o form of discourse is privileged over others because its form is predominantly argumentative," Fisher claims—an argument that might not sit well with those of you who labored long for your high school or college debate teams. "No matter how strictly a case is argued—scientifically, philosophically, or legally—it will always be a story, an interpretation of some aspect of the world that is historically and culturally grounded and shaped by human personality" (49). As I tell my students, "Anyone can narrative." As any skilled politician will affirm, you win more adherents with narrative than with logic. The narrator, or storyteller, exercises power, elevating and conferring meaning on the pieces of information that are (and are not) included in the story.

Sonja Foss wrote that narrative "functions as an argument to view and understand the world in a particular way" (49). It enables the researcher to explore and define "a coherent world in which social action occurs" (Berdayes and Berdayes 1998, 109). Narrative analysis allows the researcher to explore assumptions at work in the narrative. Studying a narrative also enables the researcher to isolate and explore the "linguistic and cultural resources" (109) drawn on by its creators, and how these resources persuade the reader to accept the narrative as a realistic portrayal of events and people.

Not that all stories are completely true, or used for positive purposes. Fisher argues that a story must "ring true" for a listener, but that doesn't always mean that every fact is accurate—instead, they are reliable. Characters in a story have to be believable, and those listening to the story have to accept that the characters act on the basis of sound values. But for every warm and fuzzy tale we tell around the Thanksgiving dinner table about how simple and unspoiled life was when we were kids, a negative story about you, or told by you about someone else, is out there, demeaning that person or putting that person in his or her place. Narratives can act as a constraint on interaction, especially if we choose to deploy a limited range of narratives in our day-to-day dealings with someone.

Folks who explore their family histories, for example, do so primarily in order to leave behind a compelling story about their family for their children and grandchildren—a "legacy" of sorts, something we all seem to want to do these days. In creating these stories, folks often leave out troubling information about their ancestors, and highlight the ancestors who led very successful—or at least very colorful—lives. The stories often revolve around what philosopher Martin Saar (2002) calls "paradigmatic moments" in our ancestors' lives. As with any significant story, these tales shape the way we understand ourselves, and how others see us. The authors want other members of their families to be "struck by the lightning of instantaneous insight into what they are and what they might want to be," Saar claims (240).

While the typical focus of narrative analysis is a single story, it is possible to explore a number of stories that cohere and form a larger story—a metanarrative or "metastory," as Berdayes and Berdayes claim (1998, 113). I take this approach in order "to generate a more inclusive perspective, and to expand the possibilities and range of debate" about the meaning of pick-up games for these folks. This approach enables the researcher to achieve a clearer understanding of the culture that produces the narrative.

Narrative analysis is driven by an exploration of setting, characters, the role and features of the narrator, events, time frame (the period of time during which major events occur), causal relations (the cause and effect relationships evident in the narrative), audience, and major themes (Foss, 402–404). While the results, such as they are, of my analysis are not generalizable, they provide a rich case study of the motivations that sustain this particular group. What follows, then, is an analysis of the narrative—perhaps "metanarrative" is a better word—that emerges from the pick-up game experiences shared by these individuals.

NOT ALL "BEER AND SKITTLES"

Before we embark on our journey, a few disclaimers and points of order. First, it will soon become clear to you—if it isn't already—that I hold positive, sometimes overly romanticized memories about my pick-up game experiences. There are days, especially as life in an academic department becomes more complex, when all I want to do is grab the gloves and baseball that I always keep in the back of my car and beg someone to play catch. It is my hope on those days that a few tosses will transport me back to the tree-lined street on which I grew up, and wash all of my troubles away.

But as many of the folks who provided stories for this book will attest, not all of their pick-up game experiences were positive or enlightening. Nor were mine. For starters, I knocked out one of my brother's upper front teeth when he was about six years old during a game of catch/baseball in front of our house. His "adult" teeth never came in straight, a development for which I still, nearly forty years later, feel responsible. Next, in my futile effort to someday join the New York Mets pitching staff (or infield) and, during the winter, the top line of the Buffalo Sabres, I broke every window on two sides of our garage. My dad eventually gave up making me pay out of my allowance—earned largely from working for him, fixing pipe organs—to have them fixed.

And not every game on Kensington Terrace ended with us basking in adolescent reverie, either. Our hockey fights were real, as were our dalliances with "chin music" during baseball season. Many games of "running bases" deteriorated into rugby scrums on our front yard. We often uttered more profane words than non-profane words on any given day, and our cultural and ethnic sensitivity often left quite a bit to be desired.

But I would still trade a two-hour committee meeting for the chance to play an extended game of catch, or touch football, any day of the week—that is, if my body would allow it.

I will do my absolute best to keep my romantic ramblings to a minimum, and to allow the meaning these experiences have for the book's contributors to do the talking. I will, however, use my pick-up game experiences to begin each chapter, as a way of easing into the primary themes that will be discussed. In no way am I advocating a wholesale abandonment of organized sports and total immersion in unstructured play. Nor do I harbor the illusion that pick-up games are no longer played. Children still make up games, and still just play—except in the city of Fairfax City, Virginia—baseball, hockey, and kick the can on the streets of our communities. Officials of Fairfax City passed a law in 2002 banning play in the city's streets. "We want to send a message that it is not okay to play in the street," City Manager Robert Sisson told the *Washington Post* (Whoriskey 2002). Sounding remarkably like an overprotective parent, Sisson said that if the city allowed kids to play on one street, "children might go to school and talk with their classmates about 'it's no problem—you can play in the street.'"

Fairfax City is not alone in its efforts to combat the scourge of street play. In the state of Wisconsin, it is against the law (Section 346.78 of the state code), claims the City of Milwaukee's Web site, to play in streets or alleys (http://www.ci.mil.wi.us). Further, you can't skateboard, ride your unicycle, or propel your toboggan down a street or alley—you can do all of those things in city crosswalks, however. Traverse City, Michigan, has a similar law, passed in 1976 (http://www.ci.traverse-city.mi.us/streetord/1020.pdf). Their city officials are more specific: "No person shall play ball or any other game" on a city street or in a city alley. Officials are a bit nicer in Springfield, Massachusetts (www.springfieldpolice.net); there, you will be fined only if your conduct in the street "interferes with its use by others."

Kids in the city of Massapequa Park, New York (www.ci.massapequa-park.ny.us/ordrev1), are not allowed to play soccer or hockey in the streets, or put up a basketball hoop near a street, since its net would no doubt be snagged by one of the town's obviously quite tall street sweepers. Section 70 of the municipal code in Warwick, Rhode Island, forbids "the playing of baseball, practicing with a baseball and throwing of balls, stones and other missiles" (now, where did I put that ICBM?). It turns out that you can't fly a kite (even if the wind is right) or play ball on the streets of Cleveland (Cleveland Codified Ordinances Section

411.04), and if police there catch you using a basketball hoop in an unauthorized fashion on a city street—twice—the hoop, pole, the whole thing, will be confiscated (http://caselaw.lp.findlaw.com/clevelandcodes).

You can't "coast" or use your sled on the streets of Hawarden, Iowa (http://www.cityofhawarden.com/citycode). "Coasting" is also prohibited in Lakewood, Ohio (www.lkwdpl.org/city/code/ch311.htm), as are rousing games of "quoits," a cousin of horseshoes, where players toss heavy rings into a small pit, hoping to get as close as possible to the pin, or "hob" (www.quoits.info).

How did this happen? You might as well ban putting up Christmas trees and menorahs during the holiday season. Ah, but I shouldn't be so indignant; many of these laws (or their precursors) were on the books when I was a kid; I just disobeyed them, and the police in my hometown rarely enforced them. My reaction, heightened for emphasis, highlights the pitfalls of over-romanticizing pick-up game experiences, pitfalls that we will have to overcome throughout our journey. So I'll drop, for the time being, my new theory that these laws are clearly the product of a recently hatched conspiracy among real estate agents, township associations, league officials, and sporting goods manufacturers. It's one thing to restrict play in order to protect the safety of children; it's another thing entirely to do it because residents of our many cul-de-sacs fear a drop in property value and the juvenile delinquency that catch and street hockey—and the mere presence of sidewalks, which are disappearing from our communities—will inevitably cause. I can't help but feel that this is yet another victory for structure, for homogeneity, for commerce. Have we all become my uncle, who used to shut the lights off and close the curtains when members of the local Jehovah's Witnesses church would visit the neighborhood?

1

Less Time Spent Schmoozing

The porch attached to my family's three-bedroom colonial in northern New Jersey was for many years the center of our social universe. Any activity—productive, antisocial, or aimless—typically started on its rickety (until the late 1970s, when my parents finally had it rebuilt, and the house sided) stairs. My brother and I began and ended our days, particularly in the summer when school was out, shooting the breeze on the porch—arguing, dreaming, planning, and later, as adolescents, bullshitting.

The porch was also the place where friends would show up, often unannounced, but usually after a phone call made from the fire engine red desktop phone in our living room. Chris Young, a fireplug-shaped redhead, would come down from his house, located at the top of a hill on Prospect Street. The Taylor brothers, Chris and Steve, would swing by from their nearly identical three-bedroom colonial next door. Joe Kuhl would cruise over on the three-speed bike he seemed to be constantly rebuilding. They all had perfectly good porches, but we rarely used any of them as a base of operations.

The porch also served as a primitive pitch-back for me as I tried desperately to copy my favorite Mets pitchers. The middle step was a strike; once, I even spray-painted what I thought was a reasonable approximation of a strike zone on the steps. No wonder it almost collapsed. Mom and dad were not thrilled with my attempts to improve my pitching precision. I had more success—and was less embarrassed by the imaginary tryouts and games I would host—in the backyard, pitching against the side of our garage.

It was on the porch that Chris Young and I decided on a boring August night in 1983 that it might be nice to hop in the car the next day and drive, for the hell of it, to Ottawa, Canada's capital. Neither one of us had been there; it had a football team and a little history, which for us, at twenty-two, was enough. We ended up having to retrace our steps and retake photos of Ottawa's parliament complex when I realized that I didn't have any film in the camera on the first day of our journey. It was on the porch where, as children, my brother and I set up our imaginary Matchbox-based cities, using cardboard boxes obtained from my dad after a regular delivery of pipe organ parts. It was on the porch that I basked (and wallowed) in my first serious case of puppy love, over a girl who lived around the corner, and who could play baseball as well, if not better, than most of my friends and me. And it was on the porch that we would end most summer nights—road-testing our profanity, and exchanging stories about feats of bravado that never actually happened. One feat did happen: we became so bored one evening that six of us picked up Steve's tiny Honda and placed it gingerly on the sidewalk in front of his house.

So much for romance.

We couldn't know that we were engaged in what noted sociologist Robert Putnam has called "schmoozing," in his best-selling book *Bowling Alone*. Pick-up games certainly fall under the same heading. Those who "schmooze" spend a great deal of time involved in informal social activities—less structured, less purposeful, and more spontaneous and flexible than the "machers" in a community. "Machers," notes Putnam, are more likely to become involved with, among other activities, politics, charitable work, and clubs (93).

Where "machers" do most of their work in middle age, "schmoozers" are most active as young adults. Children and growing community obligations cut into the time available for informal social connections—visiting a neighbor on the spur of the moment, sending a greeting card, or writing a personal letter. Putnam posits that we may not feel comfortable just stopping by to see a neighbor. We still visit neighbors, but the ties we have to them are far weaker than a generation ago. Perhaps more significantly, we simply have less time, which has caused us to see the time we do have as valuable, and not worth spending on what we believe are unproductive activities.

Still, despite the sharp decline in the number of individuals who "schmooze"—down from 65 percent in 1965 to 39 percent in 1995 (106)—these informal activities are still significant sources of social support. Surveys done in the late 1980s revealed that half of us had friends over for an evening, and that two-thirds of us had visited a friend. The vast majority of us had gotten together with a friend during the last month. We commit a half-hour a week to the organizations to which we belong, yet spend three hours per week visiting friends (97). We get together with friends twice as often as we attend the meeting of an organization.

Despite these promising statistics, the amount of "connecting" we do with friends has dropped significantly. We entertain friends less often, and are not nearly as willing as in the past to make new friends, Putnam notes. Dining out is less popular; we prefer to stay home and entertain. While the number of full-service restaurants has fallen by a quarter and the number of bars and luncheonettes by one-half, the number of fast food restaurants opening between 1970 and 1998 has doubled. Finally, we do not picnic as much as we used to (100). In short, there are fewer "hangouts" for us to visit just to sit and talk—not that we would, anyway. We seem to like our pockets of privacy.

Putnam explains that we don't make up for these changes by spending more time with our families. A little more than one-third of us report that our families eat dinner together. This is certainly not a new finding. Still, many forms of "family togetherness" (101) are fading from the scene: we vacation together less often, and even watch television together less often.

Recreational activities that revolve around social contacts such as playing cards (bridge, specifically) have been replaced by solitary avocations such as inline skating, jogging, walking, and (for the young folks) video games, Putnam notes. We watch sports more often than we play them. We watch people play musical instruments more often than we attempt to learn to play them. Young people are giving up more popular team sports such as baseball and football, part of an overall decline in sports participation by kids. Americans sixty and older, however, are spending twice as much time in exercise classes, and are walking more than their younger counterparts (110).

And what about our so-called "confessional culture," where we fall over each other to confess sins, are constantly accessible, thanks to technology, and share our lives on reality television? The 2004 General Social Survey revealed that we each only have two close friends—folks with whom we feel comfortable actually confessing. This is down from three in 1985. When asked, we are significantly less likely to name someone not related to us when listing the members of our "inner circle" (Hurlbert 2006, 15). Maybe, speculates Ann Hurlbert of the *New York Times*, we've simply upped our standards for what she calls "genuine closeness"—we come in contact with so many people that we've become quite discriminating when it comes to creating close friendships. A recent survey by the Pew Internet and American Life

Project found that we maintain what the survey's writers called "core ties" with fifteen people—to whom we turn for help with major problems—and "significant ties" with sixteen others. It's tougher to stay in touch with everyone as a personal network expands. E-mail, notes the Pew study, helps us break even—we regularly contact the same number of "core ties" and "significant ties" even as we connect with more people (4).

Putnam offers several possible reasons for why "we have been pulled apart from one another and from our communities over the last third of the century" (27). Much is written about how busy we are, but this is only a partial explanation. The increase in the number of two-career families is also on the list of modestly important factors. We spend more time in our cars, commuting to socially segregated, "physically fragmented" communities (215). And when we're not commuting, we're watching more television—"watching it more habitually, more pervasively, and more often alone"—than our parents. We favor entertainment over news programming—the latter being the kind of programming that might promote civic engagement, Putnam argues (246). But would those who isolate themselves by watching so much TV suddenly become active community leaders if TV was taken away? Putnam claims the answer to this question is unclear.

Turning our attention to children, let me suggest a few other as yet unexplored possibilities, which will be discussed in detail in ensuing chapters. First, children's experiences are more structured, thanks in part to overindulgent, competitive parents who want to ensure their children's future success. Second, the federal government's controversial No Child Left Behind initiative has introduced even more structure into their lives, with its focus on test-taking and student (and teacher) accountability. The pressure felt by educators to prove to the government that their schools are adequate has led nearly 40 percent of school districts across the country to eliminate recess—a fond memory for many of us, but most important as an opportunity for free play. The push to improve student performance has also led some to call for kids to go to school all year round, with shorter breaks. We now insist that children learn to read before they get to kindergarten—time better spent, contend Hirsh-Pasek and Michnick-Golinkoff (2003, 8) on unstructured play and on learning to interact with one's peers. It is clear that our anxiety about performance affects our children. Nearly 5 percent of children in the United States suffer from significant bouts of depression. Anxiety in children and adolescents, particularly when it comes to taking tests, is a growing problem. And an increasing number of children report suffering from phobias (Hirsh-Pasek and Michnick-Golinkoff, 9).

Finally, the popularity of "zero tolerance" policies, where students are strictly disciplined, often for innocent mistakes and minor errors in judgment, may also be chipping away at the desire of young people to engage in behavior that is even slightly outside the norm. The National Center for Education Statistics (NCES) reports that three-quarters of the nation's public schools have zero tolerance policies that cover a variety of student offenses, from violence to possession of weapons. Officials have also made it harder to leave school grounds during the school day, and now typically enforce strict visitor sign-in procedures.

But there is no evidence, suggests Russell Skiba of the Indiana Education Policy Center (2000), that creation and enforcement of zero tolerance policies has made our schools safer (15). Skiba has called on school officials to adopt an "early response" model of student discipline that "relies upon a more graduated system of consequences that encourages a more moderate response to less serious behavior" (15). Thus, it seems reasonable to suggest that "zero tolerance" policies have also deprived students of at least one more significant experience: learning from minor mistakes.

FEWER OPPORTUNITIES FOR FREE PLAY?

Devoting so much energy to ensuring that children perform well in school or on the athletic field has come with an additional cost: the marginalization of unstructured play. Allen Guttmann (1988) argues that this change took place gradually during the early part of the twentieth century. The Progressive Era saw the launch of the playground movement, a concerted effort by community activists and "genteel reformers," writes Guttmann, "to bring children's play under the control of reform-minded adults" (83). Unchecked population growth in American cities was a major problem. Wealthier individuals waited to get involved until community residents had laid the groundwork for the movement.

The goal of both groups was to "control the behavior of lower-class immigrant children," as Guttmann notes. The benefits they saw in organized play are similar to the ones we ram down the throats of children today: making them better people and productive citizens, and preparing them for the "work rhythms and social demands of a dynamic and complex urban-industrial civilization" (84). In short: getting them ready for a job. To others, the loss of opportunities for unstructured play signaled "the switch from the notion of abandon, where body and mind range freely in time/space, to the rigorously enforced game rules that control body and mind, regimenting them to the iron cage of military and industrial disciplines" (Aronowitz, quoted by Guttmann, 84).

By the late 1880s, private benefactors provided the necessary funding to open two parks in New York City: Seward Park and Hamilton Fish Park. Luther Gulick, the director of physical education for the city's schools, soon launched the Public Schools Athletic League, which as a complement to its roster of competitions offered participants "secular sermons on good sportsmanship and fair play" (Guttmann, 85). Most of the reformers bought into the idea, advanced by noted psychologist G. Stanley Hall, that the child should be viewed as a "primitive." But rather than try to prevent children and adolescents from getting out of control during what Joseph Lee, founder of the Massachusetts Civic League, called in 1915 the "Big Injun" stage, their energies should be controlled through structured play, Hall argued. Hall, Gulick, and others somewhat blithely saw the playground as a hotbed of "individualism and cooperation" (87). They believed that the antisocial, sometimes destructive behavior seen in the streets of American cities at the time could be ameliorated simply by introducing children and adolescents to the joys of team play.

Not everyone was convinced, however. Cary Goodman, executive director of a New York–based group called Directions for Our Youth, whose focus is lowering the dropout rate in New York City's public schools, argues that the introduction of team play on such a broad scale sucked the social life right out of New York's neighborhoods, particularly those on the lower east side of Manhattan. Consider author Jane Leavy's (2002) description of life in the Lafayette section of neighboring Brooklyn, boyhood home of pitching great Sandy Koufax.

> Everyone played stickball, punchball, square ball, Gi-Gi ball. The streets and playgrounds were multicultural before there was a word for it. Diversity was a fact, not a goal. Political correctness was preached only by Mao Tse-tung. Italians were guineas. Jews were born with silver spoons in their mouths. Nobody took offense. (30)

Like the members of so many of today's councils and committees on education, early-twentieth-century reformers wanted to produce efficient cogs in a corporate machine, not fulfilled individuals. "How many tens of thousands of children were readied for the robotized Taylorized factory system as a result of accommodating their time sense to time schedules, play directors, and a stopwatch?" Goodman asks in his book, *Choosing Sides* (quoted in Guttmann 1988, 90).

But Guttmann contends that Goodman's view is a bit naïve. "It is important not to become too misty-eyed about nineteenth-century play," he writes (90), especially since there is a dearth of research about how play shaped the personalities of children and adolescents in the late nineteenth century and early twentieth century. "[I]t is foolish simply to assert that a romp in the woods or stickball in the street was socially superior to playground basketball or fifteen minutes on the teeter-totter," Guttmann argues (90). Reformers such as Hall and Gulick were simply doing what reformers do, he claims: trying to improve what they believed was a troubling situation by introducing their values into the mix.

Still, I contend that a great deal of effort has been expended by parents, educators, school and sports league officials, and the media, to attempt to persuade us that playing just for the sake of playing—without structure, without a set of goals, is unproductive, and even potentially damaging to children. Hirsh-Pasek and Michnick-Golinkoff (2003) remind us that we did not even acknowledge that childhood was a separate stage in one's life until the nineteenth century. They claim that it was the philosopher Jean-Jacques Rousseau who inspired many to see children as having their "own way of seeing, thinking, and feeling" (5).

By the middle of the twentieth century, a cadre of newly-minted child psychologists began studying the behaviors of children in earnest. They soon convinced men and women that being parents "required special knowledge and training," write Hirsh-Pasek and Michnick-Golinkoff. Parents soon started tapping the purported wisdom of child development experts. Some political leaders feared that parents had placed too much faith in their expertise (6). Child development soon became a thriving industry. Authors laid on the guilt as families, particularly the growing number of families where both parents worked, struggled to ensure that their children would not be left behind. "The focus on engineering our children's intellectual development had spiraled out of control," write Hirsh-Pasek and Michnick-Golinkoff (6). Trying to cram as many activities as possible into a child's schedule creates unneeded stress. More importantly, "by making children dependent on others to schedule and entertain them, we deprive them of the pleasures of creating their own games and the sense of mastery and independence they will need to enjoy running their own lives" (11).

Shooting the breeze with your parents or trading stories of exaggerated exploits on my old front porch are as valuable to a child's development as a summer reading list or an academic camp, say researchers (Hirsh-Pasek and Michnick-Golinkoff 2003, 11). Just telling a parent about the day's events enables children to "construct and interpret the stories of their lives." The child can more easily make sense of life, and can improve his or her memory along the way.

The marginalization of unstructured play and of "hanging out" has blurred the line between childhood and adulthood, argued famed media critic Neil Postman. Children are not making up their own games, he argued; instead, these games are being professionalized at an alarming rate. "There is no fooling around, no peculiar rules invented to suit the moment, no protection from the judgment of spectators," Postman contended (129). Children often play without joy or spontaneity, and are often subjected to harsh criticism by parents, coaches, and spectators. Instead of being allowed to play just for the sake of playing, children are often goaded into playing for "some external purpose, such as renown, money, physical conditioning, upward mobility, national pride," Postman wrote. As a result, we are less able to see play from a child's perspective.

Echoing Guttmann, Lynott and Logue (1993) challenge Postman's view, and highlight a potential obstacle in our path: proceeding under the assumption that there was a "Golden Age of Childhood," as described by Postman and others (i.e., Elkind 1981), where children "were innocent, carefree, and protected" (477). The history of childhood, the authors write, is complex, and reveals more peril (in the form of disease, high infant mortality rates, and unregulated child labor practices) than the so-called "Hurried Child" authors acknowledge. Further, they take issue with Elkind's rejection of these problems since earlier societies did not recognize childhood as a phase of life. Thus, "childhood had to be 'invented' before it could be threatened with disappearance; as such, children could not be 'hurried' when they were not yet recognized as children," Lynott and Logue claim (477). There is also disagreement among these authors of when the "Golden Age" occurred.

But the amount of time spent just playing is declining. Hofferth and Sandberg (2001) explain that between 1981 and 1997, the amount of time spent on free play by children in the United States dropped by about 25 percent. Their finding is echoed by a Harris poll commissioned by KaBOOM, an organization dedicated to helping kids rediscover the joys of play by providing more "playspaces" throughout the country—a prospect no doubt embraced by their chief sponsor, Home Depot, which supplies much of the material for this endeavor. Three-fourths of the pediatricians surveyed for KaBOOM reported that over the last five years, the amount of time spent by their patients on unstructured play had declined. Not that kids would have any time to play if they wanted to, at least according to a University of Michigan Institute of Social Research Study which revealed that children between the ages of three and eleven lost twelve hours a week of free time between 1981 and 1997 (Murphy 2005).

Too many organized activities in a child's life is a chief cause of this decline, write Burdette and Whitaker (2005). And when children do find time for unstructured play, they typically watch television or play video games, the authors explain. Patients contacted for the KaBOOM study also cited the elimination of recess by more than 40 percent of the nation's school districts (Kieff 2001). Under considerable pressure from government officials to show sustained academic achievement, many schools in the United States have taken recess out of their students' schedules.

Educators argue that students' academic performance will improve if they invest more time in their studies. Parents typically accept this notion, possibly because the benefits of play are not immediately realized. It sounds reasonable: more time spent on a task will cause children to learn more. Very often, however, parents push for good grades, not for lasting knowledge. In fact, as some theorists have pointed out, children "learn more when their efforts are distributed over time rather than concentrated into longer periods" (Kieff 2001, 319). When inserted between demanding tasks, recess enables children to pay more attention. They get bored with the classroom setting and need a little novelty. Eventually, however, they get bored with recess, and need to head back into the classroom, which they then see as novel, writes Pellegrini (1991).

Lost in all of this, suggest Burdette and Whitaker, are vital opportunities for children to develop problem-solving skills and nurture their own creativity. Play also may cause a child's mood to improve (49). A less constrained outdoor play setting may also encourage "executive functioning"; children permitted to play become good planners and organize tasks effectively. Unstructured play also gives kids the chance to hone their social skills. "This is because all play with others requires solving some form of social problem, such as deciding what to play, who can play, when to start, when to stop, and the rules of engagement," Burdette and Whitaker note (48). This is just the kind of social connectedness discussed by Putnam—yet researchers have barely explored the influences that enable children to develop sound social connections as adults, influences nurtured during free play. The authors also speculate that children who engage frequently in free play are more likely to develop a strong sense of empathy. There has been a push back, with organizations such as the American Association for the Child's Right to Play marshaling forces in nearly all fifty states who advocate the reinstatement of recess.

The results of a recent study by the Society for Research in Child Development (SRCD) suggest that our worry about stressed-out, always active children may be misplaced. The SRCD found that four in ten kids between the ages of five and eighteen have no activities at all on their agendas. Structured activities consume only five hours of their time each week. Only a handful of kids (between 3 and 6 percent) are engaged in activities for twenty hours a week or more.

But the discussion of the study in an October 2006 issue of *Newsweek* (McGinn 2006, 43) sheds critical light on the news media's approach to covering this issue. After quoting the study's lead author, Joseph Mahoney of Yale University's Department of Psychology, as saying that the news media is at least partly to blame for arousing the concerns of parents and educators about overscheduled kids, the story reassures readers that all of that running around does pay off: "[T]he more activities they do, the better kids stack up on measures of educational achievement and psychological adjustment," writes Daniel McGinn, the *Newsweek* reporter. The photo that accompanied the article showed a nine-year-old girl admiring a medal she had won at a gymnastics competition.

Critics of the study point to the authors' reliance on the kids logging information about their activities in diaries, as well as the study's failure to discuss the impact of the time spent traveling between lessons and games. McGinn notes that the SRCD study "doesn't sway" educators, physicians, and psychologists "who've advocated against activity-creep." McGinn's approach suggests that these folks are intransigent—he later calls them "doubters." But to be fair, McGinn does acknowledge (toward the end of the story) that the study's findings, though far from conclusive, offer support for the idea that "every child is different—and some will absolutely do better with less" (43). McGinn describes the decision by a Michigan woman to cut back on her children's activities. She "feels as though her 6-year-old twins . . . are the only kids in town who don't take skiing and ice-skating lessons," McGinn writes. "There is nothing wrong," the woman contends, "with cuddling up on the couch with Mom and Dad."

As we will discuss in a later chapter, such an approach to covering this very important issue suggests that parents who decide to limit their children's activities must be ready to defend going against the conventional wisdom, which changes with glacial dispatch, and that experts who offer valid points about the benefits to children of fewer structured activities are still far outside the mainstream.

A final point: the article also fails to provide an "in-between" for parents who might be grappling with this question. Either your kid takes lessons on three instruments, plays two sports, and participates in the a range of after-school activities, or else they sit in front of the TV or play video games. Making up games, or sitting on your front porch until one comes to you, is not an option.

TO PROPITIATE THE GODS

Before discussing these trends further, let's explore a few definitions of "play." Educators, physicians, and school psychologists agree that "free" or "unstructured" play greatly benefits children and adolescents. Burdette and Whitaker (2005) define "play" as "the spontaneous activity in which children engage to amuse and occupy themselves" (46). Noted scholar Johan Huizinga argued in 1970 that play is indeed a significant activity. Participants derive meaning from play; it enables them to "transcend" the pressures of day-to-day life. Most attempts by social and behavioral scientists to study play have fallen short because of the failure to highlight play's "profoundly aesthetic quality" (2). Scholars have developed a number of what Huizinga believes are limited explanations for why we play: it is a release for pent-up energy; a training ground for life's more serious work; an "exercise in restraint"; an expression of our desire to crush the competition, to borrow a phrase from the sports pages.

But more is clearly going on, Huizinga argues—fun for its own sake, to be precise. "Why does the baby crow with pleasure? Why does the gambler lose himself in his passion? Why is a huge crowd roused to frenzy by a football match?" he asks. Our desire to play, and the meaning we derive from play, "find no explanation in biological analysis" (2). Participants rarely see play as work; they *voluntarily* engage in play only for the enjoyment it brings. Play, writes Huizinga, is "free"—it represents *freedom* for participants to spontaneously immerse themselves in a world apart from real life. "It is rather a stepping out of 'real' life into a temporary sphere of activity with a disposition all of its own," he argues (8).

Participants are generally quite serious about play, which should come as good news to parents and coaches who believe that unstructured play is aimless and unproductive. Our devotion to the twin gods of achievement and progress, where we try to "explain every advance in culture in terms of a 'special purpose'" (Frobenius, quoted in Huizinga, 16), is certainly not new, but we certainly have a hard time coming out from behind our devotion to view it the least bit critically. "The consciousness of play being 'only a pretend,'" Huizinga writes, "does not by any means prevent from proceeding with the utmost seriousness, with an absorption, a devotion that passes into rapture and, temporarily at least, completely abolishes that troublesome 'only' feeling" (8).

We didn't play hockey and baseball particularly well on Kensington Terrace, but we cared deeply about playing—about sustaining the significance of the play. We wanted to play well, and we wanted to win, but it was more important to immerse ourselves in the game, made-up or not. Games would often last for hours—after dark on weekday nights, and entire weekend afternoons. And, if Huizinga is correct, we actually gained something from the experience: an enhanced ability to make sense of the world. He cites Plato, who argued that "life must be lived as play, playing certain games, making sacrifices, singing and dancing, and then a man will be able to propitiate the gods, and defend himself against his enemies, and win in the contest" (19).

Not that we were serious all the time, or that we would have been able to recognize that we were serious. I'm not sure we engaged in any god-propitiating—and we certainly didn't include a lot of sacrifices among our pick-up game rituals. I must also resist the desire to pass off warm and fuzzy recollections of childhood as mileposts of genuine personal development. But I can say this: remembering the meaning derived from these experiences has helped me to trust my own instincts a bit more readily. The simplicity of these experiences is a reassuring counterpoint to the gaggle of would-be "experts" that clog our television screens with regurgitations of common sense designed to persuade us we don't have any. The answers (discussed in more detail when we look at what my respondents took away from their pick-up game experiences) don't necessarily come from the games, or from the people; they come from the fact that we engaged in these activities on our own. We screwed up a lot, and rarely found lasting answers to our surprisingly significant questions—but we did the emotional and intellectual scrounging. We weren't being hauled off to a lesson or a game or a camp every five minutes—we had to come up with and sustain relationships and activities, if only to pass the time and to prevent mind-numbing boredom from setting in. We made our own fun—sacrilege in our "all fun must be packaged and researched" culture. Actually, that's too simple, not to mention unfair to today's parents; it is more accurate to say that we have come to believe that fun must somehow still be productive—to be productive, play must be rooted in consumption. Making a city out of old shoeboxes with my five-year-old son is somehow less impactful than if we bought him a DVD about how to build a city out of old shoeboxes.

At times, the games we played became greater, more significant, than their players. What we did not recognize was how absorbed we typically were by the games. As Huizinga asserts, the game "can at any time wholly run away with the players" (8). But this is not absorption in the "climb the corporate ladder no matter what the impact on family and friends" sense with which we are so familiar. We're talking about joy, claims Huizinga—joy that can create "tension," but also "elation" (21). One thing is for sure: the variation in our skill levels was more than offset by the effort we put into the games, whatever their rules. And on those occasions when one of us achieved a resonant "crack of the bat," or a throw from the outfield landed on the fly in the catcher's mitt, our play truly did, as Huizinga postulates, "rise to heights of beauty and sublimity that leave seriousness far behind."

Of particular relevance to our journey is Huizinga's notion that play is *disinterested*; that is, play "stands outside the immediate satisfaction of wants and appetites" (9). It is a respite—an "interlude" between daily activities. It provides an opportunity to stop, for the moment, our constant evaluation of activities on the basis of what we might gain from them. We talk incessantly about how participating in sports, for example, teaches sportsmanship and teamwork. We hear little else about the experience from parents, coaches, and young athletes. It is increasingly rare to hear a professional athlete talk at length about his or her love of the game; even more rare to hear discussions of "fun." Without question, these are important attributes. But wringing every last drop of development from our activities—not to mention the constant reminders how the activity makes us a better person—can get tiring. It should be enough to do something because you selfishly enjoy it, because it transports, rather than transforms, you. As Huizinga notes, play "has no moral function" (6). This, I would argue, is a good thing. Not every experience should be thought of as a "teachable moment;" the most significant impact from an experience often comes when we allow children and adolescents to figure it out—to learn the moral lessons—for themselves. At the very least, we should give them a temporary respite from viewing experiences as packaged bundles ready to be consumed and collected.

Our games were contained, played in discrete blocks of time. We would remember what had happened in previous games, but the most resonant experiences came when we were able to block out school, our parents, our siblings, troubling world events, adolescent feats and foibles. As one of the contributors to the book eloquently said, "It was a world of our own." We did not have to aspire, please anyone else, or manage our time. We did not have to take part in an organized program; we did the organizing. As Sennett notes, "Children learn to believe in the expressivity of impersonal behavior, when it is structured by made-up rules" (315). Children who play express themselves through "the remaking and the perfecting of those rules to give greater pleasure and promote greater sociability with others." The involvement of adults in all aspects of play has caused the focus to shift to the pursuit of what Sennett calls "a deeper life" (315), marked by superficial introspection and the ongoing assessment of the motives (and personalities) of others. Our behavior sometimes suggests to children that casual friendships have no value, and should be avoided.

Sennett theorizes that the goal of play is not instant gratification. Children generally don't want games to end—they want to delay the completion of a game as long as possible. In many cases, children do not seek to dominate play; they also often change the rules in order to maintain what we might call a "level playing field" for all players, regardless of ability. A child involved in play purposely delays his or her "mastery over others and creates a fictive community of common powers," Sennett contends (319). They do all of this in order to keep themselves "free of the outside, non-play world."

As will be discussed in the next chapter, such "seclusion," to use Huizinga's word, is impossible today. "Play begins, and then at a certain moment, it is 'over,'" Huizinga writes (9). It is self-contained. You play for a period of time, then decide to end the game. But the experience stays with the participants—"a treasure to be retained by the memory" (10)—as long, if not longer, than memories of an experience with organized sports. Participants also easily pick up where they left off. The game will continue tomorrow, or next week.

Play almost always takes place on a "consecrated spot"—and typically in secret. These were our games, nobody else's. "We were different and do things differently," suggests Huizinga, as if writing a slogan for our group. As we will discuss further in the next chapter, participation in sports, at all levels, has become jarringly homogeneous. Truly eccentric players have been moved aside by players who radiate packaged strangeness. Everywhere you look, athletes, at all levels, look, sound, and gesture the same way. Little leaguers mimic big leaguers, right down to their batter's box rituals. We did this, too, but never with such purpose. Where we played games to escape "ordinary life," (12), these kids and today's professional athletes make games seem like an inexorable part of ordinary life. It seems that they are closer to actually believing they are Albert Pujols, Lisa Leslie, or Peyton Manning than we were. Goaded by their parents, many simply don't think that they are engaged in "representative acts" (Huizinga, 15). They seem to think that someday, come hell or high water, they will be engaged in "real, purposive action."

For us, the "consecrated spots" were the porch, my backyard (which I kept neatly manicured, like the infield at Shea Stadium; I was training for a job on the grounds crew in case the first baseman's job wasn't open), our garage, whose east-facing wall served as the site for many an imaginary one-person World Series victory, and, yes, "the hump" in front of my house. "All are temporary worlds within the ordinary world," Huizinga writes, "dedicated to the performance of an act apart" (10). I remember the "hump" and the garage wall more fondly than the tennis courts and baseball fields at the nearby park, although my friends and I spent many hours there. As Huizinga notes, a dedicated space such as our garage wall "continues to shed its radiance on the ordinary world outside, a wholesome influence working security, order and prosperity for the whole community until the sacred play-season comes round again" (14). When warm days in February hinted that spring—and spring training—was near, I headed to the wall with my mitt and baseball, not the park. I drew a new strike zone on the wall, and knocked away the paint chips. We could have played touch football at the much roomier local park more often than we did, but somehow, games of five-on-five, played on crisp fall days with a "steady" quarterback, wearing doctored jerseys with duct tape used to make numbers, and with everyone trying to dodge parked and moving cars, simply meant more to us.

Today, children are expected to be totally immersed in whatever activities they undertake. They are expected to rehash and deconstruct their performance on the field. Further, the crush of a full schedule seems to leave them little time to go off and play—to make up and manipulate their own rules. They are not permitted to experience the self-distance Sennett describes. What the sports and games mean to them is of less importance than what they can gain from their participation in them. Far from an "interlude," participation in sports becomes a low hum in their lives. Instead of "adorning" life, to use Huizinga's word, it can consume or overwhelm one's life. The tear-streaked faces and often vacant stares of the players on the team that lost the 2006 Little League World Series support this view. The players were clearly sad about losing, but they also seemed to be crushed by the pressure to win caused by the accelerated professionalization of a child's game.

Yet many parents, egged on by some of these same professionals, and fresh from their child's most recent practice, game, or lesson, are giving their children fewer chances to "have fun" or "hang out." Scared that allowing children to make their own fun will somehow send their children spiraling toward juvenile delinquency, or worse, mediocrity, they complain that play doesn't teach anything, and doesn't instill a sense of order. Yet Huizinga contends that order is a necessity for play—"it creates order, *is* order," he writes (10). It may not be the expression of order that parents are after, but it is order nonetheless. Flouting the rules set up so carefully by the participants "robs it of its character and makes it worthless," argues Huizinga. And just because the games aren't professionalized within an inch of their lives doesn't mean there isn't tension. The outcomes of our makeshift games were uncertain. To paraphrase Charlie Brown, we all wanted to be the hero, not the goat, when the makeshift game was on the line. There were just more ways to win—resourcefulness, in the *MacGyver* sense, was often as important as physical prowess. When we played Running Bases, for example, you had to know how far away a "dropped" ball could roll so that you could entice a runner to try to make it to the other base.

There was no rule book to refer to, but failure to follow what rules we had was met with consternation, or as much consternation as a bunch of twelve-year-olds can muster. There were some common complaints: rushing the quarterback without having first completed the required number of "Mississippis"; using a cleverly manipulated stick to pull the blade of the goalie's stick out of the way of an oncoming shot; our lame attempts at loading up a baseball—and nobody ever came up with a satisfactory, mutually agreeable definition of pass interference.

Cheating was bad, but questioning the validity of the rules—usually expressed using some variation of the phrase "this is bullshit," followed by an abrupt departure—was more serious. Huizinga's description of play suggests that these transgressions highlighted the "fragility" of our games. Perhaps more troubling—although I'm not sure we realized this at the time—acting like what Huizinga (and my grandmother) calls a "spoil sport" also pierces the illusion of play.

The treatment of professional athletes by fans supports this view. For the most part, fans have shown marked indifference to reports that Barry Bonds and other professional baseball players have for some time, it seems, used steroids and other substances, to enhance their performance. There was some outcry, too, when we learned that Sammy Sosa of the Chicago Cubs, the only major league player ever to hit sixty home runs in a season three times, corked his bat. After the requisite amounts of indignation and hand-wringing, we collectively shrugged our shoulders, and went back to supporting our teams.

But our dissatisfaction is far more pronounced when an athlete has the audacity (in our minds, anyway) to withhold services until the team capitulates to the athlete's contract demands. Holdouts are viewed as pariahs who threaten not only their team's potential success, but also the very fabric of the game. It doesn't help an athlete's case when ill-advised comments are made about having to have more money in order to feed one's family, but these individuals are most certainly banished, symbolically anyway, from their sports with more dispatch than an athlete who throws a spitball or overinflates a football to make it fly farther when it (not the athlete) is punted. As a colleague pointed out in an early review of this book (2007), however, the banishment "lasts only until the sins are forgotten." Forgotten or shared: Baseball fans still get a chuckle about the cleverness exhibited by admitted spitballer Gaylord Perry. We know he did it. He knows he did it. The fact that we were all in on his "secret" made it OK—rebellious, as my colleague pointed out.

The most serious sin one of us could commit was leaving, for whatever reason, what Huizinga calls the "play-community" (12). Leaving to play an organized sport—as I did briefly in the summer of 1979 when, as an incoming senior, I tried out for my high school's football team—was a pretty serious breach of the play-community faith. Even *suggesting* that after all of our "practice," it might be worth a try to play a season of Little League, or skate in an organized hockey program, was viewed as heresy, as if Tucker Carlson told Rush Limbaugh of his hidden interest in joining the Green Party.

2

Does Anybody Play Anymore?

In the fall of 2005, after months of trying, and countless visits to the message board at the Web site set up to publicize goings on in my hometown in northern New Jersey, I finally found Bob Zipse. Now a John Deere sales manager living in Canada, Bobby was, during the 1970s and early 1980s at least, the person in the world I most admired—mainly because he taught me how to play, or to improve my performance in, a laundry list of sports. We started with football when I was ten or eleven (and he was twelve or thirteen), worked our way through various track and field events (the evergreen hedge in our front yard never grew higher than four feet after I knocked off its crown using it for a practice hurdle), and ended up, right before I went away to college in 1979, with lacrosse. For the record, I still can throw a tight spiral fifty yards—exactly once without crumbling to the ground in pain.

If Bob was outside on our tree-lined suburban street, playing something with his friends, he would almost always let my friends and me join in. On many occasions, what appeared to be his democratic nature would lead to everyone in the neighborhood joining for a massive, sprawling game of baseball, touch football, or lacrosse. There was an implied pecking order—he and his friends were more skilled than we were, and they would often make that point abundantly clear, at times keeping the ball away from us with consummate skill and checking or tackling us with extra gusto. But if we hung in there, and tried to improve, they eventually would compliment us.

Professional sports never had a better ambassador—or a better salesperson. The interest in sports stoked by Bob repeatedly led me to ask my parents to help me buy (or buy outright) what I needed to play. Mitts, soccer balls, lacrosse sticks, my first pair of Nikes—all were bought, partially at Bob's urging, but mostly because I needed them in order to learn how to play properly. Still, Bob had a tangible impact on the fiscal health of the area's sporting goods stores, the biggest of which at the time was the now defunct Herman's World of Sporting Goods.

In the winter, we would wait for passing cars to compress the snow, and then play hockey. Plastic blades, purchased at Herman's, or the more local Masco Sports in nearby South Orange, New Jersey, would be attached with nails, or with screws, to shafts of broken hockey sticks. Eventually, I tired of how much the blades would wiggle, and moved on to a "real" hockey stick, as befitted my imagined status as our league's leading scorer. I favored the Sher-Wood 5500 for its stiffness and the curve of its blade, which allowed me to crank up a nasty wrist shot. When the snow was particularly smooth, we would approximate skating in our sneakers—no boots; too much tread. We would slowly shuffle the net (mentioned in the introduction) from the garage up our short and bumpy driveway to a spot directly in front of my house. We first tried to use an official NHL puck; after discovering that it wouldn't travel with requisite speed, we moved on to a convex (on both sides) Mylec street hockey puck, which skittered quickly along the pseudo-ice. But it was the Mylec warm-weather street hockey ball (the orange one, not the cold-weather yellow ball) that produced the most speed—and the most erratic shots, more than one of which ended up going through nearby windows.

In the summer, we would play some form of baseball, doing our best to get around the "hump" in our street. A telephone pole in front of the Krayers' house served as first base; the oil in the wood often left a sticky, dark residue on our hands. The concrete slab that marked the intersection of our next-door neighbor's walk and sidewalk was third base—you had to navigate the hump and go over the curb to get there. Second base was usually a mitt, a flat stone, piece of wood, an errant leaf, or a hubcap—whatever we could lay our hands on. But it had to be flat—we preferred not to move the base just because a car came by.

Our left field fence—until we got a little older—was a row of hedges bordering the DiLorenzo's front yard, which was situated beyond Lincoln Place, the street perpendicular to ours. By the time I was twelve, and had grown to 5-9 and 220 pounds, it had become my "short porch"—actually, it became everyone's short porch. We soon stationed a fielder behind the fence. The position required agility—the player would not want to risk getting caught standing in the yard by Mr. DiLorenzo. Outfielders started in the street in front of their house, and then dashed over at the crack of the bat. I broke at least one window in their house, and struck the side of the house countless times, as I still like to tell people today.

At first, we used tennis balls; they made an almost breathy, but resonant thump when struck by a bat. On summer days and nights when we felt particularly adventurous, we'd use baseballs. By now, we were pitching overhand to each other. Our struggle with the new style sent many of the tennis balls and baseballs foul into Mrs. DiJianne's thriving pachysandra—her version of Charlie Brown's kite-eating tree. At least twenty balls and pucks would vanish there every summer, never to be seen again—that is, until we got up the nerve to creep into the yard to gently—and sometimes not so gently—pick and paw through the pachysandra with our sticks and bats.

Until he went away to college, Bob was our ringleader—our negotiator with angry neighbors whose hedges had just been compromised or early evening post-dinner calm shattered by our raucous play, our agent, our lawyer, our teacher. I can't be sure if he truly loved having to hang around with younger kids, or if he ever became frustrated at having to repeatedly teach us the finer points of play. He never expected anything in return, and seemed to derive a great deal of satisfaction from seeing one of us properly execute a pitching motion, cradle a lacrosse ball, or punt with ample hang time.

And, even though we all dreamed—OK, I dreamed—about playing a sport professionally, there was a sense of realism in the group that, barring a miracle more stupendous than the U.S. hockey team's win over the Russians during the 1980 Winter Olympics, loving a sport was as far as we would go. We learned how to play from each other—from Bob, mostly. We'd try something new. We sucked. We probably could have benefited from taking part in an organized league, or trying out for a school team, but we improved nonetheless. We broke windows, crashed into each other, never kept score, hit cars, improved our physical condition, got faster, stronger, hit and threw further—all on our own. In my case, I still love most of the sports we played—and my brother, whom I had to literally drag outside to play with us, now reports that he is a diehard New York Mets fan. Go figure. We had no goals, and our ambitions, such as they were, were in other areas. We argued, fought, checked illegally, and sometimes threw at each other's heads. We had fun—and we didn't have fun. We had also formed a community of sorts—we didn't know it, of course. It was largely temporary—there were lasting friendships that existed apart from the games. Taking part in our ad hoc community required little emotional investment.

JAMMING

Our exploits on Kensington Terrace are an extended example of what Eric Eisenberg would call "jamming," or "personally involving, minimally disclosive exchanges between individuals" (1990, 139). The risk of creating revisionist history runs through this book and the stories I have gathered, but I do clearly remember this: we didn't play baseball, pepper our goalie with ten-foot slap shots and dodge the "hump" as part of a broader strategy to get to know each other. Conversations that took place during our games were limited to school, baseball players and other athletes we liked, girls we didn't have the nerve to talk to, and the creation of the games themselves—along with a liberal sprinkling of profanity. We didn't share a lot about ourselves—our hopes, our dreams, our relationships with our parents—with one another.

For all of the time we spent together, I knew only a little about Bob Zipse. Likewise, he probably knew very little about me. I knew that he was the first adolescent person on our block to own a mini-bike (which he let me ride by myself without any cajoling), that he had three sisters (the oldest a nurse) and a brother, a pilot who flew for United Airlines, and that his mother put up the same lights, in the same configuration, around their front door every Christmas, but that was about it. We were not close—but it didn't matter when he was teaching me, or one of my friends, how to flick a wrist shot, or when he was slapping a tag on me during a rousing game of "running bases." When we played on the street, my close friends were often there (including one who my students refuse to believe is named Joe Kuhl), but we wanted to play, not reflect or share ideas about the state of our 1970s world.

Eisenberg argues that despite this lack of closeness, these experiences are significant, especially today, when we seem to be interacting less frequently with folks with whom we are not intimately connected, and more frequently, but with less depth, with the people to whom technology so readily connects us. If the mass media are any guide, we think we are intimate with many people. We have become quite skilled—and quite ready—to reveal, to share. We reflect at the drop of a hat—to each other, to our therapists, to Dr. Phil and Oprah. This is all well and good, but Eisenberg reminds us that encounters with people we are not close to can also play a significant role in shaping the self.

Our tendency to shy away from contact with casual acquaintances is caused partially by our belief that these interactions are "phony, staged, and unfulfilling in comparison with 'deeper' relationships" (Eisenberg, 140). As a result, we spend more time judging each other on the basis of "the desirability of their personalities or motives" than on the "results of their actions." Think about our criteria for electing a president, or even a state senator: we prefer good-looking people who entertain us, and who don't bore us with reams of information about major issues. Then think about how to make it in broadcast journalism: sure, it's an idea overblown by scholars and critics, but one doesn't become a news anchor unless he or she is visually appealing—"telegenic" is the term. Solid reporting skills, relaying the truth—even a basic grasp of the language—are less important.

Much of this occurs, Eisenberg contends, thanks to what we will for the moment call the "privatization of meaning." The individual experiences people, places, and events, and then constructs and nurtures meaning about them—this process is at the heart of this book. You develop and "own" the meaning you hold, say, for your grandmother, or your first kiss. Another group of scholars (i.e., Bakhtin et al., 1982) argues that we actually "rent" meaning, which gives it more of a community flavor. You, or a friend, might choose to share stories about your grandmothers, and then make a connection through the similarities (and differences) in your experiences. The social aspects of communication are more important than what you intended when you sent a letter or an IM to someone. Knowledge, claims Gergen (1985, 270), is not "something people possess in their heads, but rather, something people *do* together" (emphasis in original). Thus, it is more illustrative of the relationship to explore the meanings that emerge from interaction rather than those that reside solely in the head of an individual.

Even with the immense popularity of Web sites such as Myspace.com, and in the face of fear mongering from our elected leaders, done in the guise of alerting us to Internet predators, we still feel that we truly need to get to know someone before we can move down the road to a more intimate connection, or to the formation of a community. Ironically, however, we spend so much time talking about ourselves that we damage our ability to, in the words of John Lennon, "come together." We get so caught up in self-revelation that we forget why we've come together in the first place, as Richard Sennett (1978) might argue. Instead of exploring the origin of our feelings, Sennett contends, we spend too much time explaining our feelings to other people. Our capacity for public expression actually suffers as we continue on our "search for a selfhood" (Sennett, 314). We have, Eisenberg argues, lost our "appreciation for the emotional rewards of public life" (140). We are left isolated and unable to interact productively. As a result, we embrace group situations where "homogeneity of values" is a good thing—where dissenting ideas are squelched, and where differences in personality are submerged.

We also now tend to hoard information, as if just having it improves our social standing. We don't share what we've hoarded, unless there is something to be gained. The information may not counter our isolation, but at least we have it. Our avarice is not surprising, since we now seem to treat even innocuous facts as precious commodities. In 2005, for example, Senator Rick Santorum of Pennsylvania, proposed privatizing the National Weather Service in light of what he believed was the federal agency's poor performance in gauging the impact of Hurricane Katrina. His bill would have banned the NWS from providing "a public product or service that could be provided" by a corporation (Reston 2005). You and I would not have been able to turn to the government for information about the weather; we'd have to pay for it in some form. We soon learned that at least fourteen private weather companies had offices in Pennsylvania—but that's another story.

And consider the August 2006 ruling by U.S. Magistrate Judge Mary Ann Medler that the nearly eighteen million owners of fantasy baseball teams should not be forced to pay Major League Baseball for using player information and statistics. This information, the judge ruled, was not "copyrightable." While the judge recognized that players do have a right to make money from their images, the First Amendment "takes precedent over such a right" (McCarthy 2006). Having directed more than my share of anger at ESPN for having what I believed was the audacity to charge visitors to its Web site for information about possible baseball trades (part of the network's "insider" feature), I felt vindication at the judge's ruling.

The information we hoard often comes from areas in which we are truly interested—in short, we create "customized" media worlds. We can avoid ideas that make us uncomfortable or require a distastefully large amount of intellectual heavy lifting. We live in our own iPod-driven worlds, picking and choosing, cutting and pasting, and, it would seem, moving apart from each other. We believe we are exercising choice, being autonomous, when in actuality we may be isolating ourselves.

As described by the folks who contributed stories for this book, pick-up games provided us with the chance to balance "autonomy and interdependence," as Eisenberg writes (139). Too much interdependence can stifle the creativity of a group's members, while too much autonomy can lead to anarchy, or, at the very least, seemingly endless personality-driven battles, and to the group accomplishing little (142). Many of the folks who shared their stories seemed to have achieved what one writer called "a sense of mutual presence" (Wentworth 1980, 103). We didn't always like the people we played with out on Kensington Terrace; our games saw their share of what sportscasters call "chin music" and mini-brawls. We fought, got over it, and continued to play. We were, to borrow Eisenberg's word, "compatible." That was enough. No exaggerated, fawning overinvolvement in each other's business for us.

We agreed to comply with some pretty arcane rules (a fly ball that dropped untouched onto the manhole cover at the intersection of Kensington Terrace and Lincoln Place was automatically a home run), even if we believed that the author of those rules was out to lunch. We had no goals, other than to play without getting injured and to avoid damaging property. Values were not freely expressed, and probably did not evolve all that much. Little time was spent discussing fair play. And although I was convinced at age fourteen that I might have a small amount of real talent for baseball, I did not have, to use a term popular with politicians, an agenda. It was enough to just play. We came together around the games. My closest friends—Joe Kuhl and Chris Tanner—were rarely involved in these games. Only Bob Zipse played organized sports (I played Little League at eight years old, and then again at fourteen). Yet when the games took place, we forgot our individual trajectories and played. As Eisenberg notes, "this perception of unity facilitates the smooth coordination of action" (145). While I harbored my Major League delusions, my younger brother was trying to figure out how to hit the most cars on the block with a single hit. But we played on.

THE PUSH TO PROFESSIONALIZE

Contrast this rather longwinded description with what it is like for a child or adolescent who plays sports today. Society has come to expect a young athlete to be totally immersed in his or her sport, with all of the quirks, and much of the fun, wrung out of the experience. Young athletes don't get to discover the "unity" described by Eisenberg—it is forced upon them. In short, you don't play at any level unless you do it in a league. Maybe it has something to do with the amount of money and time parents invest in their child's sports. Parents, notes Engh, often come to treat youth sports as a professional endeavor and believe that the money they spend now will pay off in a professional career for their son or daughter. They often become immersed in the action, following their child's soccer or baseball team as if it was the New York Yankees or Dallas Cowboys. "Each game the team wins is monumental and every loss is catastrophic," Engh writes.

Dowell and his colleagues (1999) suggest a number of possible causes for the push to professionalize youth sports: "the ascendancy of the automobile, the shrinking of open spaces, the ubiquity of the two-earner family, and the pervasive fear of crime." Faced with these developments, many upper- and middle-class families have placed their pick-up game experiences in a collective memory box, and decided that that there is a benefit to be gained only from participating in organized sports. Unorganized play just isn't productive. It's seen as a waste of valuable time. It might lead to antisocial or destructive activity.

Ironically, the confluence of these factors, and others discussed later in this chapter, is leading more young athletes to abandon sports. The National Alliance for Youth Sports (NAYS) reports that more than 70 percent of the kids who play organized sports eventually quit (Engh 2002, 3). Some simply can't keep up with a very full schedule of school, activities, and sports. Yet others zealously embrace their sports, treating them as careers, despite the fact that less than 1 percent of kids playing organized sports will qualify for a college athletic scholarship, according to the National Center for Educational Statistics (NCES). Participation in sports is not without risk: about three million children are injured while playing sports or taking part in recreational activities each year, according to statistics from Children's Hospital in Boston (2006). The nation's emergency rooms treat about 775,000 children each year for sports-related injuries. The risk of suffering a sports-related injury, say doctors, is growing.

Young athletes who stick with their sport—and more often today it is just one sport; kids, according to one school athletic director, now specialize rather than play a few sports (Dowell, Drummond, Grace, Harrington, Monroe, and Shannon 1999)—are confronted with overbearing, sometimes inept coaches, misbehaving parents, and often raucous attendees at their games. The Minnesota Amateur Sports Commission noted in a recent study that more than 40 percent of kids who completed a Commission survey reported that adults had either called them names or insulted them as the kids were playing in a game. More than 17 percent reported that they had been hit or kicked by an adult during a game (Engh, 5).

But Gregg Heinzmann, director of the Youth Sports Research Council, cautions against exaggerating the frequency of "sports rage" incidents (2002). Several of these events, in particular the murder of Michael Costin by Thomas Junta in 2000 after Costin's son had endured some rough play during a youth hockey game, have been the subject of extensive news media coverage, which contributes to the impression that there has been a recent rash of violent episodes connected to youth sports. Still, when Mark Downs Jr., a Pennsylvania construction worker and T-ball coach, in August 2005 offered one of his players $25 to hit a developmentally disabled nine-year-old boy from another team and knock him out of a game, it's hard not to be concerned for the safety of young athletes and not to question the stability and motives of parents and coaches. For the record, Downs was convicted in September 2006 of criminal conspiracy to commit simple assault and corruption of minors ("T-Ball Coach" 2006, 26).

But just as serious as the aggressiveness directed toward young athletes are the unrealistic expectations often set by parents for their children. Much has already been written about the tendency of parents to live their lives vicariously through their children. Some kids take up a sport just to please their parents. Many parents push their kids to excel in a sport out of frustration for their own failures, and then co-opt any success their kids have as a sort of redemption. Others see their child's athletic performance as a direct reflection of their parenting abilities (Engh, 56). Still others believe that success in Little League or on a soccer travel team will continue in college and as a professional athlete, despite overwhelming evidence that only a few young athletes ever make it that far. They often see athletics as a sure ticket to fame. Parents seem to feel that they can't leave their children alone to chart their own sports path—they might screw up, or change their minds, or blow their big chance, even though they likely won't have one—which, by the way, is OK and not the end of the world.

Parents and coaches start evaluating a young athlete's ability as early as age five (Bigelow, Moroney, and Hall 2001, 35). Recruiters now pursue very young players for eventual spots on high school teams. Coaches siphon off the very talented kids to "elite" teams and well-funded popular leagues. They convince young players that they won't have fun playing a sport unless they constantly strive to improve. Some players bypass high school athletics altogether in favor of club teams (Dowell et al. 1999). Premature classification of kids has led a number of youth sports officials, such as former professional athlete Bob Bigelow, to call for the elimination of "elite" teams (41) until the athletes reach seventh grade. The potential for harming a young athlete is just too strong. Elite teams "erode the self-confidence of the children who aren't selected" and "ramp up the pressure on the anointed ones" (46). Stocking a youth team with players often resembles the NFL or NBA draft, complete with scouting reports and draft-day trades. This leads Bigelow to conclude that only individuals with no connections to a league or its players should evaluate athletes.

From all of this comes an *expected path for participation* in youth sports, one that is endorsed by society and amplified by the news media. For starters, sports are to be participated in somewhere other than one's neighborhood. Many of the folks who contributed stories for this book wistfully noted that they rarely see kids playing in their yards, or out on the street. Today, truly meaningful, productive participation in sports (as we now define it) can only happen in facilities—often well-heeled facilities—designed solely for competition. Sports have moved almost completely out of the community.

Instead, young athletes compete in what Ritzer and Stillman (2001) would call "cathedrals," which unify participants and spectators in a view of sport as a means of consumption, rather than of self-fulfillment. Watching our sons and daughters play on the street, or in a substandard field behind their school just wouldn't cut it, the authors suggest. New, impressive facilities marginalize the places where children used to play—and, I would argue, as well as the ability to create play without consuming—in other words, no more using hubcaps for bases. As Ritzer and Stillman explain, "Consumers are not drawn, at least for very long" to places "that lack enchantment, especially for non-routine consumption" (87).

High schools across the country with thriving, and sometimes not so thriving, athletic programs are pouring millions of dollars into new sports facilities. To cover the cost of construction, a growing number of high schools are selling naming rights to their new stadiums and arenas (Wieberg 2004). They often reap the benefits of targeted state tax increases, and tap private donors and well-heeled booster clubs for money. In some cases, they also dip into already stretched school budgets. Even after the Georgia legislature slashed the state's 2005 education budget by $180 million, school officials in Valdosta, Georgia, spent more than $400,000 on the high school's football program in 2005, much of it financed by a small sales tax increase (Wieberg 2004).

My recent visit to Turner Field in Atlanta provides additional supporting evidence for the work of Ritzer and Stillman. Those who work for professional sports franchises labor to make sure that the audience is entertained, or at least distracted, nearly every second—from the huge video screen in right-center field, to scantily clad young women dancing on the dugout roof between innings. I found little opportunity to truly concentrate on the game. This could be advancing age talking, but I wasn't able to collect my thoughts, or take away much meaning from being there. If pressed, there was little I could place in my internal memory box. There was simply too much going on. Like many other minor league teams, our local single-A team, the Wilmington Blue Rocks, each game serves up the "Dirtiest Car in the Lot" contest, the "dizzy bat race," and babies racing across a mattress into their parents' waiting arms. The roster of promotions in Wilmington is not without originality; a highlight at Rocks games is an employee dressed as a dancing stalk of celery who emerges and runs around behind home plate whenever the home team scores.

Officials in cities whose professional sports franchises have threatened to leave if new stadiums were not constructed would claim that our enchantment indeed often does not last. As Ritzer and Stillman note, facilities in our supposedly postmodern world must regularly be "re-enchanted" (88) if our loyalty and our consumption are to continue. But it has reached the point where we now require youth sports—once unvarnished and pleasantly amateurish—to take the form of a "spectacle," as Guy Debord (1994) might argue. Partaking of a spectacle helps the viewers forget their troubles as they are transported into a world that is "vibrant and controlling," Ritzer and Stillman note (89). Parents who have spent a great deal of time and money to propel their child's involvement in a sport can forget all of this and soak in the pro-like environment.

Movement away from the community and the rush to build top facilities means participation in sports is *contained*—separate and apart from the community. Sports have lost much of their public flavor. Young athletes experience sports away from home and community. Their parents transport them, often long distances, to and from their games. There develops a faux closeness within a tight circle of coaches, trainers, league officials. I can only imagine that this gets suffocating for young players. A spot on a "travel" team carries more prestige—and more cost—than playing in a recreational league. Athletes often play on fields and in arenas constructed—sometimes at great expense—for the use of their league alone. They interact with teammates, coaches, and their parents in the stands, and then head home. They practice—a lot, having been convinced that hours of structured practice is the only way to improve performance to a level that may lead to a shot at a professional career. While many young athletes follow their own workout regimens, a growing number of them have private coaches. Even summer sports camps have been transformed from havens for play into essential stopovers on the road to enhanced performance (Sheff 2006, E-1). The number of sports camps tracked on the Web site Mysummercamps.com has quadrupled in less than three years—from five hundred in 2003 to 2,100 in 2006. The obsession with improvement, notes an NCAA women's soccer coach, "helps kids at every level meet their goals, whether it's getting off the bench or on their select or varsity teams."

If even more practice and preparation are required, athletes can take advantage of facilities like the Suwanee Sports Academy in Georgia, whose massive multimillion-dollar facility caters to serious young athletes, and whose curriculum includes interaction with onetime professional athletes such as former NBA star Mark Price. The introduction from the "About Us" section of the Academy's Web page welcomes visitors to this sports "cathedral":

> As soon as you walk through the doors, you know you're someplace special. This is the place where serious athletes come to compete. It is also the place where you and your family can come to learn and improve your skills. We are a true world-class, multi-sport facility dedicated to sports development, training and competition. (www.ssasports.com)

Coming to the facility, which includes "seven NBA regulation basketball courts and 11 volleyball courts," will benefit the athlete far more than trying to improve their play in underequipped hometown leagues, or on their own:

> If you want to compete in a league, tournament or competition, you'll find the environment is always clean, safe and climate controlled. All activities are organized and begin and end when they are scheduled. It is a flexible space used to host events of many types with seating for up to 5,000 spectators. Our real expertise lies in our ability to organize and execute national, regional and local competitions and sporting events at competitive levels players expect. (www.ssasports.com)

As a result, it seems reasonable to argue that young athletes now have roughly the same experience with sports—intense, focused, propelled by consumption of the right gear. At every level, sports are commodified spectacles. There is little room left in their sports experience for what Flanagan (1985) calls "functional ambiguity." The training is the same, the equipment is the same, the mannerisms are the same, the motions and actions performed by young athletes are the same. True, we used to mimic our favorite athletes (I was a right-handed Willie Stargell wannabe; I struggled to perfect his windmilling batting stance), but it seems, nearly thirty years later, that we did so to try to set ourselves apart, not draw attention to our similarities. But a little bit of what Flanagan calls "indeterminacy" is good in an otherwise totally structured, homogenous activity. Without it, it may be that young athletes are now less able than in years past to "project their private, most intense emotions and meanings" into their participation in a sport (Myerhoff 1975, 55–56). The outcomes of the games are sometimes still up in the air until the last out or last seconds, but all of the behaviors—by players, coaches, officials, and fans, are remarkably similar, game after game, until the whistle blows, or the last out is recorded.

Acting primarily to please a headstrong coach or an overindulgent parent, or to attain their own goals, they may hide how they feel about taking part in a sport—or not feel anything at all. As Eisenberg notes, "strong cultures can stifle autonomy and impede adaptability" (145). Further, the range of possible meanings of the sport for the players is limited. This is a shame, especially when one reads the descriptions of what playing pick-up games meant to my contributors—and when one reads an account of the life of a professional athlete who fondly remembers throwing the ball around in front of his or her house. Michelle Akers, star of the 1999 World Cup–winning U.S. women's soccer team, recalled pretending to be Pittsburgh Steelers great "Mean Joe" Greene as she tried to break up "Hail Mary" passes from her father to her brother (2000, 47). "I didn't care that he was a defensive lineman," she wrote. "I just figured I could do anything because he was big, mean, and tough" (47).

Describing his hardscrabble childhood in Alabama, Hank Aaron, Major League Baseball's one-time career home run leader, remembers devoting all of his energies to baseball. At times this wasn't easy; but Aaron exuded the autonomy and adaptability discussed by Eisenberg: "If nobody was around to get up a game or have a catch with, I'd find ways to play by myself. I could spend hours hitting a ball with a stick or throwing it on the roof and hitting or catching it when it came down" (Aaron and Wheeler 1991, 10). Aaron claimed that he became so proficient at this ad hoc game, that he could throw the ball "over the house and run around and catch it before it hit the ground on the other side." Without the money to buy equipment, Aaron and his friends made their own. Baseballs were fashioned by "wrapping nylon hose around an old golf ball." Rags tied together, the grips from a set of handlebars, and even crushed cans worked about as well, Aaron recalled.

Like Aaron, baseball great Lou Gehrig used games played in the Washington Heights section of Manhattan at the turn of the twentieth century as an escape; in Gehrig's case, he was escaping a doting mother, who "fed him like he were a runt, as if every bite he took were an immunization, as if every ounce of flesh on his chunky frame might provide further protection from the invisible germs choking New York City's air," writes Gehrig biographer Jonathan Eig (2005, 11) as she struggled to come to grips with the deaths of Lou's infant brother and sister. When Lou Gehrig made it outside, he "burst forth like a furloughed soldier, starved for recreation. He played marbles, hitched sleigh rides, and threw snowballs at anything that moved" on a nearby hill, Eig notes. Gehrig had "an arm like a slingshot," which he would need to convince the boys in his neighborhood to look past his small size and allow him to play baseball (11).

Tyrone "Muggsy" Bogues, the shortest person, at 5-3, ever to play in the National Basketball Association, took a slightly different route to being included in local pick-up games. He and his friends devised their own games by tying milk crates to a chain-link fence at a playground near his Baltimore home. "We would be dunking into these milk crates and wondering how tall we'd get, thinking we'd be tall enough to dunk into the real goals, pretending we were throwing it down like Dr. J [basketball great Julius Erving]," Bogues recalled in his autobiography (Bogues and Levine 1994). Refusing to be consumed by the taunts of others, Bogues and his friends "made sure that we showed off, and that the older kids saw what we could do" (36). The older kids came around, and began to pick Bogues. "Everyone in the neighborhood saw me differently. The little fella could *play*" (emphasis in original), he wrote.

The experiences of these athletes reinforce two key ideas: first, that unstructured play can empower children and adolescents to come up with solutions for problems on their own. Second, unstructured play can provide a valuable "interlude" in what for a strikingly large number of young people from families with the means to afford activities are crammed daily schedules. Professionalizing sports to the point where unstructured games seem to have little or no value takes these experiences away from kids.

MASTERING ITS PARTICIPANTS

Also damaged is the potential for the young athlete to have "jamming" experiences of the kind described by Eisenberg. While "jamming" experiences typically are structured and regulated by a clear set of rules, participants often come away feeling that the game transcends their participation in it. Similarly, while the contributors to this book fondly remembered the games they played or the rules they created to govern their play, they often placed more emphasis on the non-sports-related lessons they took away from these experiences. As Gadamer suggests, the game sometimes ends up mastering its participants (1988, 92).

Clearly, today's young athletes are expected to do their best to master the games they play, but the game will *always* be more significant than the athlete—especially when the athlete challenges its significance, or the authority of a coach, manager, or owner by engaging in nonconformist behavior, anything that might affect the team's performance. Vince Carter, a longtime NBA star now with the New Jersey Nets, in 2003 decided to attend graduation ceremonies at the University of North Carolina so that he could pick up his degree in person. Carter's decision came right before his former team, the Toronto Raptors, were preparing for a playoff game against the Philadelphia 76ers. Carter made it back in time for the game, but journalists who covered the game suggested that his absence from the team—even for such a short period of time—caused his performance to suffer, which damaged the team, and may have caused Carter to miss a crucial shot late in the game. The treatment of Carter reveals that we tolerate, even embrace self-consciousness in our professional athletes only when it's entertaining—Deion Sanders springs to mind here—but not when it leads a player to challenge the cultural authority of the game, not to mention the authority we think we have as fans to shape the contours of a player's career.

Because "jamming" participants limit the amount of information they share about themselves, they are able to achieve the balance between autonomy and interdependence discussed earlier. They can, as Myerhoff explains, experience "organization and ecstasy" that flow when individuals direct "full attention toward the other" (Eisenberg, 147) while recognizing and respecting individuality. More important for our journey, they are able to use games as an escape from their daily travails and to "lose the self-consciousness that can intrude on everyday life," as Eisenberg notes (149). Focusing too much on individual exploits "shifts our criteria for evaluating people's behavior away from the results of their action, toward the desirability of their personalities or motives" (Eisenberg, 140)—perhaps the ultimate irony in our results-driven culture.

Maybe the most valuable thing to take from my pick-up game experiences at this point is the fact that we left the game on the field—on the street, on the tennis court. Sure, we would brag about scoring ten goals or a home run, but the games we played did not consume us. They were only a part of our days. For many young athletes, the sport is all there is—or academics are all there is—or working is all there is. Even very young athletes describe their involvement with sports as their "passion" or their "life." Children talk about their school "careers." Thanks at least in part to the constant availability of information about sports, we can now totally immerse ourselves in them. This is what is expected of us by society, so why should we expect anything less from young athletes? We talk constantly about sports—from the water cooler to e-mail to the abrasive, often ill-informed ranting that passes for sports talk radio. There is little chance to catch one's breath. We professionalize even those activities with which we would pass the hours as children. In 2006, we witnessed the birth of a professional "rock-paper-scissors" league.

The media are no help—they amplify the "expected path of participation" in sports mentioned earlier by lionizing those individuals who preach total devotion to sport, and marginalizing those in athletics who take a less intense approach. This stems in part from the fact that reporters and commentators have grown used to talking about sports in narrow, black and white terms—lots of heroes and villains, daunting challenges, upstarts, and underdogs. Individuals who don't come properly packaged or who are not easily digestible do not get a lot of attention. In fairness to those athletes who have enjoyed the benefits of proper packaging, fans rarely get to learn anything about them that doesn't mesh with the script carefully written by league and team officials, a script with which most sports journalists are afraid to tinker. Sports journalists would also have us believe that participation in sports is a required rite of passage, or at least a hobby, for nearly everyone. And when you play, don't do it unless you are committed to giving it all that you've got. A recent series of Gatorade commercials asks, "Is *it* in you?"

Who really wins? Sporting goods manufacturers. The National Sporting Goods Association (NSGA) projects that in 2006, we will spend more than $53 billion on sports equipment, apparel, and footwear—up from a little over $51 billion in 2005 (www.nsga.com). They depend on our ongoing belief in the notion that only the best equipment will do when it comes to playing sports. This goes way beyond a parent complaining about paying $300 for an aluminum bat or my pining for a time where we needed just a ball and a bat. "In my day," as baseball immortal Honus Wagner (voiced by an actor) reminds viewers in a recent commercial for DHL, an international package delivery service, "we didn't have bases, we had rocks." We expect athletes of all stripes, sports, and performance levels to use the "right" equipment—the most up to date, technologically advanced ball or bat, glove or stick, pad or helmet. No tape, screws, and nails for this crowd.

To paraphrase Ritzer and Stillman, when it comes to sports, we have allowed the dominant institutions (teams, leagues, manufacturers) to redefine "enchantment" for us. Heading down to the baseball field with your glove hanging from the barrel of your bat is wam and fuzzy, but it is also quaint and outdated, according to their formula. We wear exquisitely accurate replica jerseys, and revel in "throwback" stadiums such as Camden Yards, but wouldn't want to spend half an inning watching a game in its amenity-free predecessor, Memorial Stadium—that is, if it were still standing. I mean, come on—*bench seats*?

3

The Consecrated Spots

When I turned forty in 2001, Sheila must have known that I was secretly longing to revisit my old neighborhood. The celebration she concocted for me was amazing; first, she took me to dinner at one of New York's top restaurants. Then, she bought me tickets for a New York Mets game at Shea Stadium in Queens. It was a marvelous day, complete with a bumpy but scintillating ride to the stadium on the Number 7 train from midtown Manhattan to Flushing. The day after the game, I asked Sheila if she would mind stopping in Maplewood for a quick look around. She quickly agreed. We drove—twice, no three times—past the house on Kensington Terrace. I explained, for what must have been the fiftieth time, about the "hump" and the confused construction of our makeshift hockey net. We bought lunch at a frantic bagel shop, located downtown in Maplewood Village in a building that previously housed Bert Miller's, my favorite record (yes, record) store.

We took our lunches over to the park, and ate on a recently renovated wood bench with white stone arms behind and across a small creek from the main branch of Maplewood's library. Maybe it was the start of a midlife crisis, or the culmination of a week's worth of looking up old friends and classmates on several high school reunion Web sites (which still send me perfunctorily warm and fuzzy e-mails), but I was in heaven. I told Sheila about our pick-up baseball and football games in the park, about the annual stocking of goldfish in the nearby kidney-shaped pond, about playing games of *Chase* (based on a short-lived 1970s action series on NBC) in the park on our bikes, about skidding down the hill overlooking the softball fields during one of these games and crashing while riding my Raleigh ten-speed. I told her about how we managed to play cohesive games of football and baseball with just a few people—usually Chris Young, my brother Richard, and one or both of the Taylor brothers. We also eventually allowed the young DiJianne brothers to play with us. We liked to lord it over them, but we really needed more players. The games probably sounded to Sheila more organized than they actually were; when we played baseball, for example, the goal was to consecutively field so many balls (usually ten) cleanly in order to get a time at bat. One misplay meant you started over at "one."

From our bench behind the library, we could see the natural amphitheater on the side of the park nearest the train station. As we finished our bagel-based sandwiches and small bags of chips, I told Sheila about the movies I saw there; many of them, including *Hooper* and *Gator,* starred Burt Reynolds. To this day, I can't pass by a showing of *Smokey and the Bandit* on television without stopping by to fantasize about summer nights spent darting and speeding around the suburbs in our cars. Combinations of my parents, brother, friends, and I plopped down in the amphitheater on old blankets or bed sheets and craned our necks to see the massive screen, strung in front of a cluster of pine trees.

But I probably spent most of our lunchtime conversation reminiscing about the township's ad hoc ice skating pond. Each December, Maplewood's firefighters would slowly flood a depression about the size of a football field located on the north side of the park. The pond sat directly behind left and center field for one of the park's five softball diamonds. Playing the outfield in early spring was particularly treacherous while the pond was being drained. If it was a particularly cold winter, the water would freeze over to the point we could skate on it in a couple of weeks. More temperate winters meant a longer wait before we could hit the ice.

On cold autumn days, I start to smell the bonfires that we would stoke in large green oil drums using branches from nearby maple trees, scrounged pieces of wood, and broken hockey stick shafts. Nearly every day after school in the winter, I would journey to the pond, lace up my tattered leather skates over two pairs of socks, and place my shoes or sneakers about six feet apart on the ice to approximate the width of a NHL goal—without the actual goal, of course.

I spent most of my time on the ice skating unsteadily and practicing my stick handling, and during temperate winters avoiding the soft, slushy spots in the ice. The township didn't put up a sign to warn skaters about this eventuality until I was in high school, although even the shortest skater would only go in up to the knees if the ice completely gave way. Actual games of hockey were few, but there was a great deal of NHL player emulation, mostly done in the vain attempt to impress the female skaters.

The "pond" was the site of my one genuine hockey injury—a badly cut lip courtesy of a stick wielded at my face by one of my best friends at the time. I told Sheila about how I repeatedly wiped my lip on the sleeve of my powder blue down coat until the blood turned the sleeve a disgusting shade of brown. But this part of my story had a decided "badge of honor" flavor to it. I tried to be sensitive to her distaste for my injury, and her empathy for my mother's distaste for my injury (she spotted the bloody sleeve as I tried to stash the coat in the hall closet—an act she rarely saw from me), but I reveled in my one-time toughness. I had played the rest of the afternoon and on into the night with my bloody lip.

Before getting back on the highway and heading home to Delaware, we made one last pass through my old neighborhood. Sheila noted in amazement how near my house was to my elementary and high schools, and said she was struck by how architecturally sophisticated these buildings were. "It must have been so nice growing up here," she said more than once. I had to agree. As we passed Columbia High School for the last time before heading home, I recounted for Sheila what being dismissed from school was like for kids in my neighborhood. The phrase "organized bedlam" sums it up nicely. Kids heading home dotted the landscape. We typically poured out of the school, headed for home, a snack, and reruns of *F Troop* (in my case, anyway). When I was in junior high school, I spent a good portion of this time rolling repeatedly down a hill adjacent to the school with two friends, in the attempt to see if who could make it down the hill the fastest without careening into the nearby street.

While my walk home between kindergarten and sixth grade, and ninth and twelfth grades, took about five minutes, I still remember talking, joking, and playing around with my friends. Some fairly significant socialization took place during these walks—bragging, bullshitting, and talking about girls, at the very least. Sometimes we would alter our route slightly; we'd head to the local corner store for a Freez-a-Pop or a soda. When I was in high school, the cramped but very happening Ralph's Luncheonette on Valley Street, and the slightly less cramped Roman Gourmet in the center of town, were prime post-education hangouts.

An undercurrent in my midlife memories was the fact that my friends and I *walked* (or ran, and sometimes rode our bikes) to do all of this. No cars involved. Very often, there was no discernible transition between the walk home from school and playing—we'd toss our books on the porch, begin procrastinating about doing our homework, and grab the bats and gloves, or the sticks and puck. Nearly every day, I walked downtown or to the A&P or to the King's supermarket in Maplewood Village to pick up groceries for dinner. My mom and dad weren't much for long-term shopping.

I was shocked to learn recently that only 10 percent of kids walk to school (Battiata 2004, W8). This represents a sharp drop from an earlier figure of 70 percent. The rest hitch a daily ride with a family member, drive themselves (if they're old enough), or travel via school bus. Perhaps more troubling, we walk without a purpose in mind—to accomplish something beyond aerobic exercise and draining the batteries on our iPods—only 5 percent of the time. The pedestrian, it seems, is fast becoming an endangered species. In a cruel irony, pedestrians account for more than 13 percent of traffic fatalities in the United States. In Delaware, where I live today, that figure is 15.4 percent. While I in no way wish to minimize the tragedy of these incidents, they are fairly isolated. In an odd twist, residents in at least a few communities across the country are pushing local leaders to do away with at least one potential solution to the problem: sidewalks.

Joseph Berger of the *New York Times* discovered in July 2006 that many residents of Edgemont, New York, a small town near Scarsdale, want nothing to do with the cost of installing and maintaining sidewalks. Perhaps more telling, installing sidewalks would pierce the illusion harbored by many residents that they are totally disconnected from nearby urban areas. "If you put a sidewalk in front of my house," one resident told Berger, "you're making it look more like Queens" (2006, 14-WC). They revel in the almost bucolic splendor of their neighborhoods. "Urban amenities like sidewalks," wrote one resident of the Arden Park section of Sacramento, California (Carmichael 2006, G1), would despoil this environment—even if kids have to navigate gingerly on their bikes around parked cars and residents wait until times of the day with less traffic to take their walks.

At issue in Edgemont, writes Berger, is the proposed installation of a sidewalk that would enable children to walk to the Seely Place School. Ensuring the safety of children, not to mention enabling them to play, seems like a worthwhile goal, especially since commuters have discovered that the road next to which the sidewalk would be built offers a quick shortcut to downtown Edgemont.

But the bottom line for residents is, well, the bottom line. They balk at the possibility that the borough will make them pay for the new sidewalks. They balk at the prospect of having to shovel the new sidewalks. They balk at the possibility that segments of a fence or hedges on their land will have to make way for the new sidewalks. A township official noted that residents "get almost violent if you threaten to take those obstructions away." Sounding like the well-known, but often inaccurate television journalist (and avowed libertarian) John Stossel, the official claims that the debate boils down to one question: "Does government have the will to impose a sidewalk on a neighborhood that doesn't want it?"

Margaret Geosits of Emmaus, Pennsylvania, believes strenuously that the answer to this question is no. She is challenging the denial by the city council of a requested exemption to a relatively new ordinance requiring residents to install sidewalks. City officials ordered more than two hundred residents to have sidewalks installed by the year 2009. A Lehigh County judge upheld the council's decision (Kraft 2006, B4). Geosits sued on behalf of ten residents whose homes are located on the north side of a busy street in Emmaus. While Geosits claims that the proposed sidewalks would not connect her street to places worth walking to, the nearly eighteen thousand vehicles per day that pass her home would seem to justify some measure of protection for pedestrians.

As with the laws banning playing in the streets, it's worth taking a moment to consider how we've gotten to this point. Part of the blame rests on the explosion in home construction, or more accurately, the arrangement of those homes as they are constructed. Duany, Plater-Zyberk, and Speck (2000) explain that our "sprawling, repetitive, and forgettable landscape" of subdivisions, cul-de-sacs, and McMansions have caused many to rethink the appeal of life in the suburbs. Reliance on single-use zoning codes, combined with our love of driving and our unstinting devotion to the idea that buying a home—the largest possible home—is the pinnacle of success, has transformed communities into "uncoordinated agglomerations" of land parcels "with little pedestrian life and even less civic identification, connected only by an overtaxed network of roadways" (12). For pedestrians, in short, this means, fewer sidewalks.

For kids, this means almost less autonomy; they have to beg their parents to drive them to school, to visit friends, to their lessons and games, and to shop. As Sheila pointed out, they less frequently knock on the back door of a friend's house and actually have to interact with the friend's parents. Duany, Plater-Zyberk, and Speck contend that this leaves children "frozen in a form of infancy, utterly dependent on others, bereft of the ability to introduce variety into their own lives, robbed of the opportunity to make choices and exercise judgment" (117). Eventually, those children become teenagers, most of whom obtain driver's licenses and head out on America's roads. In their first year behind the wheel, write Duany, Plater-Zyberk, and Speck, more than 40 percent of them will have accidents that require police involvement (120).

Of the almost $495 million spent between 1998 and 2001 on federally funded "surface transportation" projects in my home state of Delaware, just 2 percent went to projects that centered around pedestrians and bicycling. Californians who like to walk and ride fared even worse; the Surface Transportation Policy Project (STPP) reports that California spent 0.6 percent of its federal transportation money on pedestrian and bicycling-related projects.

Since I lived so close to school, driving was out of the question—except for my brother, who decided that three blocks was too far to travel on foot. He became quite well known among local police officers thanks to his impressive accumulation of parking tickets. Today, in my suburban neighborhood, after-school life, and to a lesser extent, weekend life, is similarly subdued. Folks still work on their cars, and we see kids playing from time to time, but it's hard not to think that most of them are somewhere else doing something else. Our neighborhood at times seems only to be a conduit, a way station, for passage to other activities. Aside from the two or three young boys from down the street who skateboard, Big Gulps in hand, or ride their bikes past our house, and the teenaged young men who play street hockey in their driveway from time to time, the life of leisure in our little segment of Maple Glen Hill is quiet.

About a half-mile or so away, our town's beautifully manicured soccer fields are alive with activity. Players of all ages, boys and girls, run obediently between tiny orange cones in preparation for the games on their ambitious schedule. From spring until late fall, we can hear the cheers and screams of players and parents from our front porch. We spill out into the streets to watch the Fourth of July fireworks display each year (visible over the trees behind our houses), but that's about it. We don't venture out together into our little piece of public space that much.

Some would argue that we're scared of venturing. The late George Gerbner, among the most revered scholars in the field of communication, suggested as much as he compiled data during for more than three decades for his groundbreaking cultivation analyses. He found that people who frequently watched television believed that the world was a more dangerous place than it actually was. The news media, particularly since the September 11 attacks, have become unabashed fearmongers, reporting minor threats and miscommunications as if Armageddon were just around the corner. News organizations devote disproportionately large amounts of time and space to reporting child abductions, using inaccurate statistics to drive their inflammatory accounts. Barry Glassner (1999) explains that fewer than five thousand children are abducted each year, and that most of these children are returned to their families. This is a far cry from the estimated 800,000 child abductions reported recently in *Time* magazine.

Anthropologist Setha Low (2001) suggests that it is this unsupported fear of crime that has sent growing numbers of people into gated communities around the United States. Having concluded that their old neighborhoods "aren't what they used to be," (55), largely thanks to what they believe is the unchecked flow of "others" (primarily African Americans and Latinos), they flee in search of safety, even though, as Low points out, the "others" can easily get through the gates—and some do regularly to complete their work as day laborers.

This "fear flight," as one of Low's subjects from gated communities in New York and San Antonio called it, revolves around a striking willingness to trade the familiarity of neighborhoods where they had spent, in many cases, most of their lives, for protection from, as Low puts it, the "dangers perceived as overwhelming them" (55). The key word, of course, is *perceived*. What's particularly troubling about Low's research is that most of the individuals who have bought homes in gated communities would never return to their old neighborhoods.

ARE "INTERLUDES" STILL POSSIBLE?

The answer to my question is a resounding "maybe," at least among the folks who responded to my request for stories. Younger respondents were nearly as nostalgic as the older respondents for a return to less hectic days and less structured games. Not all of the younger respondents felt that they were contained or repressed by organized sports, but others did develop a love for a sport or sports without playing on a sponsored team or in an organized league. An eighteen-year-old woman explained with noticeable fondness that she was fortunate to grow up in a tree-lined suburb of Philadelphia, "with trees in my nice yard, and a basketball hoop in my driveway." Offering at least some support for the American Academy of Pediatrics' recent report about the importance of unstructured play, she remembered that her street was almost always "littered with kids," perfect for playing sports. "The southeastern Pennsylvania climate was perfect for fun, no matter what the time of year," she said.

The description offered by Matt of the Toronto suburb in which he grew up, is a little less romantic. "The entire place was brand new construction, and from above would have looked much like a cookie-cutter grid," wrote Matt, now nearly thirty. "Green electricity boxes on every block, due to buried power lines. Strategically placed trees, but none large enough to have shade." He quickly added, "None of this is to be negative at all; it was a very nice place to live."

Several young respondents (younger than thirty, anyway) described their hometowns and neighborhoods using nostalgic language that would seem to have come from someone a little older, and that suggests that the act of "consecration" is alive and well, even in the nondescript, sometimes overbuilt suburbs. Jodi, in her early twenties, described living in a town "that the Cleavers lived in on the show *Leave it to Beaver*." She and her family lived on a dead end street "where every neighbor was friendly." Block parties were a regular community event. Describing activity perhaps more true to current form, Jodi recalled that the entire town was "obsessed with sports," and that even very young children were "immersed" in sports and their activities. Dana, also twenty-two, fondly recalled backyard baseball games played with her brother and sister and kids from their Whippany, New Jersey, neighborhood. Some of the younger respondents took a more pragmatic view of what could be gained from playing pick-up games; they saw the games as a way to hone their skills, and prepare them for the so-called real world. We'll explore that more in the final chapter.

The importance of pick-up games in one's life could be determined by a neighborhood's demographic makeup. Ken, a graduate student and goalie for a local college soccer team, said that when he lived in St. Louis as a child, his home or the home of one of his friends was their primary location. Ken and his best friends at the time—"big, tough fifth graders [Ken said he was a few years younger than his counterparts] who lived a few townhouses down from me"—would play indoor soccer in his basement, "denting the faux-wood paneling and once even breaking through it with an elbow," he said, adding that the elbow was probably his, "having been pushed through with fifth-grade force."

When Ken and his family moved to Houston, the terrain changed. The development in which Ken lived was the nation's largest and fastest growing at the time. As a result, Ken had many potential playmates, and pick-up games—a "vast potpourri," he called it—from which to choose. Ken's description of the games he played recalls Eisenberg's description of "jamming." He and his friends never started a game over; "We picked up where we had the previous week (during the school year) or the previous day (during the summer)," he wrote. Individual performance and winning were less important than playing the game and enjoying oneself. Stated another way, the game transcended the participation of Ken and his friends.

Chris, a college student from a Philadelphia suburb, waxed nearly poetic about his pick-up game experiences: "As the cold weather sets in around me, and the city noises rumble on in the background, I long for Saturday football games [played] at Beaver Creek, the elementary school in my hometown." Unable to find a suitable football field, Chris and his friends convened at a local soccer field. It was "imperfect," Chris wrote, but they were able to play thanks to the lines chalked on the field. "Every drive started from the goal line, and midfield was a first down," he recalled. Jeff, now in his early twenties, wrote just as effusively about his home: "Because my house was on the edge of the cookie cutter development, my backyard opened up to the grass fields surrounding the church and school," he wrote, referring to St. Ephrem's Elementary School in Bensalem, Pennsylvania. "The grass was my home for the entire summer. Rain, not roads, mini-malls, or construction, was the only thing to stop me from bliss."

MY "MELTING POT"

The stories shared by my older respondents revealed equal parts reverence, indifference, and unease for the neighborhoods and improvised locations where they played pick-up games. Some remembered their "consecrated spots" with fondness; others saw them only as a backdrop for their games, and still others offered negative, sometimes biting comments about these locations. Not surprisingly, much of this anger seems to stem from the fact that a respondent's family was poor. But a recurring theme across many of the descriptions is how respondents managed to have fun despite some hardscrabble surroundings and, often, a complete lack of equipment, which we will explore further in the next chapter. It took a great deal of imagination to turn a vacant lot or street into Yankee Stadium or center ice at Madison Square Garden. Even more important, perhaps, is the fact that the games were often the creations of respondents, not of a coach or a video game maker. It was no surprise, then, to read in these stories that the game itself was more important than the surroundings—in some cases, even more important than the other participants.

Still, compelling games need an appropriate setting, one that exists completely apart from the world of parents and schoolwork, as Huizinga might argue. Again, it is not my contention that kids and teenagers have stopped using their imaginations; there are simply more organized and pre-packaged options out there for them in which to partake, options which by and large are provided for them, rather than created by them. Trips to the mall, a soccer game, a trumpet lesson—all are valuable activities, but children don't create the environment in which they take place.

Maxine, now in her forties, grew up in the northeastern part of Philadelphia—the "northeast" as most residents know it. Like many of the respondents, she remembered her blue-collar, middle-class neighborhood as being ethnically diverse. More significantly, perhaps, Maxine, like most of the respondents who mentioned diversity, stressed that her neighbors coexisted harmoniously, often helping one another out. Made up of what she called "classic Philadelphia row homes," the neighborhood offered kids a wide range of venues for their games. "In between the two rows of houses was a grassy lot where we played ball games, climbed trees, dug holes in the dirt, built snowmen in the winter and picked blackberries in the summer," Maxine recalled. Nearby Tacony Creek Park was the site of winter ice skating on the creek, sled riding, and "hunting for salamanders, frogs, boxer turtles, and caterpillars during the summer months."

A respondent who grew up in nearby Juniata Park had similar memories. Before the respondent became a teenager, the neighborhood was close-knit. "We had block parties, and neighbors helped each other," the respondent noted. By seventh grade, however, the neighborhood had deteriorated to the point where the respondent's family decided to move. "Sadly—and I joke with my parents about it—I left all of my friends to move to a different part of the Northeast, about twenty-five minutes away."

And in North Philadelphia, which does not enjoy a positive reputation, Cherrell grew up happily, within walking distance of Fairmount Park and the Philadelphia Zoo. "The neighborhood was a great place to grow up," she wrote. "All the kids on my block knew each other so we all played together." Bike rides around a nearby reservoir, and ad hoc basketball tournaments at a nearby playground filled the days. "I grew up in the best part of North Philadelphia, in my opinion," she said. The "real fun," said Cherrell, happened at night, when the kids had to stay near their homes. She and her friends played dodge ball, hide and seek, and tag, along with their own variation on "red light-green light."

Mark, now in his late fifties, grew up in Paterson, New Jersey, and attended East Side High School, made famous (years after he was there) in the movie *Stand By Me*, starring Morgan Freeman as Joe Clark, the school's domineering principal. Mark soon turned to the local YMCA—

"my 'melting pot' and the silently acknowledged 'safe zone' in the middle of what seemed like all the neighborhoods." It was there, he said, that "the interracial bonding and positive interactions took place." Mark continues to frequent the YMCA in nearby Montclair, New Jersey, an experience that has "enabled me to have peripheral and close friendships with a racially diverse group of people."

In Greenville, Texas, where John grew up in the late 1940s, there was much progress to be made. He lived on a street with other affluent families. But "go two blocks north and one would find the black section of town, completely segregated." Travel one block south, "and you were in a low-income white section of town." Greenville, he said, "was definitely a part of the Old South." A sign posted on Main Street read "Blackest Land, Whitest People."

A vacant lot that marked the boundary between white and African American sections of town served as the backdrop for games of sandlot baseball, John said. Tracks owned by the Southern Pacific railroad became the "fence" for the field. "The lot sloped a bit down as you faced out on our diamond and small rivulets cut holes in the ground, which made fielding tricky," he said. On the rough terrain played integrated teams. "This was a place where we white and black kids got up our own games," he recalled, "and this was in the late nineteen-forties."

Nick, an editor from suburban Philadelphia, described playing "a perfunctory method of hockey" in the driveway of his home in Riverdale, New Jersey, a working-class suburb of New York City. The driveway was forty feet wide, and its surface "was packed with real fine grey dust," Nick recalled. Most of the time, the driveway contained the truck driven by Nick's father for his job. But Nick and his closest friends, then in their early twenties, converted the driveway and two adjoining, connected garages into a hockey rink. A floodlight between the garages bathed night games in light. They strung the net—first made from wood, then an almost threadbare blanket—between the structures. "We had to make do—this was nineteen seventy-two," he said.

Using a Wiffle Ball as a puck, the game was played with two players per side—two on offense, two defending the goal. When there was snow on the ground, players could almost create the illusion that they were skating. A series of two-on-ones ensued; the defenseman tried to gain control of the ball and shoot it away from the net. If the ball reached the curb on the other side of the driveway, Nick said, it was a "clear"—ten "clears" meant a change of possession. The offense tried to score as many goals as possible before the defense accumulated the requisite number of clears.

"Pretty damn clever of me," said Nick of the game he helped to create, although he suspected that his creativity was lost on his neighbors. "Noticing a bunch of twenty-two-year-olds doing this, they probably wondered about our arrested development," he said.

Avoiding confrontations with angry neighbors tested the ingenuity of some respondents. John, a college professor from Delaware, played baseball nearly every day during the season in a vacant lot near his home in Fountain Springs, Pennsylvania. A woman—John referred to her as a "spinster" who was "legendary for her eccentric ways"—owned a house that was located to the third base side of home plate in what was foul territory. "Invariably, one foul ball would end up over the fence," John recalled.

Since John already knew the woman—he regularly mowed her lawn and helped her with errands—he "was the one always elected to knock on her door to retrieve the ball—a character-building experience to put it mildly." Another enticing target for John and his friends was the large picture window in the front of John's house. A teammate once came perilously close to shattering the window with a line drive. "My life literally flashed before my eyes, as I watched its arrow-like trajectory," John said.

Eric, who was a graduate student at a large private Pennsylvania university when he wrote and submitted his story, recalled that his house in Lancaster, Pennsylvania, where his parents still live, served as the "neighborhood playground." Outfitted with a driveway basketball hoop, the house "has a nice side yard that is perfect for football and Wiffle Ball," Eric said. Hockey was Eric's focus for a significant chunk of time as a teenager. Teaming up with a next door neighbor who shared his love for the game, they fashioned their own net and pooled their money to buy sticks and two complete sets of goalie equipment. "We used to fight over who got to play goalie," Eric said. Eric's dad resisted his son's pleas to install lights on the roof of their house so that he and his buddies could continue to play into the night. "He didn't want the neighbors to complain," Eric recalled. Even without the extra light, the games were a significant part of his adolescence.

Not everyone endeavored to curtail pick-up game activity. Ingrid, an English instructor, recalled that the folks from whom she and her husband bought their home had forbidden kids from playing on their lawn. Ingrid said she quickly changed that rule, encouraging neighborhood kids to play in the family's large backyard. "It's as big as a baseball field," she noted. "Soon, all boys on the street, and some from other streets, were in our backyard, regularly, from the time school let out until it was dark." Not the best recipe for maintaining a lawn, "but the yard was filled with children's voices and laughter."

Hallee, now in her early thirties, also painted a happy picture of play on the northeast Philadelphia block where she grew up. Parents concerned that cars moved too recklessly down the street asked the city to erect a "Deaf Children Playing" sign, even though not a single hearing impaired child lived on the street, Hallee recalled. "There were tons of kids on the street," she said, "many of whom became my elementary school pals and 'walking' companions." Hallee remembered a palpable "feeling of family" on the block. Folks "loved each other or hated each other," as so many families do from time to time. "We all knew each other by name, and our next door neighbor had a copy of our house key," she said. Sometimes, as Jennifer, a Delaware resident, explained, you often had to play with the folks you could find. In her neighborhood in the late 1960s, "parents didn't drive kids all over creation and you couldn't be too choosy about who you played with," she said. Contrast this willingness to play with whoever was available when one was outside with the popularity of arranged play dates.

Hallee's world at the time was contained and easily managed. After school, a snack, and finishing her homework, she would immediately head outside to meet her friends. Echoing Huizinga, Hallee said that her block was the "right place" to play "because we were all there—there were sidewalks to run on and trees to climb in. There were [electrical] wires and walls to throw balls at and fences to climb over," she said—all within shouting distance of her house, an important feature when an additional snack or a trip to the bathroom was necessary.

VENTURING FORTH

Other respondents would venture out into their neighborhoods and the surrounding areas in search of fun. Neither Noelle nor her friend Megan had a pool, so they developed a game they would come to call "find the sprinkler." During hot summer days, they would ride their bikes through their neighborhood in Wilkes-Barre, Pennsylvania, searching for sprinklers, which they would then ride through in order to stay cool. But their most important stop, Noelle said, was a train trestle located midway between her house and the tennis courts where she and Megan developed their tennis skills. The courts, while well kept, did not provide an environment conducive to honing their skills. "We could never get a good rally going," Noelle recalled. "Plus, neither one of us could serve."

After making sure that no cars were parked under the trestle, the games began. "One of us would hit the ball against the wall. If it came back to us, we hit it. If it made it to the other person's side, they would hit it against the wall." No score was kept, and the number of bounces taken by the ball after it struck the wall did not matter. Nor was there any "out" call. "We could hit the ball as many times as we wanted. It was the nicest tennis game around," Noelle said.

Twice during her story, Noelle reflected about the amount of imagination it took for her and Megan to develop their variation on tennis. "Who would have thought to use the big stone wall holding up the train track as a tennis backdrop," she asked. "Gosh, I was a lot more creative in those days."

A field belonging to a nursing home became the site for regular spring and summer touch football games, wrote a respondent from Cheltenham, a Philadelphia suburb. "There were trees all along the sides" of the field, "so we would play between them," he recalled. "There was one tree that always had branches the protruded out so far that we would always play in the same direction away from the tree."

Not all of these venues were as inviting as the trestle or even the field near the nursing home. Diann, who was raised in Bergen County, New Jersey, remembered playing rousing games of kick the can near trolley tracks, in a churchyard, and in a nearby cemetery. "At night the cemetery and the trolley tracks really creeped me out," she said. Mike, who grew up in a working class neighborhood in Chester, Pennsylvania, then well known for its industry (including the Baldwin Locomotive Works and the Scott Paper Company), remembered playing touch football on a section of a shipyard parking lot. The lot "was not our preferred choice, as there were often broken beer bottles and other assorted debris to contend with," he said. But since the shipyard workers preferred to park their cars closer to the street, this "makeshift field" was almost always available to Mike and his friends. Eventually, as they got older, they were able to "banish" a new cadre of young neighborhood kids to the lot and take over a well-appointed nearby playground, access to which had been denied to them by older kids who had moved out of the neighborhood.

A lack of players meant that Mike and his friends would "spend hours just passing and punting the football over the rows of swings on the other side of the playground, trying to develop passing arms and kicking legs." They would move their games to the surrounding streets if the playground was occupied, a choice made particularly tenuous by the number of blind intersections in the vicinity. The street was bordered on one side by a railroad embankment. "If you were running a pass pattern, you literally had to run into and across intersections where you really couldn't see a car coming from the embankment side until it was too late," Mike recalled. No one was ever struck by a car (there were a few close calls, Mike said), but an onlooker soon called police, who dispatched a patrol car "to keep us from turning the street into our stadium," Mike noted.

At the risk of veering off into my sometimes romanticized memories of pick-up games on Kensington Terrace, I identified with Mike's claim that avoiding oncoming cars and sidestepping shards of glass made this "one of the most enjoyable periods of my life." Families in Mike's neighborhood lacked the financial wherewithal to provide their kids with the latest toys or sporting equipment. "We were having such good times . . . that nobody seemed to notice or care that, by some standards, we were 'deprived,'" Mike said.

While my parents were for the most part able to keep my brother and me from feeling deprived (except when we desperately wanted, in my case, a new mitt or hockey stick, or in his, the latest Matchbox cars), the most meaningful use of our toys and equipment (the uses I remember most vividly, at least) came during the games that we created. To go completely off the romantic deep end for a moment, I cringe when I talk to a student who remembers buying Matchboxes as a child and keeping them as collectibles. My mind immediately flashes back to Richard and me building imaginary cities under our beds and constructing ramshackle ramps in our back yard in order to determine whether the small cars could be made to fly like the cars that did the stunt jumps in our favorite police shows.

For David, who grew up in a "blue-collar" Evansville, Indiana, neighborhood in the late 1960s, even harsh winters could not dampen the camaraderie that developed among him and his friends. "All the kids in my neighborhood lived outside as much as possible," he recalled. Kate, twenty-seven, said that it was her mother's limit on the amount of television she and her sister could watch (less than one hour per day) that at least partially fueled their desire to be outside. Their South Jersey neighborhood "was full of kids my age," she said, adding that she and her sister "instantly became friends with everyone."

Snowy winters brought out the creativity in Marion, from New Jersey, and her friends. She lived at the bottom of a hill in an area "someplace between rural [and] suburbia—no farms but people still had chickens and ducks." A neighbor "had a goat—a mean critter you wouldn't want to turn your back on," she recalled.

After-school typically meant sled riding, but the activity required extensive preparation. The hill was a dirt road traveled by residents on their way to and from work. To make it up the hill, they would install chains on their tires, and fling ashes on to the road to improve traction. "Well, ashes and sleigh riding don't mix," Marion recalled, "so the first order of business was to cover up all the ashes" with snow. "We were a very industrious bunch," she noted proudly. By the next morning, the ashes had again been spread on the road.

What struck me about Marion's description of this ritual was her comment that nobody from the neighborhood ever prevented her and her friends from restoring the road to riding condition, despite the fact that they had to go through their own traction ritual because of the kids. This brings us back to our discussion of expectations for how young people play. A number of respondents recalled that their parents expected them to go outside—and stay outside—to play from the time they came home from school until dinner was ready. John, a university professor from Mississippi, said that he expected his friends (and they him) to be outside, ready to play. Organized activities on his suburban block in the 1970s were the exception. "These games would go on until enough kids were called inside for dinner, and in season, might resume after," he said.

Not having to clear every action with your parents empowered many of the contributors. Richard, a history professor, grew up on "one of those narrow, in-between streets that dominate" parts of Philadelphia. Because the yards on his block were small—it was possible to tend them "with a watering can," Richard remembered—players had to make do with the street. The years immediately after World War II saw few cars make their way through the streets of Richard's neighborhood. Players occasionally had to make way for a horse-drawn milk wagon. The situation was made more tenuous "if the horse decided to relieve himself on third base or on the midfield stripe," Richard explained.

A CLOSED SOCIETY

Kids on Richard's block near 60th Street and Chester Avenue in southwest Philadelphia became quite territorial, often excluding potential players from even adjoining streets. "We were a closed society," he said. "If you didn't live on Belmar, you didn't play on Belmar."

Players on Belmar Terrace frequently ran into one snag: "the street had a slight downhill grade and ended with a sewer on each side." Errant throws quickly gathered speed and often ended up plunging into the sewer. Friendly public works employees would periodically pop the sewer grates to perform regular cleanings, and would return the lost balls to Richard and his friends. On Kensington Terrace, after much trial and error—and bruised fingers—we determined that even a heavy sewer grate could be lifted, after repeated wiggling, with a strategically placed hockey stick blade.

Richard's mother, however, was not pleased with her son's plan to recycle and reuse his quarry. Upon learning of his plan to wash a dozen recovered balls, "she shrieked, gave me a lesson on municipal sanitation, and threw me in the bath," Richard recalled. Undeterred, Richard and his friends arranged "more secretive" recovery operations.

Soon, Richard's pick-up game options would increase. His family moved to Ellwood City, Pennsylvania, a small town in western Pennsylvania, when he was eleven. "Lawns, empty lots, and even fields" supplanted narrow Belmar Terrace. With enough players, a genuine game of baseball could be played. Balls and strikes were even called—"if we could co-opt some unsuspecting onlooker." As Richard recalled, "We had the entire town to choose from; it was never a long walk (or bike ride) from one part of the town to the park. A few well-placed phone calls could produce a great game in less than an hour." Of particular significance for our journey is that it was Richard who placed the calls. He and his friends organized the games, no matter the venue.

Sometimes the cost borne by parents for encouraging extended play was a bit steep. Sandy, who grew up in South Africa, said that his mother "was a great one for wanting us to be outside on a nice day." Crushed flowers, broken windows, and trampled bushes were simply "the price she had to pay," for active children.

Jennifer, also from Delaware, received a surprise when she recently visited the field on which she played so many games of kickball as a child. "I was amazed at how small it was," she said—the same reaction that I had during my visit to Kensington Terrace with Sheila in 2001. How could this small space contain all of that activity, I wondered. Like the marathon baseball and street hockey games on Kensington Terrace, the games of kickball in which Jennifer participated were true neighborhood events. "It was the only time everyone in the neighborhood played together," Jennifer recalled. Of particular relevance for our journey, it was a world entirely of the kids' making. "No parent ever ventured to the kickball field," she said.

Frank, a college professor who grew up during the 1960s in a suburb of New York City, recalled a similar lack of parental involvement in the pick-up games he and his friends played in a nearby park. Independence—creating a world of one's own—was of the utmost importance, and it was that attribute that fueled the fondness expressed by so many of the respondents for the playgrounds and parks of their youth.

"The park was a great place," Frank said. "It was such a feeling of independence. We would just go down there, and we would just tell our parents, 'We're going down to the park' and that would be it. And then we wouldn't see them again all day." Frank's family vacationed once a year for a week, but the trips were too structured. "It was almost stifling," Frank said. Further, family vacations did not produce the kind of emotional reaction produced by heading to the park for a game of baseball or basketball. "When you got to the park, it was your environment. You could curse if you wanted to, you would smoke every once in a while, and that was like a freeing thing," he said.

Fortunately for Frank, the structure he experienced and resisted during family vacations did not typically carry over to days when games were planned. Dinner was typically served at around 6:45, when Frank's father returned home from work, so Frank had to be home (technically) at 6:30. "I look back and I thought, 'Well, I can't eat dinner with everybody—I just can't. I have to go and play," he recalled thinking. Frank expressed gratitude to his mother, who would serve his dinner at 6 p.m. so that he could get to the park on time. Unlike many of today's parents, who seem intent on accounting for every last second of their children's time, Frank's mother subtly encouraged his independence. "I think she realized it could be a lot worse. We could be smoking and not playing sports, or drinking, even though that wasn't an issue in those days," Frank contended.

Even when the activity was little more than hanging out, recalled Will, who grew up in southeast London in the early 1970s, he and his friends, caught up in a "strong sense of a small, street community of young people," never experienced fear. "Though there was some sense of danger, that you could get into fights or get chased by other kids who took a dislike to you," he said, "and a sense of risk about adults (strangers or friends of your family) who would tell you off or report you, we had no notion . . . of any real danger from adults." They simply didn't worry about child molesters or pedophiles, as our children are taught from a young age to do today. Their main concern was having their game of "playing out" being prematurely curtailed by the local park police—the "parkies," as Will called them.

Will would ask his parents if he could "play out" after dinner—it was a catchall description encompassing a range of activities engaged in on the streets of their neighborhood, including "petty vandalism, knocking on people's doors and running away [which Will and his friends called 'Knock Down Ginger'], being cheeky to passers-by, throwing things, or playing dares by running in front of cars"—not the stuff that made for a smooth relationship with his parents. For his parents, the term *playing out* had "a slightly common, working-class connotation," Will said. They viewed his activity as "wasteful and a bit delinquent." Playing in the park, however, was fine with them.

The fact that Frank's mother approved of his pick-up game play may have stemmed from how close Frank's family was to other Catholic families in their neighborhood. "I think she liked most of our friends, and she certainly knew their parents very well," Frank noted. It was at this point in our interview that Frank confirmed for me the importance of compiling stories for this book. After describing his mother's willingness to allow him to play, Frank offered an even more emphatic assessment of the value of pick-up games: "There was no better feeling, I think for me, than to go out on a hot, humid night and play basketball, and just get filthy, and then walk down to the Seven-Eleven or one of the delis, and get something to drink, and then just go home." To be clear, Frank did not disparage today's organized leagues; he simply sees making up your own games as a healthy complement to more structured play, if only so that the love for sports continues as one gets older. This ongoing love, Frank contends, will not be sustained by controlled involvement in a sport.

ACTS OF ACQUISITION

For some respondents, finding a place to play required a bold act of acquisition. John, who grew up in Garwood, New Jersey, remembered that he and a group of six friends "staked out" their field near a local elementary school. "The footprint of the site was perfect for what we needed," he said. The games on their list included stickball, soccer, a variation on Australian Rules football, and Wiffle Ball. "That schoolyard was our whole life for about ten years," John said. One of his friends, who now lives in another part of the state, conveyed the impression to his children that the schoolyard in Garwood was a pretty grand place—"like one of those modern sports complexes." When he brought his kids to the schoolyard for a visit, they were "shocked when they finally got to see the famous Washington School of their father's childhood," John recalled. One of his friend's sons remembered his dad's boast that the yard was home to numerous fields, but wasn't able to locate them. "I told him they were there—he just wasn't looking hard enough," John said. Clearly the Washington Elementary School yard was not "enchanted" enough, to use a term explored in the previous chapter, to catch his attention, having been exposed primarily to the packaged, structured, contained side of sports.

Even when a place offered little in the way of actual equipment, pick-up games continued. Tonia, in her mid-twenties, grew up in Mint Hill, North Carolina, "a rural town that offered the parking lot of Hardees to teenagers and a municipal park anchored down by broken, rusted swings to its children." Just as powerful as the memories shared by respondents is the fondness they still feel for their childhood hometowns. Tonia said she "cannot image the place as anything but the soft sleepy place that must be as still as it was when I made my escape to college." Tonia's comments suggests that there might have been a time—as there was for me in my early twenties—when she could not wait to leave her hometown. Where once the relative simplicity of experience was a catalyst for moving on, it now has a strong appeal.

Similarly, many respondents, as suggested by Dana's comments, recall a degree of closeness among residents of their hometowns that probably didn't exist. Maxine, who grew up in northeast Philadelphia during the 1960s and 1970s, explained that hers was "a neighborhood where people sat out front on their steps or patio chairs when the weather was nice and talked with each other." Parents would maintain a kind of benign surveillance of children besides their own. They would divulge your whereabouts, Maxine said, "if they saw you across the boulevard (Roosevelt Boulevard, one of Philadelphia's busiest roads, which runs right through the northeastern part of the city) or too far away from home or hanging out with certain people." Kids would get angry with the adults who ratted them out, but temporary consternation was the price for keeping track of the kids. Visiting the National Aquarium in Baltimore recently with my wife and son, we spotted a child tethered to his parents by a colorful, but short leash. My wife's look said it all: If that were me, I would have chewed through it by now. Sadly, the little girl seemed resigned to her fate.

The tendency to overestimate how much we knew our neighbors suggests, perhaps, that we're not all that happy with the isolation and hurriedness that seems to color so many lives. We might enjoy it if talking over the back fence came back into vogue, and kids traipsed all over everyone's yards.

CONCLUSIONS

So maybe this particular type of "schmoozing," to borrow Putnam's term, is still around. It is quite comforting to find that the desire to carve out "interludes" during our increasingly busy lives is strong—even more comforting to find it burning so strongly in young people, who, according to the experts, are so consumed by multiple activities that their imaginations have shriveled from lack of use. Despite being raised often in "cookie-cutter" developments and being shuttled from row to row, column to column on their spreadsheet schedules, children and young adults are still playing.

But before we call Barry Glassner and ask if he would include "the overscheduled child" in his next book of overblown and overstated societal fears, a small red flag: one gets the sense reading the stories of younger respondents that they indeed are not being allowed to roam around to find fun. They are content to play in their front yards and venture to the boundaries of their cul-de-sacs, but there is an implied reluctance in many of their stories to go further—to, as Joe Kuhl and I did in 1973, ride our bikes four towns over so that I could show him where I went to church. We didn't tell our parents about our journey, which covered about ten miles, round trip, and took about two hours. Were we scared? A little—we were twelve. Were our parents mad once we told them about the trip with a phone call (on a pay phone, no less) from the A&P at which my mom bought our groceries? A little. Did we get over our fear and our parents their anger? Yes.

But we learned that we could do it—on our own.

Many of the older respondents whose stories I've excerpted for this chapter wish this freedom for the young charges in their neighborhoods. A story from one of my older respondents (now seventy) uniquely underscores this point: as a college student, he got a job supervising an after-school program at a Milwaukee junior high school. Administrators wanted the boys, whom Barry (my respondent) described as "very tough," to "play nicely at such sports as basketball and soccer." Wanting none of either sport, the boys soon convinced Barry to allow them to play a particularly aggressive version of dodge ball. "After a while," Barry wrote, "I abandoned the official agenda and . . . looked the other way while the boys pummeled one another with the soccer ball. God, how they loved me for it."

4

No Purpose in Mind

When I try to describe for colleagues and members of my extended family that as kids, my friends and I used to play made-up games based on the television shows *Emergency* and *SWAT*, I get more than a few quizzical looks, not to mention a few thinly veiled expressions of concern for my sanity. *Emergency*, which aired on NBC in the mid-1970s, followed the exploits of two Los Angeles County paramedics and a group of doctors and nurses who worked in a nearby emergency room ("Rampart Base") that experienced destruction and mayhem in far more limited doses than viewers see these days on *ER*. Trivia fans might remember that among the cast members of *Emergency* was Bobby Troup (Dr. Joe Early), better known for writing the song "Route 66," made famous by Nat King Cole.

SWAT, which aired on ABC in 1975 and 1976, took viewers inside the lives of a fictional Special Weapons and Tactics unit based in what appeared to be a California city. Leading the squad was Lieutenant "Hondo" Harrelson, played by veteran television actor Steve Forrest. Robert Urich, who went on to star as private investigator Dan Tanna in *Vegas* and as the title character in *Spenser: For Hire,* played team member Jim Street in the series. The titles of a few episodes convey the show's rather aggressive flavor: "Death Score," "Deadly Tide (Parts 1 and 2)," and "Murder by Fire."

Long tree branches (rifles), our bikes (the vehicles), and the ability to climb fences and onto roofs were the only equipment needed for *SWAT*—that and a bootlegged (from the speaker on our television) copy of the *SWAT* theme, which was a big hit in 1976 for composer Barry DeVorzon and the short-lived disco band Rhythm Heritage. If we were out of earshot, humming the song, or even letting it play in our heads was enough. Not only did it propel the action, it may have also kept our minds off the fact that we were teenagers running around our neighborhood with tree branches doing our best to rescue imaginary hostages and get the best of imaginary enemies in imaginary gun battles—but this may be a bout of harsh reflection thirty years after the fact.

My family's ramshackle garage served as SWAT headquarters. My friends and I parked our bikes in a perfect row. I seem to recall that we even made sure that the front wheels were either facing the same direction, or that they were pointed forward—the faster to move out on calls. We received our calls to action from an inexhaustible supply of flimsy walkie-talkies, a beat-up old telephone that we kept in our "squad room," or the citizens band radio in my dad's station wagon (with the engine off, of course). We were pretty democratic about assigning "villain" and "hero" roles. I was tall enough (about 5-10 at the time) to step gingerly, rather than climb, over the five-foot-high fence that surrounded our back yard, which gave me a decent head start if I was playing one of the criminals.

The game based on *Emergency* was a bit more involved. First, we had to decide which of our bicycles was best suited to be Squad 51, occupied by the paramedics played by actors Randolph Mantooth (John Gage) and Kevin Tighe (Roy DeSoto). Although I'm pretty sure that riding any more than two people on my trusty Raleigh ten-speed would have been a surefire recipe for shattering injury, I'm more sure that we gave it at least one try. While the preparations for the game were complex, the object of *Emergency* was simple: one of us, usually Chris Young (who went on to become a member of the fire department's reserve in my hometown) would pretend he was the Los Angeles County dispatcher; his imitation of the Plectron, a three-tone buzzer signal that would send Squad 51 to a fictional accident, explosion, or other calamity, was also our cue to start. After he, or I, or my brother, relayed the location, we'd be off. I usually ended up on the back seat of his aging, creaky tandem bike, which served as the pumper. I guess "off" might be a bit optimistic. At the time, both Chris and I were proud members of the Paramedics club at Maplewood Junior High School (advised by a tall, eloquent science teacher named David Sanders), so I knew how to stock my fishing tackle box/medical kit: a little rubbing alcohol, a few bandages, and Band-Aids. Thanks to some filched twine, I was able to get the box to sit behind me on the bike—bungee cords would have made this so much easier.

My brother informed me in an e-mail just before Christmas 2006 that it was he who played Roy DeSoto, the character who typically drove Squad 51 in episodes of the show. "We would ride to the scene of the emergency making siren noises, truck brake noises," my brother recalled. "Somebody should have locked us up then." Once our duty was done, we'd return to the driveway, back our bikes in like they did with the vehicles on the show, and wait for the next call to come. "Quite a bit of imagination on our part, now that I think about it," Richard noted with some pride.

Accurately mimicking the actors and the dangerous scenarios was as important to us as running through the neighborhood—not a surprising assessment of the behavior of a half-dozen semi-creative adolescents, to be sure. It was thrilling to cut through backyards and hold up what passed for traffic in Maplewood. The Band-Aids and stolen hydrogen peroxide came in handy; on more than one occasion, we actually suffered minor injuries en route to one of our fictional calls, or while engaged in a make-believe hostage situation behind my garage.

As I write this, I'm struck by how clearly it all comes back to me, although, to be sure, there are some gaps in my memory. The details of the games are fuzzy, but I can, with a little assistance from my brother, get the plotlines and dialogue from the shows just right. What I share, though, with many of the respondents who contributed stories for the book is an almost unbridled enthusiasm for games both made up and learned. This enthusiasm came through in two ways; in the emotional intensity reflected in some of the responses ("Tons!" was one such response to the question "Did you make up any games?") and the depth of their descriptions, which typically came complete with a full breakdown of rules and regulations.

I also share my respondents' inability to put our collective fingers on why these games and forms of play were so important to us, or who taught them to us. Valerie, who grew up near Buffalo, surmised, "The older kids in the neighborhood (our babysitters) passed down some of the games. Sometimes when they were bored, they would play with us." Noted play theorist Brian Sutton-Smith would probably not be surprised; he argues that despite progress in identifying and elaborating the many ways in which we describe play, both individually and culturally, it may be that play is done for no reason at all, other than that it feels good. As Garry Chick (1998) noted, there is little evidence to support the three primary functions typically ascribed to play: physical, social, and cognitive training (9). The fact that we play less as adults than we did as children shoots a fairly large hole in the hypothesis that play prepares us for a future far more complicated than childhood, Chick contends. The idea that play stimulates a child's development is probably sound, Sutton-Smith claims (36), but not in all cases. As he notes, "play is seldom the only determinant of any of the important forms of learning that occur in young children" (41).

Many of the scholars and medical professionals whose work is cited in earlier chapters are unwilling, Sutton-Smith suggests, to discard or even look critically at the tendency to describe play while being faithful to a "rhetoric of progress." As a result, their attempts to quantify the impact of play may end up causing the skills supposedly learned during play to move from our fantasy worlds to everyday life. Sutton-Smith calls this the "tutorial stimulation effect" (40). Improved or mastered skills have as much, or more, to do with the bond formed between child and teacher than the attractiveness of a particular kind of play, Sutton-Smith argues. Further, parents who believe that play is beneficial are more likely to engage in play activities with their children (45).

For most of the twentieth century, Sutton-Smith writes, scholars, educators, and play theorists held fast to a "play ethos," which revolves around the assertion that play stimulates development. Writing in the late 1990s, Sutton-Smith acknowledged that he and his colleagues might have been a bit overzealous "in assuming many functions for play, and in assuming that these functions were essential" (42). Children do benefit from play, he notes. We play more complex games as we get older; we are able to do so thanks to the improvements to our social skills we picked up while playing simpler games as kids. However, this does not mean that we play primarily for its developmental benefits. Evidence accumulated thus far does not suggest a causal relationship, Sutton-Smith notes, even though the skills we pick up while playing and while acting socially and exercising our brains probably do "share and transfer back and forth" (42).

Play often becomes more about the goals of a therapist or a teacher than it does the happiness of a child. They may use play to control children, or to reinforce positive behavior. Adults also use play as a motivational tool. Children are more likely to behave as an adult wishes them to if a dose of time for play is used as an incentive. But the real joy seems to come when children are allowed to pursue their own goals, if indeed they have any.

Dr. Lenore Terr, a clinical professor of psychiatry at the University of California at San Francisco who has worked extensively with young victims of physical and sexual abuse, claims that play enables us to gain a sense of control over our worlds, an element missing, claims Jackson (2001) from computer games, which highlight "the randomness of life" (144). Merely surviving the frantic journey through a computer game is a victory, she notes. In older forms of play, notes Terr, we make up the rules, the language, and move the play toward an outcome (quoted in Marano 1999).

Sutton-Smith notes that some may develop skills through play that enable them to pursue careers as professional athletes (43). The desire to play, if not the mastery of play, also enables children to develop lasting friendships. It can also ease the tensions often felt by children on the playground, but Sutton-Smith acknowledges that it is not clear whether lessons learned on the playground stem from skills picked up while playing there. Complicating matters is the tendency of researchers to concentrate on a child's relationship with his or her parents rather than with other children (44).

But while there is much uncertainty about what is gained by play, one theory about play described by Sutton-Smith has considerable support: "Successful play experience increase the potential for continued happy playing." A thorough exploration of play may begin with the assertion that play does not have to have a function, or serve a purpose. How is it possible, as Jackson suggests, that we play to "prepare for the future in a world of constant flux" while also endeavoring to "live for the moment, having fun?" (145). Is play always a stop on the path to social, emotional, or even financial success? Isn't it enough that we enjoy it?

We may play creatively and engage others while doing so; we may be happy playing by ourselves; we may play in order only to keep the world out; we may play to satisfy an addictive craving—we may avoid play altogether, as Sutton-Smith suggests. Most important for our journey is the realization by scholars that the most valuable aspect of play may lie in an individual's reasons for playing. Most, if not all, of the respondents who shared their stories with me acknowledged that the impact of past play is still felt, but few explained that impact in terms of developmental gains. And in looking back at our games of *SWAT* and *Emergency*, it is difficult to argue that any of my abilities were honed by pretending that a thin roll of burlap strapping affixed haphazardly to the back of Chris Young's bike was in fact a fire hose.

Chick, like Sutton-Smith, believes that play prepares for more play, rather than for a career in business or a stint in the major leagues. Being "playful" is an attribute to be nurtured, he contends, if only because it makes for more fulfilling, and less violent, relationships (20) between significant others. But as with so many of the hypotheses we have explored thus far, little evidence exists to support Chick's claims.

EVERY CONCEIVABLE FASHION

Marc, who grew up in Paterson, New Jersey, during the late 1950s and early 1960s, recalled that he and his friends "constantly" played touch football "on one of the less busy streets behind my house." A respondent who grew up near Winnipeg, Manitoba, told about playing "hockey in every conceivable fashion." A third respondent, who was eighteen at the time he submitted his story, noted that he and his friends played "tons of games," which included "freeze tag," and, eventually, a game called "fireball," known in other parts of the country as "butt ball." Players line up against a long wall ("the bigger the wall, the better"). The thrower throws the ball—tennis balls used in elementary school gave way to racquetballs in middle school ("they sting much worse and leave generous welts," wrote the respondent)—so that it bounces off of the wall, and had to catch the rebound with one hand.

"Break any of these rules, and you must immediately run as fast as you can away from the ball to touch the wall before someone picks it up and throws it at you," recalled the respondent, who grew up in Pittsburgh's Squirrel Hill neighborhood. Attempts to marry advanced tag and "cops and robbers" were foiled by the harsh asphalt playing surface.

Then there's "Ledgey," the game played by Glynn and his friends. An India rubber ball was thrown at a four-foot sloped ledge "that ran the circumference" of a nearby school. "Standing fifteen to twenty feet away, one threw for the ledge and tried to loft the trajectory of the bounce high in the air," he recalled. The opposing player tried to catch the ball; if successful, he or she would throw—"a bit like jai alai in that respect." But if the player missed, the India ball—"notorious for the energy they had"—would roll about a city block away from the players, thanks to the slope in the adjoining playground. No score was kept, Glynn recalled, and there were few rules, little arguing among players, and no parental involvement. The only required skill was being able to hit the ledge. Players developed pinpoint aim. "Oh the joy of hearing the 'thunk' of that ball and watching it arc lazily in the sky in the cool shade of that red brick building," Glynn recalled fondly.

A number of respondents described year-round quasi-schedules of games. "I played every possible game you could think of," wrote a male respondent who grew up in Indianapolis, "depending on who was around to play with and what they wanted to play." He enthusiastically detailed playing "every ball game possible, every hide and seek and chase and tag and run and jump and fall and roll game." The respondent, now in his forties, particularly loved "playing follow the leader in the woods or riding our bikes exploring everywhere possible."

Bikes were not only used for exploring. In the mid-1970s, my friends and I went through a prolonged Evel Knievel phase, as the noted daredevil jumped his motorcycle over the fountains at Caesar's Palace in Las Vegas, stacks of cars and buses, and eventually made his failed try to traverse the Snake River Canyon in a rocket-propelled motorbike. We'd lay a row of garbage cans on their sides, or pile up old tires to give us something to jump. Ramps were constructed out of flattened appliance boxes or sheets of plywood supported by everything from milk boxes to old pieces of furniture.

Successful jumps were rare, as we could never really get up enough speed to make it over the assembled detritus. Using a ten-speed bike should have been out of the question, but we did make awkward jump attempts with our Raleigh and Sears models. Raleigh's "Chopper" model, manufactured to look like Peter Fonda's chopper in *Easy Rider,* looked like it was up to the task, but its disproportionately small front tire made for some very rough pseudo-landings and bent front forks and rims. Eventually, the public's interest—and ours—in Evel faded, and we moved on to more intricate, but only slightly less dangerous, chase-oriented games. John, who grew up in central New Jersey in the 1970s, remembered creating a bicycle-driven version of polo. "I don't remember that we made the goals from," he said, "but we would use Wiffle Ball bats to hit a drugstore kickball from our bikes." Neighbors would come to watch their games, but eventually excessive wear and tear to their bikes caused John and his friends to give up the game.

One respondent who grew up on Long Island in the 1970s went us one better. In winter, he and his friends would search for a large, icy parking lot—perfect for performing acrobatic tricks on their bicycles. In one, "you could get off your bike and slide alongside it for distance," he recalled. Skilled riders—the respondent among them—developed a risky "dismount" that would likely send many of today's parents into paroxysms of shock and disbelief. "I would ride the bike full speed and then dismount the bike for the slide and then to a back flip over the hedge landing flat on my back on the cement on the other side of the bushes," the respondent, now nearly fifty, recalled. And why? "All because I could (I think my kids are smarter than that!)."

And if a recent survey by the National Sporting Goods Association (NSGA) is an accurate barometer of childhood activities, his kids—most kids—are also spending significantly less time on their bikes (Cauchon 2005). Nearly 70 percent of kids between the ages of seven and eleven rode a bike at least six times a year, the NSGA found. By 2005, the percentage had dropped to 47 percent. In addition, nearly three million fewer bicycles were sold in 2004 (9.8 million) than in 2000 (12.4 million), according to *Bicycle Industry and Retailer News.* While a comment from Marc Sani, the magazine's publisher is at least a little self-serving, it does highlight the resonance of the pick-up games narrative: "Bikes used to be empowering for children. My parents didn't care where I went as long as I was home for supper." Today, argues Sani, "parents are afraid to let kids out at night."

While I am certain that kids still manage to sneak out of their homes and play outside after dark, the respondents who offered enthusiastic recollections of pick-up game experiences support Sani's comment. Describing a game called "first base," a respondent from the Juniata Park section of Philadelphia, noted proudly, "Yes, we played in the street," as if thumbing their noses at overprotective parents. "It was like *Wayne's World*. We would just move when a car came and would shout, 'game ON' once the car was out of sight."

David, who grew up in the 1950s in Massachusetts said he "lived to play" Rolly-Polly on his dead end street in the "flats" of Norwood, Massachusetts. Games typically got off to a frantic start. "Someone would yell first ups; there would be a brief dispute over who actually yelled first, and then all but the batter would scurry for a position on the black top," David recalled.

Once everyone had found a spot, the batter would toss the ball in the air and hit it "as hard as possible to the waiting fielders." The batter then laid the bat down in the street, perpendicular to his or her feet. If a fielder caught the ball on the fly, he or she took over as the batter. Fielders who cleanly collected ground balls would stop in their tracks, then turn and roll the ball toward the bat. "If the ball struck the bat and did not pop up so it could be caught by the batter, the fielder would become the batter," David said. However, if the ball did pop up off of the bat, and the batter caught it on the fly, the batter kept hitting.

A respondent from Durham, North Carolina, who grew up in the early 1960s offered two slight variations on Rolly-Polly. If a player caught the ball and was close to the bat in the estimation of the other players, "the bat would be placed vertically," the respondent noted, to make it harder to hit. If the player was even closer to the bat, the hitter was allowed to yell "peanuts!" and then begin bouncing the ball in front of the bat in an attempt to disrupt the opponent's concentration.

The primary appeal of Rolly-Polly, David said, was that any number of players could play. Further, "baseball gloves were permitted, but not required," he said. The only downside was the tendency of players to break windows in nearby houses. The game's simplicity, along with the fact nobody won or lost, would probably make it unattractive to today's children, David speculates, children who have most likely been raised by parents well acquainted with the "play as progress" theme outlined by Sutton-Smith. There was no real point to the game, nothing to be gained. It was fun.

Mary grew up in Clifton, New Jersey, during the 1960s. She and her friends concocted several interesting variations on hopscotch, one of which included an element today's parents might not be pleased with. Using chalk, they would draw a large rectangle, with a number of smaller squares around it. They wrote something different in each square—"cigarettes," for example, or "cars." Players tossed a rock, and then hopped to the square in which it landed. "Then you had to name as many of that category as you could. When you stopped, the next person had to do better than that," Mary recalled. "It was tough. Imagine naming cigarettes! But we all could, because most of the moms and dads smoked them."

Dana, whom we met in chapter 3, described four-on-four baseball games played with her siblings and "and a random mix of boys and girls" from their neighborhood in Whippany, New Jersey. Players had to bring "whatever aluminum bats and baseballs they could find in their house(s)." After breaking some windows, Dana recalled, her mother "demoted us to tennis balls." Players compiled statistics for each game, in the hopes of winning the coveted Most Valuable Player (MVP) or the equally coveted title of Home Run Derby champion. "The trophy was nothing more than a paper covered Tic-Tac box or coffee can decorated for the specified *[sic]* honor," Dana recalled. "However, to us these boxes were bragging rights for a summer of hard work."

The impromptu spirit lives on. Rebecca, also from Massachusetts, grew up in a neighborhood whose demographic makeup was not conducive to playing pick-up games. "My two sisters and I were alone in our neighborhood of mainly elderly folks," she recalled. Her current neighborhood is home to many young children who regularly play pick-up games, despite their involvement in a range of activities. "Two or three [hockey] nets are on the side of road," Rebecca said, ready for games of street hockey. Her neighbors constructed a "goalie" from plywood and placed it in front of the net. The goalie is decked out in "hybrid hockey/lacrosse gear" and features a wig. "It freaks people out when they drive [by]," Rebecca noted.

A recent snowstorm provided Rebecca and her husband with an opportunity to rediscover the revelry of play. After completing the mandatory shoveling, they took part in a snowball fight with their children. Rebecca recalled: "It was terrific fun, practicing surprise tactics and laughing with them." They took playful control of the situation, as Terr might note. "We created rules, like no aiming at heads, children under five, cars or houses." Further, "children under five were allowed clear shots at bigger kids (and Mom and Dad, and teams could switch members." Much of the battle saw the kids pitted against Rebecca and her husband, "but sometimes we had some allies."

INNOCENT CRUELTY

Not all of the games described by respondents involve what experts might describe as pro-social behavior. A respondent who grew up in Maracaibo, Venezuela, recalled a game called "Quemado," or "burned." Three boxes were drawn on a concrete basketball court—two small rectangles, one larger square. Most of the students would station themselves in the larger box, with a student and the teacher occupying the smaller boxes. They would try to hit the students in the larger box with a volleyball. "We basically had to avoid it and remain inside the big box as much as we could," the respondent said. If you caught the thrown ball before it hit the floor, you could take a shot at teacher or student. "If they were hit, they had to join us in the big box," the respondent noted.

However, if a student inside the box was hit, they joined the student and teacher in the rectangles, changed allegiances, and tried to hit the kids in the bigger box. A group of students would station themselves in the larger box.

Tonia and her friends, who grew up in North Carolina, played "catching bats." Tonia acknowledged that the game was "old and violent and shameful," but it was also "my favorite thing to do in the evening." Players stuffed old socks with rocks. The socks couldn't be too shabby. "We hunted around for good sized stones and made our rock weapons," she recalled.

The optimal time for catching bats was about nine p.m. on most summer evenings, when "the sky was musty pink." Carrying their weapons, Tonia and her friends headed down a path that took them through a cornfield near her house. Players dashed after the bats, full socks in hand. At times the bats got so close, Tonia recalled, "you could make out the vampire teeth." Players would then throw their socks, which the bats would chase. As the players caught up to the bats, which by now were hovering near the socks, "one of us would take sock and swing at the bat as it hovered and flew back upward," Tonia said. The object of the game was simple: "Whoever knocked down the most bats won."

The winning player would at most have killed two or three bats. Players at the time didn't see any cruelty in their actions. "Bats were nuisances and we saw them as our enemy," Tonia said. With the passage of time, however, this perception has changed. "Detached from my hometown, I cannot comprehend this innocent cruelty. Just as I see Mint Hill as this sweet and humble haven, I have sentimentalized all the nights when we were so bored and sick and tired of small town life so that eventually we departed the south," Tonia stressed.

Tonia is certainly not the only respondent to paint a rosier or more compelling picture of what in the glare of recent educational theorizing seem like pointless activities. But her embellishment suggests that play may produce in us the ability to look back fondly, to sentimentalize, which, I would argue, enables some of us to draw lessons, even temporary ones, from either the activities themselves or the effort it took to put them together. If indeed children and adolescents today are not as inclined as their parents and grandparents were to play pick-up games, they also may be less able to rediscover the power of the pointless act.

In an e-mail sent a day after her original story, Tonia seemed to drop the circumspection and revert to sentimentality: "I realized how much I want to go back to being a kid and feeling stimulation from such a simple game," she wrote. The small town she and her friends so desperately wanted to flee was now an oasis of simplicity to be cherished. "In many ways, I wish that I had not been exposed to things outside the town so that I felt I was missing out. Today, I still feel like a bumpkin in the big city, but I have also realized that compared to my peers from large cities, I am never as bored or unsatisfied," Tonia said.

Her closing comment brings us back to the "expected path" of participation in sports—in anything, for that matter. "I understand the sanctity of silence, the outdoors, and doing 'nothing,'" she wrote. Tonia's thoughts echo Sutton-Smith's suggestion that the primary reason we play is so that we can become better players, and play some more.

Some of the games described by respondents might seem strange to kids moving from one lesson or sport to the next. Robyn, who grew up in Brooklyn, in the late 1970s and early 1980s, remembered playing "skelly," which sounds from her description like a scaled-down version of shuffleboard: "You melted crayons or candles into bottle caps to give them weight," Robyn said. Next, a grid was drawn on the pavement. Players tried to knock each others' caps into certain boxes in order to score. "Boys played more than girls," Robyn recalled, "but a few erstwhile tomboys were just as good as any guy."

A thirty-four-year-old woman from Cherry Hill, a suburb of Philadelphia, and her friends played something called "Light as a Feather/Stiff as a Board." Usually played during sleepovers, the game began when one person would lie on the ground. The rest of the players would pretend that the person had died. They would then make up a fictional story about her life. "The lead girl," the respondent recalled, "would sit at the girl's head and massage her temples while leading the chant. We would all chant 'light as a feather, stiff as a board.'" The assembled players would then use two fingers to lift the person off the ground. "It always worked. We never dropped anyone," the respondent recalled.

Looking back at the game, one element eluded the respondent. "I still don't know how we lifted people with just a couple of fingers. It's really funny that we trusted each other so much." More than one respondent recalled that neighbors and the police in their hometowns put up with, if not condoned, their activities. The respondent who described games of "Light as a Feather/Stiff as a Board" said with certainty that "no one ever yelled at us to get out the bushes or leave their flowers alone. No one every told us to keep off the grass."

A man in his early fifties who grew up in England also experienced tolerance from neighbors for games of "kick the can" that often took him and his friends through nearby gardens. "The strange thing is that . . . we actually didn't need to creep in through the hedge; the police officers coming in and out of their own building always spoke to us, never sent us away and tolerated us using the grounds of the house as our own private play space." The respondent speculated that he and his friends would not be able to get away with these acts today, and most certainly not with "the version of tree-climbing 'Tarzan Tag' we invented." Jesse, who grew up in a suburb of Philadelphia, was not as lucky in his encounters with police, although no one was ever arrested for playing "manhunt" near his elementary school. "The police would sometimes come after us to tell us that we were being 'shady,' and that we couldn't play on private property," he said.

Marian, whose sleighriding exploits we explored in chapter 3, remembered playing "cops and robbers" with friends. "Sometimes you found a stick that really looked like a Colt Forty-Five—a real treasure to save," she said. As night fell, "one mother after another could be heard calling her offspring home." Marian twice underlined the next sentence in her story for emphasis: "We weren't interfered with—but we were watched and I remember feeling safe."

Ken, a college writing instructor, said that the games concocted by him and his friends "seemed endless and timeless," an assertion reinforced by the fact that none of the players wore watches. "If it was close to dinner, individuals peeled off from the game as their inner clocks went off," Ken recalled. As with many of the respondents, Ken and his friends did not keep detailed records of their games—"just long-term remembrances of the special accomplishment, sane (a spectacular catch) or insane (throw it over the moving cars and catch it)," a game we replicated on Kensington Terrace. A respondent now in his mid-twenties remembered playing games of "guns" (where the object was to find a clip to a toy gun which had been hidden in someone's yard) "well into the night, some days for more than six hours."

The romantic in all of us would readily agree with the respondent from England. The media tell us that the world is a more dangerous place than it was when he grew up in the 1960s, and most certainly since the September 11 attacks—even though the frequency of violent crime has decreased. Overly cautious (in my eyes, anyway) parents have perhaps limited the number of opportunities for pick-up games play. More is going on, however, in what amounts to a battle of competing narrative strands. As we discussed in chapter 2, many activities that once were primarily the province of pick-up players have morphed into organized (and sometimes televised) activities. In addition, fewer children have the time available to play, immersed as they are in a sometimes frighteningly wide array of activities. We are expected, encouraged, to undertake any activity with gusto, drive, focus, leaving little mental space to do something just because we like it.

Jeff, now in his early twenties, grew up in Bensalem, a small city outside of Philadelphia. His involvement in Little League "was always full of thrills," achieved with many of his friends from St. Ephrem's Elementary School. "Ruining white baseball pants with hook slides in the red clay infields or dives in the grass in the outfields provided for some amazing moments," he said. But he was able to fully express his passion for baseball through pick-up games organized with his friend, Mike.

One game, arranged on a nearby soccer field, became another, which became another. "Soon, the summer took a pattern: Mike would call, I'd say yes, kids would show up, my mom would have the barbecue fired," Jeff recalled. If it hadn't been for the coming school year, "I would have never left that summer. Girls, music, money, and college didn't even enter our minds. Not even the major leagues were discussed." Over two-liter bottles of Coke, Jeff and his friends spent far more time discussing previous on-field exploits and choosing new teams.

Even though Jeff and his friends reassembled the following summer, they never "found the same glory," he said. "High school ball and Babe Ruth leagues dominated in the following years and the bliss of just playing took a backseat." John, a college professor from Delaware, also mourned the lost opportunities to play. "None of these organized sports," he said, "gave me as much pleasure as the pick-up games in the vacant lot," a sentiment shared by many respondents.

But during the winter before high school graduation, Jeff and his friends took "drastic steps" to put off having to separate: they took up roller hockey, fueled by a newfound devotion to the Philadelphia Flyers.

Games were played in St. Ephrem's parking lot. Jeff spent "nearly every dime I had" on goalie equipment he still owns. "The game took on new significance when one of us would bring a new stick or skates," he recalled. "Everyone felt the need to show off."

The coming of winter did not put an end to the games. "Snow could be removed by all of us pitching in with shovels," Jeff said. Games played at night actually became more popular, despite the cold. Jeff surmises that the devotion to these games stemmed from the players' desire "to keep friendships and youth alive." Soon, however, the lure of high school sports, and, eventually, the move into adulthood finally ended these games.

A comment by Jeff about trying to rekindle these friendships is particularly instructive. "We all still try to find time together but the memories of the shared times from before are often the only subjects to talk about," he said. Eisenberg might argue that these friendships only truly mattered, or mattered most, when the games were underway. Rarely did the personal lives of the players spill out on to the field, whether it was a parking lot or a soccer field serving as a baseball diamond. But will our children have experiences to get overly romantic about?

Albert, who grew up in South Philadelphia and has since gone on to become a noted writer and popular college writing instructor, took a firmly pragmatic view of the relationships formed during pick-up games. "It was a social activity, like a party to us," he said. "We'd do the party thing and go our separate ways." The ability to compartmentalize relationships made them more cordial, Albert believes. "We didn't see those guys beyond those games," he said. Athletic competition, whether it's organized or not, causes players to forget against whom they're competing. Games also caused the temporary "obliteration of friendships" that were usually reestablished once the game had ended.

For John, who attended eight different schools in four states, pick-up games served an equally pragmatic purpose. "Learning to find a way into the social circle of the neighborhood was a necessity for me," he said. "Pick-up games were a great way to 'break the ice' and become a known quantity, and start to sew the seeds of friendship." To this day, part of the preparation for relocating includes "questions about local basketball and volleyball opportunities," he said.

John overcame the fact that he was always among the smaller players trying to get picked for games in Tempe, Arizona, where he spent five years. "I was a warm body and could even up the numbers," he recalled. "That was enough to get me on the court." He soon learned that a lack of attention from fellow players could be turned into a strategy. "I became a shrewd and imaginative passer (and hope I still am) so that once I'd played with a group and fed the ball to the shooters, I had no trouble being picked the next time there was a game." He was no longer the last one chosen to play. Soon, he was exhibiting his shooting skills. "I hit my share [of shots] and enjoyed showing that passing was not my only basketball skill," he said proudly.

Albert had more personal goals for his participation in pick-up games, he said in a 2006 interview. He wanted to make his older brother proud. "He was the *one*," Albert said, "except when we were on opposite teams." More important, perhaps, was the desire shared by Albert and the other players to rise to prominent positions on what Albert called the neighborhood's "physical hierarchy." Participating in sports "positioned you on that assumed scale of toughness," he said. Not surprisingly, tougher was better. Albert "willingly, happily" ran at full speed most of the time and "embraced contact," often diving for loose balls—all to compensate for a lack of height and ability. "I walked it off when I was younger," he said. Today, however, Albert surmises that it was "too great a price" to pay for the infrequent compliments from other players.

Games of "Buck-Buck" took on a decidedly more aggressive flavor than those brought to life by Bill Cosby in his standup act and in the 1970s animated series *Fat Albert and the Cosby Kids*. The anchor would reach around and hold a telephone pole. A second player would hunch over and grab the anchor around the waist. Other team members would follow suit. Members of the team would then take turns running toward, and then jumping on the "bridge" created by the other team, in the hopes of causing it to collapse.

Dirty players would curl their knees under their bodies in flight and aim for the lower back of an opposing player, Albert said, hoping to jar the kidneys. Players would also focus their efforts on the skinniest person in the bridge. "You tried to hit the weakest link," Albert said. Players who made up the bridge tried to withstand the weight added by each jumper. The team trying to dismantle the bridge wanted to get their jumpers up as far as possible, in order to maximize the number of players on the bridge. Lighter players would jump first; heavier players last. The winning team supported the most players.

For Albert, all of this was about "establishing your maleness." He remembered Martin, a young boy raised by his aunts who endured "all kinds of ridicule" for his allegedly effeminate behavior by the area's so-called tough guys, who were being egged on, said Albert, to beat Martin up. Instead, Martin "kicked the shit" out of one of them, and was never bothered again. As a matter of fact, he was admired for taking out a bully.

For a while, Albert said, the desire to compete and to be noticed "started to go away." But, he said, the attraction of competition is strong, even for someone in his early fifties; so strong that the mileage racked up on the body is forgotten. After moving back to the city after college, Albert began playing football on a local schoolyard. It is "exactly what it sounds like: you played in a schoolyard, usually from fence to fence or fence to wall." Albert had played touch football with a group of regulars in Roosevelt Park, near the sports complex in South Philadelphia. A stint in an organized tackle football league ended when Albert tore ligaments in his ankle during the second game of the season.

Albert recalled recent pick-up games of basketball with young men twenty years his junior. He still relishes collision. He repeatedly goes into the key to contest rebounds. After a particularly bruising collision during a recent game, the player who knocked Albert to the court looked at him and said, "Looks pretty crowded in there, don't it?"—referring to the space under the basket. Albert interpreted the young man's comments this way: "get the fuck out of there . . . you don't belong in there." But back under the basket he went, just as Michael Jordan did when he returned to basketball after retiring, just as Pete Rose did when he gambled on baseball. "They still need it," Albert said. They still need the competition.

For some respondents, pick-up games were a bit more democratic, but often no less violent than what Albert described. Nick, whose description of "driveway hockey" appeared in the previous chapter, recalled that games of baseball and football played on the scruffy grass field near his house in New Jersey were "egalitarian" affairs, but mostly to ensure that the games got off the ground. Players from the neighborhood ranged in age from eight to fourteen—a few were older. Rules were adjusted so that the younger players, and those with marginal skill, could compete. "We'd slow pitch, to let them hit it," Nick recalled. Balls and strikes were not called. A twenty-four-year-old respondent who grew up in a rural community about thirty miles from Philadelphia, said that she and her friends would gather to play the organized sports in which they were all involved, but would alter the rules to facilitate play. "For instance, when we got together to play field hockey, we would have only maybe six people, so we would designate two areas for goals and then just try to shoot and make goals," she said. But as Albert suggested, there was at times a distinct pecking order, even for unorganized games. John remembered that he and his friends would "draft" the younger siblings of regular players to fill out teams for games of basketball. "It was a great honor for one of them to be picked to play with us," he said proudly. Regular pick-up game players often looked up to the kids who played in leagues, said Frank, another respondent. "We believed (wrongly) that we were not in the possession of the necessary skills that were required to be a "Little League" athlete," he said.

In Atlanta, positions of authority were key elements in games of foursquare played by a respondent. "Rules were always done away with and invented depending on who was in the king's (number 4) square," the respondent said. The queen occupied the number 3 square; the number 1 and 2 squares "were about equivalent." The king decided when a player could hold the ball or would receive a do-over. "The idea was to stay king for as long as possible," the respondent noted.

Games of two-hand touch football were, to use Nick's word, "vicious," and would end when a defensive player would deliver a particularly brutal two-handed slap or slam to an opposing player. When Nick and his friends were "feeling rugged," they would opt to play tackle football—a risky endeavor on a frozen field littered with rocks. Older kids would tackle younger kids with relish, Nick said. Quarterbacks would hand the ball off to the skinniest kids, and then "watch the panic on their faces" as an older player "crushed them to the turf." Passers had to get the ball off "before they got slaughtered."

Sometimes the injuries were self-inflicted. John recounted extremely competitive games of Wiffle Ball played on a field whose foul territory behind third base was directly adjacent to a street. "I remember once almost getting wiped out by a driver when I ran into the street; scared the daylights out of the driver, but I made the play," he said. Later, John would break his nose in an on-field collision. "To this day, people can't believe that I broke my nose playing Wiffle Ball."

Even friendly games of touch football, like those described by Chris, a college student in his early twenties, had penalties for what the group deemed over the top behavior. "There was plenty of sensationalism and showboating," Chris said of his Downingtown, Pennsylvania-based teammates, "but it was all in good humor." Besides, "if anyone got out of line, they'd get hit extra hard [the] next time they had the ball," he said.

RUN THE BASES BACKWARD

Like many of the pick-up game stories sent to me by respondents, Frank's revolved around the ingenuity of the players who had to deal with poor or nonexistent equipment, or the lack of enough players. It was almost always impossible to find eighteen kids to field two teams for baseball for games at a local Babe Ruth field. "But there were probably eight of us, or ten, or six, that would play this game . . ." Frank said. "We would pitch to ourselves," keep score in the dirt, and only hit toward left field. One final rule: "we would run the bases backward."

The game was a model of efficiency. A first baseman wasn't needed, since the third baseman was now the first baseman. Two players would be stationed in the infield, two in the outfield, Frank said. The game chewed up large chunks of time—from nine a.m. until noon (break for lunch), and then again from one till five p.m. "On vacations, especially spring vacation, in the early days, we would just all go down to the park, and play baseball, what we considered to be baseball."

When asked if they had ever given the game a name, Frank described how he tried to teach it to the players on the Little League team he coaches today. "I'd call it crazy baseball, because you'd run the bases backwards," he said. What amazed Frank was that his players could not hit the ball unless it was pitched to them. "It took them half the season to learn how to throw the ball up by yourself and hit it on your own," he said describing what players and coaches call a "fungo." Being able to hit fungoes was a valued skill on Kensington Terrace. But instead of throwing the ball up with my left hand, grabbing the bat, and hitting it, I somehow learned to toss the ball with my right hand, and get the bat back in time to grab it and swing.

No doubt Frank's players would have difficulty figuring out some of the games described by respondents. Growing up near Winnipeg, one respondent and his friends invented a game called "Nets," a freewheeling variation on soccer. Five players were designated as goalies, and stood in front of one section of a baseball backstop. The remaining players—up to a dozen in some cases—would then kick several soccer balls at them.

"The game was constant," the respondent recalled. "You would shoot as soon as you could get control of a free ball, and at any net you wanted." Shots came at the goalies from numerous angles. After allowing five goals, a goalie was permitted to become a shooter. Despite the chaotic nature of the game, players worked to ensure continuity. "Games would continue over into the next recess, yet we always seemed to remember who was in net when the bell had rung and how many goals they had against them," the respondent noted.

The ability to adapt to sometimes tricky conditions and, more important, to the number of available players, is reflected in many stories. A male respondent who grew up in Michigan but now lives in Kenya frequently plays soccer with a group of local kids who spend a lot of time at the beach. Players are required to play barefoot, and there is no goalie, only a player who "hangs back and plays defense." What happens if the ball finds its way into the ocean? Is it out of bounds? No. "It is still in play and contestable, even if you have to swim to get it," the respondent stressed. "In that event, you can use your hands to retrieve the ball until you can play with the feet."

When Jody, now in her twenties, played kickball with other kids in her "small and quaint" hometown that resembled what viewers saw on *Leave it to Beaver* (a dated popular culture reference for such a young person, by the way), the players "had various strategies to get three outs, such as if the ball was soft, you threw and hit the person" to get them out. If one team clearly was more formidable than the other, "we would create a run limit per inning," she said. For Chris's regular fall Saturday football games, played on a nearby soccer field, "the faces changed from week to week depending on who had to work or go away." On-field happenings and results did not tarnish the players' relationships. "There were no personal grudges and even the most social outcasts in school were welcome if they made it out to the field," Chris said.

At times, as in Samantha's case, the rules would be unique to the group. Frisbee contests with her friends usually turned into games of "full-contact Frisbee, football, volleyball, and rugby," she recalled. All of the games came only with the rules she and her friends, fellow college undergraduates, made up. As a result, "we'd throw the ball or Frisbee around, tackle each other, and throw it to someone else. All in all, we were incredibly unorganized."

Sometimes it took a blatant act of defiance to keep the game going. John, who masterminded the games of "bike polo" discussed earlier, recalled that games of stickball played with friends would often end prematurely if enough balls were fouled off and on to the roof of the school behind home plate. "It was an 'out' if that happened, but that didn't help us if it was our last ball," he said almost ruefully. About once a year, the school's janitor would appear on the roof and toss down all of the lost balls—"about two hundred balls of all types." But John and his friends often grew impatient with the janitor. "Every once in a while we couldn't wait and would borrow our friend's father's extension ladder and go up there ourselves—fortunately we were never caught," he recalled.

Cherrell, who grew up in North Philadelphia near Fairmount Park, played a game called "graduation" on her front steps with her friends, a variation on the standard "eenie-meenie-miney-mo" games many of us played as kids. Players who were designated the "teacher" would put their hands behind their backs and conceal a pebble in one of them. "One by one, the teacher would ask them what hand the pebble was in," Cherrell recalled. "If they got it right, they took a step down to the next grade." Players started on the top step, which represented first grade. "If they got it wrong they would stay in their current grade." The game went on until a player reached the last step, fifth grade, and was deemed ready to graduate.

The graduates of Cherrell's school might have found themselves prepared for an occupation-oriented game described by the respondent from North Carolina. Now in her fifties and living in Virginia, she and her friends back in Durham would play a game they called "bum-bum-bum." She was fairly certain that she would be the only respondent to describe the game.

Players would line up on two sides behind lines. "One group would stay behind the line while other group would decide on an occupation they would pantomime," the respondent recalled. The "occupation" group would then begin marching and chanting "bum, bum, bum—here we come—all the way from Washington." The group whose players stayed behind their line asked their occupation, to which the occupation group would reply "most any old thing." The "behind the line" group would then direct their opponents to "get to work."

In a scene that recalls games of "charades," members of the occupation group would then "act out the occupation," the respondent recalled. If an opponent successfully identified the occupation, the other team would scatter and try to run back to safety behind their line. "If a player was caught," noted the respondent, "she would then join the other team. The object would be to capture all players." Players who took part in "Crusaders," a game created by Rachel and her friends in their suburban Chicago neighborhood, had a similar goal. "Kids were either Saracens or Moors," she recalled. "We'd go through the forest preserves (big big nature parks at the edges of the suburbs) and we'd pick each other off with bows and arrows," which were actually "water guns, spitballs, or berries." The armored (with homemade armor) troops would actually march to the "holylands (the tennis courts outside of the forest preserve)," she said.

A respondent who grew up in Ohio was a key architect of fort-based games in her neighborhood that revolved around "creating a network of paths and tunnels in the undergrowth along the steep bank of the lake." The most significant thrill derived from playing "was watching grownups walk by and listening to them knowing they couldn't see us (or catch us, as our father tried but failed to do)." He was simply too large to make his way through the tunnels, she said.

For some, the goal of pick-up play was to get closer to a potential significant other. A twenty-three-year-old respondent who grew up in a "deteriorating steel town in western Pennsylvania, remembered a version of hide and seek called "Spot" played with a flashlight. "It was more of a chance to kiss your girlfriend/boyfriend," he said. Games of kickball gave Jennifer, who grew up and still lives in Delaware, the chance to get closer to the object of her affection, Johnny, and the "equally handsome and athletic" Jack. "The teams would fight over who got to have them," Jennifer recalled. "Then there was my unathletic friend Joanne and I—the teams would fight over not having us," she said.

Jennifer and Joanne developed a lasting friendship as time went on. They learned profanity while sitting in "jail"—part of a game called "relivio" that began with everyone in contact with a base until someone shouted "relivio!" Players would scatter, trying not to get caught by someone from the other team. "If they caught you, they had to say 'caught, caught, caught, one, two, three, no breaks, no breaks' while touching you," Jennifer recalled. Players could escape "jail" only when a teammate managed to get to the jail and touch you. If the chasing team jailed all of their opponents, they won. Eventually, Joanne moved to a neighborhood where the hot game was "flashlight tag"—like "relivio," a game described with relish by many respondents. "We were older, early teens, and this made an even better excuse for being around the guys," she said.

CONCLUSIONS

It is probably inaccurate to say that most parents would not allow their children to participate in the controlled mayhem that passes for a number of the games described by respondents. Even I cringe (and retrospectively ache a little) when I read about repeatedly skinned knees, kidney-busting "buck buck" jumps and kids climbing to the roof of a large building to retrieve stickballs. I am confident that there are parents out there who believe that a little controlled mayhem is a good thing, an antidote, perhaps, to the fatigue that must come for at least some kids after a week's worth of immersion in structured activities.

Still, at the same time it is invigorating to read about these exploits, positive and negative, conformist and destructive. Doing so brings us back to what has become the book's main theme: the attractiveness of being left alone to make up your own fun, as corny as that sounds. The stories shared by respondents are vivid support for Sutton-Smith's contention that the main benefit to be gained by play is the ability to play again, perhaps with more skill. The stories described and analyzed here almost always appear to be told in a kind of experiential vacuum, as if the rest of the world—then and now—has decamped from inside our heads. The joy and giddiness—even the anguish and disgust expressed by a few respondents—were (and in some cases, still are) derived while operating with almost complete independence.

For me, the most powerful irony in these stories is that many of these folks are the ones who are now imploring their children to get more involved in activities that take them away from home. One friend of mine goes so far as to insist that his daughter and son, who already have calendars teeming with activities, call up their friends on weekend nights, so that they won't be left out of the adolescent social scene. Just staying inside and watching TV or reading won't cut it.

None of this should be taken to mean that children and adolescents have stopped using their imaginations or have lost the ability to make up games. Stories contributed by younger respondents suggest that their imaginations are alive and well, if tempered somewhat by fits of pragmatism. What they seek to gain from play (described in detail in a later chapter) echoes the "rhetoric of progress" described (and criticized) by Sutton-Smith. They focus on the skills that they have added to their arsenals thanks to pick-up games, rather than more abstract lessons about getting along with others or embracing the diverse makeup of the group with whom you play.

And as for us older folks? Our imaginations are still functioning; although we have to try harder to really break through the structure, get down on our butts and knees, and play. We're not doomed to a half-life (or quarter-life) marked by endless homogeneity and a diminished capacity to think on our feet. One of the great joys of my life is making up games with my seven-year-old son—the Wiffle Ball rolling through the mailing tube game, the roll the Hot Wheels down the ramp made of cardboard boxes game, the "Daddy Tunnel" game (where he proudly and happily rides his scooter underneath the tunnel created by my legs), and so on.

It simply takes more effort to get our minds to the point that we can do this. At times I don't want to—I huff and sigh sometimes when my son rolls one of his cars my way. We have to mentally dodge the commitments and the structure and the fear in order to even for a little while rediscover the state of mind described eloquently by Frank, who fondly remembers long ago pick-up baseball games: "In our minds we were Nolan Ryan, Don Sutton, Duke Snider, or even Babe Ruth. We always got the critical ninth inning bases loaded two out up by one full count strike, which of course won the World Series. The friendships that developed on those mythical play sessions still bring a warm feeling to my heart and fullness to my soul." All of the opportunities to play organized sports, put together, he said, "pale in comparison to our own personalized field of dreams."

The key words in that sentence? "Our own."

5

Out of Necessity

My parents bought me a full set of catcher's gear when I was eleven or twelve. Catcher was the first position I played in Little League, but my coach soon moved me to first base once it became clear that my body was in business for itself as far as height was concerned—I was 5-10 by the time I reached sixth grade. It took real effort to curl my body up behind the plate—that and I was always afraid a foul ball would take off a finger or two. I enjoyed playing first base, but yearned (and still yearn) to play third base or the outfield, where I thought I could finally deploy those game-saving diving catches I practiced for hours every day after school in my backyard, or at the park.

But what to do with my catcher's gear? We first put it to use on Kensington Terrace for times when we'd try to "trick out" (as the young folks say) our games of baseball or "running bases." Then again, there was typically no home plate to block, and very few of our players slid on the concrete—although now and then, in long pants, it was tried. The solution? We turned it into goalie gear. This was before the folks that manufactured Mylec street hockey equipment came out with plastic and foam street hockey goalie pads—or at least it was before we knew about or could afford them. Until then, our designated goalie, usually Chris Taylor, would strap on the abbreviated gear, typically over the tattered, stained denim jacket he wore—even in the dead of winter—and go "between the pipes," which, if you have been following the story so far, were made of scrap wood. A baseball mitt became a catching glove; another became the goalie's "blocker"—an awkward fit, since Chris used that hand to also hold the goalie stick.

For a while, the lack of "real" goalie pads was not a handicap for Chris. True, he couldn't close the "five hole" (the space between the goalie's legs) with any consistency, but he could dash out from the net and slide, often twenty or thirty feet, into the legs of the shooter, thanks to the already slick but by now worn down plastic covering of the leg pads. Eventually, my parents would front me the money for a set of Mylec pads, so my old catcher's gear stayed with Chris for most of our adolescent winters. That is, until one day when we decided to move our bulky net to the backyard of Russell French, our best player. Russell had the hair of former Canadiens great Guy LaFleur; it always seemed to flutter behind him, as if he were going full speed on the Montreal Forum ice. With the net in place a few feet behind the back wall of Russell's house, we commenced practice.

Russell lined up a few hockey balls and pucks about twenty-five feet from Chris, and began to blast slap shots at him. As I recall, Russell either took it easy on the first few shots, or Chris showed no fear—probably a little bit of both. But having little luck scoring on Chris, by now sliding around with exaggerated confidence on the leg/goalie pads, Russell grew angry and mustered an NHL-sized windup for his next shot.

The windup alone—Russell's right hand was so high above his head that he could have placed the star on an average size Christmas tree—caused Chris to panic. You could see his eyes widen dramatically through the cage of my catcher's mask. Guessing that the puck would do significant damage regardless of where it hit him, he made a quick, but ultimately costly decision: he jumped out of the way.

A number of professional athletes have commented that significant moments in their careers—the game-winning goal in a Stanley Cup final; a walk-off homerun; a long field goal to win the Super Bowl—seem to move in slow motion. Such was the case with Russell's shot on Chris—at least for the lone onlooker: me. In planning his jump, Chris neglected to factor in the possibility that Russell would try to place the puck somewhere along the cross bar—the "top shelf," for those of you who don't follow hockey. Russell followed his plan to perfection; the puck headed briskly for the top left corner of the net. It was interrupted by Chris Taylor's crotch—the only part of his body (aside from his forearms) not protected by my catcher's gear. It was, to borrow a sportswriter's cliché, a one in a million shot.

And it caused Chris to run at least ten laps around Russell's house, screaming in pain. I remember thinking that it was a hell of a way for Russell and me to confirm the Doppler Effect we had learned about in science class.

My memories of Maplewood hockey games seem to end with Chris's pained dash around Russell's house.

AGENTS OF MATERIALISM

More than one person this past Christmas related to me stories of how they received just one or two toys for Christmas each year when they were kids, either because of financial constraints or a conscious decision made by their parents. They were happy with what they received, and hinted that their children could or should be just as happy with one or two toys. A few of these comments came from parents still relatively fresh from their Christmas buying excursions, so their thoughts may have been tinged by fatigue and their internalized terror at the thought of receiving the next round of credit card bills. In these comments, though, I sensed that behind their wistfulness they suspected they could never maneuver their children to accept their Spartan version of happiness. The horse was clearly out of the barn; I should note, however, that it probably was when my colleagues and I were children, too.

Perhaps children are by now quite comfortably ensconced in their roles as "agents of materialism," as described by Robert Wuthnow (quoted in Schor 1998, 87). They, as much as their parents, bring the values of consumerism into the family, Juliet Schor argues. As Jackson notes, kids form their first important relationships with products, not people. Adults teach them to equate consumption with happiness, and to consider the benefits of brand loyalty at a strikingly early age.

Parents, not wanting to disappoint their children, and often burdened by guilt for working too many hours, allow them to have extensive input into a wide range of buying decisions. Children have almost encyclopedic knowledge of products and marketing tactics, concoct extremely lengthy Christmas lists that they can recite upon request, and fixate on, rather than develop affection for, particular toys—a fixation at least partially driven by redundant news media coverage of each year's new "hot toy" and the tendency of reporters to treat the annual "Black Friday" dash to the malls as the most newsworthy event of Thanksgiving week, no matter what else is happening in the world.

I have also noticed that in our family the act of receiving gifts under the Christmas tree, while still marvelous and magical, is also exhausting because of the frantic passing and unwrapping of presents. Shouts and squeals of joy are punctuated by the sound of stuffing wrapping paper in trash bags. Like many couples, my wife and I have discussed enacting spending limits, on presents for each other and for our son, but we seem to blow right by these limits every year. We want to make sure that we get what the other wants. We want to make each other happy, to show our deep and abiding love for each other.

This urgency carries over and accelerates when celebrating Christmas with our extended family. Divvying up and unwrapping presents unfolds like backstage during a set change at a Broadway play—presents are tossed, wrapping seems to hang in the air; genuine, affectionate, and perfunctory "thank yous" are shouted across the room. The true test becomes making sure we don't leave any of our newfound goodies behind. We dutifully collect our gifts and almost mindlessly place them in the back of our small SUV for the ride back home. Even weeks after Christmas, it is difficult to engage—for our son as well as for us—with all of the presents we have received. Maybe, as Kathy Jackson (2001) argues, we're just too busy to allow undefined, unplanned experiences to break through the organization we value so highly.

Finally, there's the observation made by many parents, including those we count as friends, that children, especially infants and toddlers, like the toys they receive, but they *love* (and play extensively with) the boxes and wrapping in which they were packaged. If pressed, though, most of these folks (and this includes my wife and me) would shudder at the thought of giving their children only boxes and bows to play with. We would be flouting the parenting standards set and policed by ever-present educational experts, and the publishers of parenting books and magazines. Yet we sit and marvel at how much, in our son's case, these boxes and mailing tubes engage him and trigger his imagination—just as much, if not more, than the scores of toys he has received.

I share these examples to underscore how strong my memories of my catcher's gear still are. I also have vivid memories of my red, white, and blue Rawlings baseball glove (with Brooks Robinson's autograph stamped in the palm), and my first set of drums, given to me by my parents after much whining (by me, not them) when I was sixteen. Gifts such as these just mean more when you are a child. John, a college professor from Texas, still has the thirty-one-ounce J. C. Hawthorne bat he bought at Sears, autographed by former single-season home run king Roger Maris.

Maybe the push to consume has indeed changed the nature of receiving and enjoying gifts. In my travels, I have encountered children who treat the toys as a formality, as the expected completion of their well-thought-out lists to Santa. Thankfully, perhaps, children still derive great joy from getting presents, although the level of their excitement can be frightening—at least that's my tentative conclusion after seeing a hotly debated (on YouTube anyway) commercial for BMW a few Christmases back. It features a little boy, probably about seven or eight, consumed with joy at receiving a toy robot. With ferocity, he rips the wrapping paper from the box. Realizing what it is, he screams, and screams again. He rubs the box on the floor. He caresses the box lovingly, and shows it to a parent, who is videotaping the scene. The little boy is oblivious to his sister, who at first simply observes his paroxysms of delight. As the boy thrusts his hand triumphantly in the air four or five times, she joins in the celebration.

You may be thinking (quite correctly): isn't that what parents want—for their children to be happy with their gifts? Scientists have not just recently discovered that kids like to obliterate wrapping paper to get to a gift, or observed their feelings of disappointment at not getting what they want. But the degree of joy, indifference, or disappointment is troubling, at least to me, as if the only road to happiness for children goes through Consumptionland. Again, not a new thought, but the increased intensity in our gift-giving rituals leaves a simple smile and a hug in the dust. The challenge has been met, the checklist of gifts completed.

It seems reasonable to suggest that the aggressive marketing (and just as aggressive consumption) of toys has made the act of creating one's own toys seem quaint, even radical. We have been led to believe that we can educate our children only if we consume the products specially designed for that purpose, even though at least some of them, like the celebrated series of *Baby Einstein* videos and DVDs do not, despite their makers' claims, make the children who watch them learn more, or learn faster, than children who don't watch them. There simply are not many opportunities for children who want to craft their own toys. Even the impressive range of "Make Your Own Toys" Web sites I found during a recent Internet search had a distinct air of structure to them. I felt compelled to follow the instructions carefully laid out by what must be very careful people if I was to have any fun.

Necessity—and a little imagination and mimicry of NHL goalies—led us to strap my catcher's gear onto Chris. The product we needed at the time at first did not exist. Once it did come on the market, it was out of our financial reach. So we made do—mini-McGyvers before our time. But "making do" is not acceptable consumer behavior in a market-obsessed society. I can't imagine what today's marketing gurus would think of one respondent's decision to turn his father's crutches into hockey sticks. "Fortunately, my father had a couple of sets of crutches so we could play two-on-two or three-on-three since the goalie used a shovel," the respondent said.

Perhaps the famed media critic Neil Postman offers a partial explanation. He argues that in our push to prematurely nudge children toward adulthood, we have brought about the end of a more innocent conception of play. "What we have here," he wrote, "is the emergence of the idea that play is not to be done for the sake of doing it but for some external purpose, such as renown, money, physical conditioning, upward mobility, national pride. For adults, play is serious business" (1994, 131).

So serious, I believe, that we have marginalized the act of scrounging for materials and cobbling together various and sundry devices in order to play. For play to be legitimate, it must emerge from contact with consumer goods, and through participation in organized activities. This line of reasoning runs counter to at least one respondent's experience. Growing up in Dodge City, Kansas, in the 1930s, his typical path to playing was "to find an object and create a game around that object." Kids today tread a much different path, acquiring, sometimes aggressively, the object first. The games are largely planned for them. In his celebrated book, *Everything Bad is Good for You*, Steven Johnson (2006) writes, "The virtues of playing baseball and making friends on the playground and communing with nature are universally agreed on" (210). He makes this assertion to defend his extensive exploration of the purported benefits of partaking in today's complex world of popular culture.

Johnson contends, for example, that the narrative structures of television programs such as *24* and *The West Wing* are more layered and intricate than shows from the past, and require more mental energy to comprehend. Viewers must be able to make sense of the deep social networks found in these shows. Complex moral questions are posed; avid viewers develop a high level of intimacy with characters.

Similarly, love of video games is slowly enhancing, rather than eating away, as some parents claim, the brains of young people. Johnson calls this phenomenon the "sleeper curve." A game's multiple threads and complex instructions cause an increase in a player's "tolerance for planned ambiguity" (79). As players partake, their ability to recognize abstractions and to recognize patterns improves, Johnson claims (57). These games, it seems, are helping to train another generation of expert multitaskers. Instead of focusing on one stimulus, person, or happening at a time, we show off our penchant for "continuous partial attention" (61). This helps to hone one's skill for "analyzing a complex system with multiple interacting variables changing over time" (207).

Young consumers of media, claims Johnson, are more willing to collaborate with peers on projects that take them outside the dominant media corporations—hence, the fascination with YouTube and MySpace. They embrace their self-anointed status as creators of media product. They are much less passive than my generation, which apparently spent the 1970s swallowed up by our ugly Sears couches, staring blankly at hopelessly simplistic, unchallenging television shows such as

Laverne and Shirley. One paradox in Johnson's thesis troubles me: how did dumbed-down content like *Laverne and Shirley* also manage to talk down to us? (74).

I don't disagree with Johnson when he argues that children and adolescents can hone their intellectual abilities by playing today's sophisticated (at least compared to Space Invaders and Frogger, which I played) video games. But the benefits he cites are also the ones desired by today's teachers, school administrators, and college admissions folks. The skills purportedly developed by young video game denizens are precisely the skills deemed valuable today by educators who set policy, educators whose agenda is largely set by the members of the business community who have been given an excessive amount of input into that policy.

As a colleague of mine would say, the games hone a "different kind of smart," one that will enable them to flourish on a standardized test. I take issue with Johnson's claim that today's television fare is more complex than shows from the past. For every *Laverne and Shirley* on the air back in the 1970s, we had the rich dialogue and thoughtful character development of shows such as *Barney Miller* and *M*A*S*H.* We saw *All in the Family* open a national dialogue on social issues, and Mary Tyler Moore cut a new path for young women who wanted to be told that their desire for a career was not abnormal—come to think of it, we could use another show like Moore's today.

The intricacy and multiple narrative strands that propel shows such as *24* are impressive, but they actually detract from the layered relationships that Johnson describes. Sure, it takes more mental energy to handle the frenetic dialogue in an episode of *The West Wing* than it did to understand that J. R. Ewing was out to hurt or cheat every character in *Dallas,* but we learn very little about what makes the characters tick. The creator of the successful *Law and Order* television franchise has acknowledged that he purposely downplays character background and relationships in favor of plots that are "ripped from the headlines." Perhaps that approach is more satisfying for young viewers who tap a staggeringly wide array of sources for their news, but it means that we see fewer original ideas. We are better equipped to handle more ideas, to be sure.

A DIFFERENT KIND OF SMART

As for Johnson's claim that consumers of popular culture have parlayed their increased intelligence into actual production of media content, I would argue that what's at work is actually an illusion of participation.

Extensive "fan fictions" based on a television show or character, and the thousands of videos uploaded to YouTube, are often quite original and compelling, but they are typically based on content largely provided by the big media companies that all of these new skills purportedly make it so easy for us to thumb our creative noses at. We do more work, but exercise less imagination, in the creation of these new media products. Not only are we using their technology, we are using their formats, and, to a rather troubling degree, their content, to propel our ideas.

Which, believe it or not, brings us back to pick-up games. While the media content of the time was often the catalyst for our games, we adapted them to suit our temperaments and ambitions. Content provided a framework for our games of *Emergency*, for example. While I have not studied the behavior of video game players, I will offer one tentative hypothesis: more may be expected of players, but more is also given them in the first place. We filled in the blanks in our games primarily because the content left a lot of blanks for us to fill.

An active imagination is not a prerequisite for success at *Grand Theft Auto*. These games are complex, multilayered, and require players to follow intricate instructions and remember a great deal of information, but they don't call on players to create. Even when we were riding our bikes around the vicinity of Kensington Terrace on our way to our next rescue scene, we were making it up as we went along. We didn't really achieve a whole lot, other than piquing the concern and curiosity of our neighbors, but we used the television show, or the batting stance or slap shot copied from a player, as a starting point for more involved play.

One final point: Johnson's brilliantly written book underscores the significance of ideology. Sonja Foss (1996) defines ideology as "a pattern or set of ideas, assumptions, beliefs, values, or interpretations of the world by which a culture or group operates" (291). Educators and politicians have spent much time and money informing us that their ideas about education are the right ones. They have been shockingly successful, largely because their efforts touch on something relevant to most of us: educating our children. But we've come to believe that this way of approaching the challenges of educating our children is, for now at least, the most effective one; other views about how best to educate our children have been pushed to the margins of our national discourse. Despite its flaws, No Child Left Behind is now our dominant approach to education—it has become *hegemonic*. To sustain its dominance, supporters must continually downplay and criticize alternative views and approaches. This includes the less structured, more imagination-based experiences described by my respondents.

Recalling pick-up games experiences in Venezuela, one respondent said emphatically that "those have been without exception the best days of my life." As hard as it might be for today's overstimulated young people to believe, these experiences were significant. "I cannot understand how today's youth say that we did not have any fun because we did not have Nintendo, Xbox, even a computer in our room," the respondent contended. Contrast that with the fact that many of the younger folks who contributed their experiences for this book found the tools they needed for pick-up games in stores. Equipment was, with a few exceptions, readily available for them to use. At least one respondent, a young man who grew up in Ontario, Canada, was less than kind about the game preparations of his elders: "We did the old-school 'place two random objects on the ground about six feet apart' thing to make a net for street hockey," he wrote, rather dismissively.

This is not to say that younger respondents were covetous or unwilling to share the game-related fruits of their consumption. Jody, now in her mid-twenties, remembered that the responsibility for providing equipment was shared by the families in her neighborhood. "One family had hockey players so they had the nets," she said. "One family played baseball and soccer so they had the equipment for those games. Each kid was able to contribute to the pick-up games that were played." Brett, now in his early twenties, recalled how his grandfather cut the bottom out of a basket that previously held apples and "nailed it to the front of his house so that I could shoot hoops" during visits. Ironically, the folks who lived across the street from Brett's grandfather "had a real basketball hoop, but they spent more time shooting at my 'basket' than at their own."

It is possible, then, that we have come perilously close to extinguishing the sense of wonder in our children by co-opting their imaginations. All of the possible answers to all of their possible questions have been arrayed before them; no longer do they turn to adults for guidance, even if they want to. They are nearly unable to follow the natural rhythm of the seasons as a guide for when to play. "As kids," noted a respondent from Ontario, "we played certain games according to season, but nothing was written and it was a kind of osmosis that bestirred in us to start the acceptable activity for the appropriate time of year." When the time came to play, the rules were "simply known," he said. Older kids did not teach younger kids the rules—"one simply absorbed the concepts."

Their curiosity, claims Postman, in some cases gives way to cynicism (90). They are not allowed to make good on the primary functions for children of toys, suggested by Jackson (2001, 145): "to construct who we are, appreciate our personal and collective pasts, prepare for the future in a world of constant flux, and live for the moment, having fun."

Perhaps these scholars overstate this development. But to be sure, the desire to pretend, to exercise a bit of control over one's own world, has been redirected by well-meaning educators who see little value, or who have been taught to see little value, in leaving a child alone to play, or to do nothing. There must be a point to their play, a goal, something produced at the end. Their urgency flies in the face of the theories, discussed in earlier chapters, that revolve around the notion that the only goal of play should be to make more play possible. Kids thrive when allowed to make up their own rules, arrange and deploy their toys, and turn a box into a castle if a castle isn't available—or just play with it as a box.

NEVER BOUGHT BUT ALWAYS FOUND

Many of the respondents who shared their stories focused on improvisation when describing the equipment they used to play pick-up games. Nicky remembered creating membership cards for a Sports Club formed by her and some friends. The process involved "cutting poster board, gluing on printed words, and putting them in the plastic cases you can buy for valuable sports cards," she said. Marian and her friends called their organizations "one-day clubs"; members seemed interested only in the imaginative initiation rites they came up with. "Once we melted crayons in the sun, and put a different color on each finger," she recalled.

Respondents were proud that they—not their parents, or a neighbor, or a coach—had figured out how to play with little or no formal equipment. A seventy-five-year-old respondent who grew up in South Philadelphia remembered having to fashion footballs in order to play. "We would roll some old newspapers into an oblong ball and tie it with string." The makeshift ball was "heavy enough to be thrown and kicked," he said.

When not playing football, he and his friends would nail roller skates to the bottom of a crate, and then affix a plank to the front of the crate, in order to make a scooter. "The best part of all these games," he said, "is that we never had any adults to tell us how to play them and it didn't cost any money." Albert, who grew up in a housing project in South Philadelphia, remembered that the "closest I ever got to a uniform was a number written on a tee shirt with a crayon." His act of improvisation "did not make my mother too happy, since she had to wash it."

Growing up in a Chicago suburb, one respondent recalled that besides his family's basket and hoop, "everything else was improvised. Chalk for boundary lines, scraps of plywood for bases, and brooms for hockey." Not that improvisation came without cost, however. The respondent and his friends found that repairing numerous Wiffle Balls and Wiffle bats with duct tape increased their weight substantially. "Getting nailed with a line drive began to hurt," he said.

Avoiding pain was the goal of a respondent from Winnipeg, Canada, and friends. "We invented a ball-hockey ball that was simply wadded up newspaper wrapped in masking tape," the respondent said. "It wasn't as painful as one of those orange hockey balls when it hit you, and didn't bounce like a tennis ball would, so you could control it on your stick." Product comparisons were important. "Electric taped fastballs hurt," recalled a respondent who grew up in northern New Jersey. However, "the other masking tape was softer but didn't last as long." A respondent who grew up in Jackson, Michigan, played through the pain, as we expect professional athletes to do. "For a while, I wore a plastic motorcycle helmet because I got beaned in the head with a puck," he recalled. But he refused to bolster his equipment to prevent injury. "Some kids would stuff their clothes with pillows for pads, but not me," he noted proudly.

Sometimes the pain was unintentionally inflicted. Mike recalled a pair of "steel toed ripple-sole shoes" he wore during pick-up football games. "I can't remember why I got the steel toed version," he wrote, "but I do remember that I always wanted ripple-sole shoes, having had a previous pair that let me run like the wind."

The effect of the shoes on Mike's on-field performance was immediate. In one game—"the kind one normally has only in fantasies"—Mike caught a half-dozen touchdown passes. He was considerably taller than the other players, but he attributes his success to "outrunning the defenders with their puny sneakers." Mike added two long field goals and a few punts that traveled more than fifty yards to his stat sheet that day.

The opposing players continued to be oblivious to the construction of Mike's shoes "until the point that someone on the other team tried to stomp on my kicking foot and just about broke his heel" on the fortified footwear. The injury caused the players to adopt a rule requiring players to wear only "regular" shoes, which, Mike recalled, meant "Converse high-top sneakers." Without the steel toed shoes, Mike went back to having "okay, but not great, performances."

Lack of official equipment caused many respondents to alter the rules of the games—often for self-preservation. "We never had any batting helmets or catcher's equipment," wrote a respondent from my hometown, Maplewood, New Jersey. "But we were not so stupid to realize that we could kill ourselves if we permitted fast pitching and catchers." Instead, pitchers would softly lob the ball toward the hitter. "The batter would throw it back after it bounced off the backstop," the respondent recalled.

Parents of several respondents were willing, if not always active, participants in the orchestration of pick-up games. A respondent who grew up in Ohio remembered that her mother, "an avid seamstress," allowed her and her friends to make use of an "attic full of fabrics" in order to play dress-up. Older siblings of friends were also a key source of equipment, as Rachel, who was raised in a Chicago suburb during the 1970s, recalled. "The big big Catholic and Italian families usually had a ton of equipment in the garage left behind by the older kids who had gone off to college," she said. When "official" equipment found its way into the hands of a respondent, it was treated with respect. A male respondent in his late forties from Evansville, Indiana, noted that the key to success in pick-up basketball "was to have a decent leather basketball that I guarded with my life."

The descriptions of equipment suggest that pick-up game participants were not that concerned with getting the trappings just right. It was rare for the respondent from Maplewood to see a new baseball during a game. "Every now and then a kid would save his allowance to get one or a kid would get a new one for his birthday. Often we would use baseballs that were taped up." Taping up baseballs preserved them for future games of "street ball," wrote a respondent who grew up in Paterson, New Jersey, during the 1950s. Yet another respondent looked at the lack of equipment through the eyes of a psychologist: "[W]e would use the resources that we were given as boundaries." A gate was out of bounds; garbage cans were used as goalposts; magazines strapped to shins with rope became goalie pads; empty flour sacks, nearby cars, or "squashed refuse" became bases.

"The supplies usually never bought but found," wrote one respondent who grew up in the Sunset Park section of Brooklyn, New York. At times, all that it took was a flat stone and chalk for a game of hopscotch, as Marion recalled. Sometimes the items lasted only as long as the game; sometimes they were reused repeatedly. Marion and her friends preferred roller skates that clamped on to the bottom of one's shoes to "shoe skates." Not only was their size adjustable, "one pair lasted for years if you didn't leave them in the rain." Sometimes the supplies were, well, odiferous, as in the case of Bill, who, along with his friends, would deploy dried cow dung as bases on the farms near Shippensburg, Pennsylvania. "We scrounged materials from everywhere, but mostly from nearby construction sites," said a respondent who grew up in Wayne, Pennsylvania, a Philadelphia suburb. It was easy for the respondent from Winnipeg to create a steady supply of ball-hockey balls because "old newspaper and masking tape were cheap and abundant."

On Kensington Terrace, mitts that were not in use became bases, and crushed soda cans were used when hockey pucks were scarce—or if we ran out of money to buy new ones. If we feeling particularly feisty, we would collect and crush a few dozen empty soda cans and then pelt whoever was playing goalie with them. I sensed a similar level of feistiness in a story by a male respondent in his mid-thirties who grew up in rural southern Pennsylvania. "We fashioned weapons and armor (some play, some real) from whatever we could find on local farms and what we could get away with in shop class," he said.

The respondent and his friends would fan out into a nearby patch of woods "with swords made from the legs of lawn chairs hammered flat and bottles of A-Treat cherry soda we would pretend was wine." The respondent and his friends were guided on one adventure by a map created by the group "in the style of J. R. R. Tolkien." At least one respondent's adventure involved devising a primitive method of propulsion. Not satisfied with modifying a swing set to enable her and her friends to "jump off the neighbors' fence and grab the top bar" in order to "fly out in to the yard," a respondent from Columbus, Ohio, remembered rigging up makeshift cannons that fired tennis balls, thanks to the judicious use of rubbing alcohol as fuel.

STUDIES IN SELF-REGULATION

The story told by a respondent from Lynbrook, Long Island, brought back memories of my standing at the gas stove in our house, heating a plastic Mylec replacement hockey stick blade, trying to enhance the curve of the blade set by the manufacturer. Like the respondent, I had either shattered or splintered the blade on my wooden hockey stick (I used wooden sticks even when playing street hockey), and was now feeling forced to use a plastic blade. Force, and lots of it, was what it took to jam the blade on the cleanly sawn end of the stick. The respondent from Lynbrook now shares his inventive spirit with his kids. They now use "a plastic racing car with an airfoil as a football kicking tee."

Recalling my attempts at equipment modification caused me to wonder if parents today would be as sanguine as mine were upon seeing their son at the stove, gas at full tilt, trying to alter the shape of a piece of wood. If the tendency to overprotect our children didn't kick in, the desire to make sure that our young athlete had the best equipment, modified by true professionals, would. We seem to have ceded resourcefulness in this area to the folks who have created the "expected path" to participating in sports discussed in a previous chapter.

John's father was particularly resourceful during John's self-described "short-lived street hockey phase." The choice of equipment for John and his friends during their "phase" was limited to $1.99 wooden hockey sticks purchased at a local drugstore. The sticks were for players who shot left-handed; John and his friends were primarily right-handed shots. Enter John's dad.

"He covered my blade with some cork and electrical tape" to correct the directional problem. "It lasted longer than anyone else's stick," John noted proudly. John still has the handle of that same stick. "I don't know what kind of wood it was made from but it was perfectly laser straight," he said. John cut the blade off it and uses it as a straightedge for woodworking projects.

A respondent in his late thirties from Connecticut remembered that persistence was sometimes required to get the necessary materials for a game: "with kick the can, we'd bug our mom until she gave us a large coffee can that we kicked with abandon—the noisier the better." For another respondent, it took a trip to a neighboring town on bikes to buy used pieces of PVC pipe to complete the frame for a hockey net.

Often, just who was responsible for providing equipment for a game became a source of contention, said one respondent who grew up on Rockaway Peninsulas in Queens, New York. "Who would supply the stickball (a 'pennsy pinkie' or Spalding) was always a source of debates. Who brought it last, who broke it last. Same with the bat." The respondent and his friends often had to search for spare change to buy a ball, and would always be sure to "pick one with a seam that was not raised."

While not all—not even most—pick-up games were exercises in group harmony, a number of respondents recalled events that echo the writings and theories of noted play theorists and scholars, who believe, among other things, that play is a catalyst for the development of self-regulation (Bergen 2002) in children. Extensive pretend and spontaneous play also improves one's ability to use narrative to describe events, and enhances problem-solving skills.

A respondent from Indianapolis recalled raiding his father's tools and materials to fashion forts and ramps for games played by him and his friends. But it was the second part of his response to this question that underscored the impact of spontaneous play: "One kid would start something and the rest would follow along and build upon the first kid's ideas," he said. "Whatever turned out would always be the best combination of us all. Sometimes I'd lead and sometimes I'd follow, but I found out that I was best at assisting others with their ideas or concepts."

Not every attempt to cobble together the items needed to play was successful, as Diann, who grew up in Waldwick, New Jersey, remembered. She and two friends tried repeatedly to build a solid fort. "We tried sticks, sheets, paneling, etc.—anything we could find, but we never had a fort that lasted a night," she said. "We always wanted to have a secret club." A respondent, now in her fifties, recalled success with making snow forts complete with thatched roofs "made of evergreen."

Structural stability was an elusive quality in the forts built by many respondents. Trash day on Kensington Terrace often meant that we could find a spacious appliance box and convert it quickly into a fort, or a "base" for a chase game, or even a house, sometimes complete with furnishings spirited out of garages and attics. But it didn't matter, it seems to me now, whether the box would withstand our roughhousing, or even a slight push of wind. They gave us the opportunity to get away, to hide, to play in our own worlds.

The description by a respondent from Ohio of a tree house built from "wood and nails we pilfered from dad's workshop" underscores the significance of these separate spaces. "Any items we brought to the tree house were small and usually included snacks and favorite books, and weapons to hurl at the inevitable 'enemy,'" she said. For us, this meant chestnuts gathered from a tree in a yard two blocks from our house and hauled back for battle, or, if we didn't feel like dealing with Mr. Frampton, who owned the house and taught gym at what would become our high school, we settled for acorns. The respondent from Ohio remembered throwing pieces of gravel and tar—but only at the bulldozers and loaders completing paving work in her neighborhood. Pebbles and sticks were used in imaginary battles—but "the tree was the only thing that ever got injured," she said.

In southeast London, Will and his friends bought costumes and "props" (toy guns, for example) from local stores to propel their pick-up games. They fashioned bows and arrows from tree branches. The branches came in handy, too, as cover for traps dug to thwart their enemies. It was "almost [like] wilderness survival activities in a local park," Will said. The park lacked the tranquility we normally associate with the word. "It was quite wild and unruly, rather than neat," Will said. "It was next to a genuinely dangerous area with a steep hill, which was fenced off and known to be used by 'bigger boys'"—for what, Will chose not to describe.

Not every pick-up game improved our ability to self-regulate, or enhanced our ability to solve problems. Of course, as kids and adolescents, we didn't see some of our schemes and product adaptations as problems. It seemed perfectly normal to me, at fourteen, to be using the stove to bend my stick blades or stealing rolls of my dad's duct tape to cover the blades once they were properly bent. Nick recalled that he and a friend from high school converted the hallway leading to the bathroom in his house into a somewhat narrow, but sufficiently slippery, hockey rink. The goalie played on his knees, using the red pole from a mop to try and prevent the milk jug tops, used as pucks, from slipping by and passing over the threshold to the bathroom. "We would mark the shit out of the walls with the red mop," Nick recalled.

CONCLUSIONS

None of this should be taken to mean that children have ceased to use their imaginations when it comes to play. This part of our journey is meant only to offer tenuous proof for the theory that kids may not be getting many opportunities to flash what I'm sure are very robust imaginations. Part of our current ideology of play, however, is the idea that the things needed for play should be bought, not made or fabricated.

The skeptic in you should be asking: You grew up in the 1960s; consumerism was alive and well, if not as omnipresent as it is today. Didn't *you* have any toys?

I did. And I loved them—actually, I loved some of them, was indifferent to some of them, and disliked some of them. But, aside from one or two items, I don't remember that much about them. I remember far more about play that combined purchased items and the objects my friends and I would fashion. I remember the three-cornered paper footballs, my catcher's gear, and our hockey net. It was, to paraphrase the songwriter Neil Diamond, a little bit them, a little bit us.

So why did we make traps and cover them with sticks, and harbor the illusion that a pair of worn catcher's pads would provide the same amount of protection as a proper set of goalie pads? We weren't thinking, not that much anyway, about protection; we were thinking about playing, about kicking the crap out of each other, scoring ten goals, hitting a baseball farther than we had the week before, tossing a perfect spiral.

We did it because we wanted to, were motivated to, compelled to, by something inside of us. Much of the impetus for play today comes from outside the child, from external sources. Further clues may be found by applying the list of functions of play offered by Hartley, Frank, and Goldenson (1952) to the experiences we have explored in this chapter.

First, they contend that we play in order to imitate adults. Our appliance box homes and the makeshift classroom I created in our basement suggest (1) an attempt to perhaps improve on the environment I was raised in with a little independence; and (2) a career path, although neither of these thoughts flowed through my preadolescent head.

Second, the authors argue that we play in order to "play out real roles in an intense way." In some ways, the games and scenarios described by respondents are more intense, and certainly demanded of them as much energy, psychological and physical, as did their forays into organized sports. This runs counter to the news media's promotion of the idea that intensity is exhibited in the proper amount only by athletes, no matter what level of play, who take part in organized sports and activities. I played hockey on Kensington Terrace with more intensity than I ever managed to devote to my abortive high school baseball tryouts.

Third, we play to reflect our relationships and experiences. I'm not exaggerating when I say that my adolescent world revolved around sports. My devotion was tested by the complete lack of interest in sports expressed by my parents and my brother. Still, I reached out to them through sports, and to my brother through pick-up games. Further, I still love watching sports on television, and stashing away bits of information about professional athletes. I regularly visit sports-related Web sites such as baseball-reference.com, where statistics for nearly every Major League player can be accessed by name, team, and position.

Fourth, we play to express pressing needs. I was accepted, even lionized at times, for the limited sports prowess I exhibited during pick-up games on Kensington Terrace, an assessment echoed in many of the stories shared by respondents. Friends and other players remembered my long home runs and crushing body checks. This was a level of love that I certainly did not feel in the halls of my high school. And I still haven't completely satisfied the need to show off for women; my wife has seen many displays of what's left of my athletic ability. She kindly observes my games of catch with my niece and nephew, and my feeble attempts to play three-on-three basketball. She then kindly listens to me for the next two days as I complain about the havoc I have wreaked on my body.

Fifth, the authors claim play helps us release unacceptable impulses. To this day, I am better able to manage my anger when I've had the chance to fire a hockey ball at the net Sheila bought me some years back, or play the drums aggressively for an hour. Staging hockey fights on Kensington Terrace, in theory at least, meant we would be less violent elsewhere.

The authors contend that we play in order to reverse the roles we usually play in life. In my family, I was the oddball. I wanted no part of the family business, and I didn't share, with any zeal anyway, my family's love for Broadway musicals and show business. Navigating the "hump" on Kensington Terrace, I was in control, and often, in command, especially since we often included much younger kids from the neighborhood in our games. I was tall, fat—then, during high school, thin and gangly—and not particularly coordinated. I was the sports editor of my high school newspaper, an experience I truly enjoyed, but which permitted me only a passing connection to the world of athletics I longed so to be part of. When I smashed a tennis ball two hundred feet down Kensington Terrace, or threw a perfect spiral to Bob Zipse, I got a little closer to having the feelings I was sure our school's athletes were having—about competition, about performance.

Does play mirror growth, as the authors suggest? Perhaps. We slowly became more sophisticated pseudo-athletes as we got older, just as we were becoming less awkward in social situations, and more able to take care of ourselves. A few of the games that we had enjoyed a few years before, like *Emergency,* were stricken from our repertoire, replaced by other activities—most prominently tennis and its shrunken cousin, paddle tennis. We even went through a beer bottle–collecting (the beer had been consumed by others) phase. On the other hand, hanging out, but not causing or getting into much trouble, became a favorite pastime, as did planting ourselves in front of the television to watch some of the shows criticized by Johnson for their lack of sophistication, and to crank up the Atari for rousing games of Space Invaders. Perhaps we were simply being taught that cranking up our imaginations was no longer required in order to grow. By the end of end of the 1970s, our minds turned to college, women, and getting jobs—and, in my case, figuring out how not to end up working for my father.

Finally, the authors contend play helps us to work out problems and experiment with solutions. Again, the results from our games are mixed here. The problems we encountered were almost entirely game-related—how to make the net easier to carry, how to fix a broken bat, how to assign the younger kids on the block to our teams in the most unfair fashion. Like many of our respondents, however, I travel that path to new solutions. It's sometimes a treacherous journey; I still expect to find solutions too quickly, and I can drive Sheila crazy with my desire to fix a problem immediately rather than let a solution emerge. But, strangely, my teaching is less frantic. I let my students go off on their own to find answers and complete projects. I expect them to depend on their ability, however nascent, to think for themselves. Comprehending the value of this approach, at least, seems to have come from dealing with the compelling chaos of the games on Kensington Terrace.

6

Say Goodbye to Hollywood

Most of the quotes that appeared under the overly posed photos of graduating seniors in Columbia High School's class of 1979 contained pretty standard subject matter: brand spanking new abbreviations ("R.M.A." for "remember me always"); emotional and matter of fact acknowledgements of close friendships; fond, sometimes gushing remembrances of brief but passionate romantic journeys; feats of alcoholic legerdemain, and clipped episodes of relived athletic achievement.

Some folks tapped Broadway shows, Aristotle, and, perhaps, *Bartlett's Familiar Quotations,* while others, like me, decided to cobble together our own quotes. As the one-time sports editor of the school paper, where I wrote a weekly column called "The Bishop's Sermon" (clearly it should have been "homily," but I lacked even slightly sophisticated knowledge of religions), my quote emerged easily: "The sermon is over, but spreading the message has just begun." Even though the case could be made that I must have been predicting a career as a teacher, I still cringe when I read it today—it's so preachy, so ominous.

Still others culled their yearbook sentiments from lyrics written by popular musical artists of the day. A quick content analysis of the music-related quotes from the 1979 CHS yearbook revealed that the Eagles were the most frequently tapped source (eight), followed by Billy Joel (seven), and New Jersey's favorite musical son, Bruce Springsteen, with six (and apologies to Frank Sinatra and Jon Bon Jovi). In 1979, Springsteen had just started down the road to superstardom. He carried a certain "alternative rocker" cachet with many of my friends. Some told intricate stories about going to see the Boss—and consuming "mass quantities" of alcohol, like the Coneheads from *Saturday Night Live*—at the Stone Pony in Asbury Park, New Jersey. They took great pride in their perception that they had in fact "discovered" Springsteen. Jan

Gorlin, one of my best friends at the time, borrowed a lyric from Springsteen's song "Growin' Up" (from the *Greetings from Asbury Park N.J.* album) to serve as most of his quote: "I strolled all alone through the fallout zone and came out with my soul untouched." The song "Born to Run" was excerpted twice. Two other friends went a little deeper into the Springsteen catalog, pulling quotes from "It's Hard to be a Saint in the City" ("Just a backstreet gambler with the luck to lose") and "The Promised Land" ("I packed my bags and I'm headed straight into the storm").

Two folks used the Eagles song "Wasted Time" to express their hope that the three years spent at Columbia weren't—what else?—a complete waste of time. Another student, citing the song "Take It Easy," was more emphatic in his desire to escape CHS and move on with his life, reminding us that we would never again grace the worn brick and linoleum halls of CHS with our presence. One used lyrics from the song "Desperado" to express his deep concern about an uncertain post-CHS future.

Among the more popular Billy Joel selections was "Say Goodbye to Hollywood." The song's lyric contains Joel's recollections of turbulent, changing friendships. But for Columbia seniors, one excerpt was so compelling that it nudged its way under their photos:

> Life is a series of hellos and goodbyes;
> I'm afraid it's time for goodbye again.

The students who borrowed these lines weren't alone in anticipating the disappointment of losing the relationships we had formed and nurtured during high school—although we certainly would not have expressed it like that. One student actually did, though, using this quote from Joel's moving song "I've Loved These Days": "Now, before we end and then begin; we'll drink a toast to how it's been." I knew even then, for example, that the passel of five or six guys who waited with me around the corner from my homeroom on Columbia's third floor, talking about sports and the copious amounts of money Jon Dalton allegedly earned scalping New York Rangers hockey tickets, would essentially disband.

Looking back today, it becomes clear that we were for three years part of one big "jam," as Eisenberg might call it. These were not my closest friends, aside from Russell, and even his significance in my life ebbed and flowed, especially before, during, and after hockey season. We came together to get through that particular fifteen minutes, then barely saw each other during the day, and rarely made contact outside of school. As Allan (1996) notes, we rarely extended the boundaries of our friendships by bringing each other into our other "social contexts." Only Jan and Russell were regular visitors to my house, for example, for often-short sessions of sports-related discussion. That level of access and intimacy was reserved for closer friends such as Chris Young and Joe Kuhl and our rousing games of *Emergency* and Kensington Terrace baseball. Even as a teenager, I could see in Joe the persistence, devotion to family, and strength of character that he still exhibits today. Pahl (2000) explains that friends like Joe "enlarge and extend each other's moral experience" (22). In the hallway around the corner from room A-303, on the other hand, we engaged in what adolescent boys to this day would never call "small talk"—lots of laughter, lying, and the redirection of nerves if one of us had a paper or quiz due on a particular day. This portion of our lives was made easier to navigate by these short sessions.

As Eisenberg suggests, we did not reveal much about ourselves beyond our shared experiences at CHS, but the interactions stemming from these relationships could be intense, whether it was an argument about whether the Mets or the Yankees was the superior team, or what I'm sure were not progressive or enlightened discussions about the girls who would pass by. But it turns out that this was a kind of coping mechanism often revealed during intense adolescent friendships. Writing in 1953, Sullivan noted that one of the key attributes of an adolescent friendship is the ability it produces to cope with "the fears and anxieties that occur during early adolescence" (quoted in Berndt 1982, 1450). Maybe we meant more to each other than we thought—then and now.

Sentiments expressed by Maura, twenty at the time she shared her story, support some of these ideas: "Kids came and went on our block, myself included, but each one knew the rules, and each one knew that unless they had a family vacation they were not allowed to leave the cul-de-sac on summer nights." Today, it seems we place more emphasis on self-revelation, in part to satisfy our competitive drives. If George Will is right, and we do live in a "confessional culture," then we now even compete at reflection. Writing in a journal, for example, has been replaced by "journaling"; practitioners have their own magazine. As Sennett notes, we tend to think that we have to practically intertwine our lives with the lives of others in order to make any headway in the world (1978, 11). What ends up happening, he argued, is that we spend so much time and energy on revelation that we forget why we came together in the first place.

It is unclear to me now whether we actually achieved anything, other than mastery of sports trivia, during these sessions. To be sure, these were purely situational friendships, but they did produce some memorable interactional magic, much of which was drawn from parts of the identities we were test-driving at the time. Mike Barrow and I would trade lines from Bugs Bunny cartoons, each trying to top the other's impressions of Bugs, Daffy, and Marvin the Martian; Dennis Martin and I would express our fervent hope that he and I could someday see the band Chicago in concert; Hal Fredericks would recount (nearly every day) almost being killed by a bus while riding his skateboard down some of Maplewood's most treacherous hills to school; Mark Wujek would try to sell us bootleg recordings (on cassette) of rock concerts he taped with the aid of his trusty stereo; and Chris Wargacki would struggle to maintain consciousness while mumbling about spending the previous night, or an entire weekend, wasted.

Maybe these friendships were more like those seen in the workplace, at least as Putnam describes them (2000, 87): casual and enjoyable, but rarely intimate. But at least we satisfied two of sociologist Robert Bellah's (1996, 115) conditions for friendship: we enjoyed each other's company, and we were useful to one another. On the third condition—sharing a commitment to a common good—we may have fallen a bit short, unless we lower our sights a bit. Our friendships were not really guided by a moral compass, or by a charitable impulse. They were, to quote Suzanne Stern-Gillet (1995), friendships more about process, where pleasure is of utmost importance, than of "activity," which is driven by a joint movement toward some sense of virtue. "Such activities," she writes (quoted in Doyle and Smith 2002), "are central to living the good life." They become "relationships between whole persons." As friends grow closer, Dahl explains, "they recognize each other's moral excellence" (22).

Yet I sometimes think of these folks with nearly the same fondness as I do my closest friends from that time in my life. I look upon them with "cheerfulness, serenity, and composure," as Adam Smith suggested in 1759. But aside from an e-mail in 2003 from Mike, I have had no contact with any of them since we graduated in 1979. I contacted Mike during a bout of Google searches driven by the realization that I had just turned forty. I learned that he is a pharmaceutical sales representative, that he lives in Nebraska, and that he clearly remembers our dueling Bugs and Daffy dialogue ("Would you like to shoot him now or wait 'til you get home?" Bugs asks a perpetually confused Elmer Fudd). And the rest of the A-303 denizens? I know very little about them, except that Chris earned a degree in social work and now runs a leather goods shop in Tennessee. Brad works at the largest hospital near my hometown, and Dennis appraises real estate in the Pocono Mountains of Pennsylvania.

As Billy Joel confirmed for us, moving on to the next stage in our individual journeys was inevitable. Most of us were headed off to college and to gainful employment. Some were headed to the proverbial "big city," where we ran the risk, Adam Smith (1776, 747) noted more than three centuries ago, of being consumed by "obscurity and darkness." We seemed to sense that our friendships would whither "in the face of competition and the demands of a market society governed by contract," as Adam Ferguson argued (Hill and McCarthy 1999). The encroaching need to earn a living caused us to start looking at each other with "considerable caution and suspicion," as Ray Paul suggests (2000, 53–58).

I was the only one within my closest circle of friends (the Taylor brothers, Joe Kuhl, Chris Young) to go to college; my "moving on" happened in a few stages during the spring and summer of 1979. My ambitions, coupled with my desire to hastily leave Maplewood, put a significant amount of emotional distance between us, a distance that I still haven't managed to travel or erase. They treated me as though I was preparing to condescend, simply by virtue of my decision to go to college—like a group of regular pick-up game players who freeze out a friend when he or she tries out for an organized league or team. My brother filled the gap for them, usurping (at least I felt that way at the time) these friendships before I ventured to Temple University in late August. Soon, new friendships born of my burgeoning interest in journalism would form, but then, as now, I missed at least the outer contours of the relationships forged on Kensington Terrace and in the hallways of CHS.

I think about Room A-303 and my old friends when I hear panicked stories from students and young members of our extended family about graduating from high school and going on to college. The application process is, to oversimplify, nerve-racking, and crawls with overzealous, avaricious consultants and coaches. I put little work into preparing for college, as my SAT scores attest. No prep courses. I applied to three schools, was admitted to all three, and chose Temple because of its proximity to Maplewood. As slipshod as my preparation was, it was *my* preparation. My parents had little to do with it. My father kindly drove me to my placement tests, and dropped me off two months later at my dorm, my old Admiral television and new hardcover Webster's dictionary in tow.

Today, parents are relentlessly involved in every stage, every nook and cranny, every millisecond, of the college selection/application/admission/attendance process. Their energy, coupled with the zealousness of college admissions professionals, has charged the process of applying to college with a troubling urgency. Armed with well-intended guidebooks and laptops, high school juniors and seniors feverishly piece together the lists of schools to which they will apply. Parents are urged to buy the correct books, visit the requisite number of college fairs, and to think of their son or daughter's college experience as just one more piece of social currency they can place on their own "shelf." One student whose application I reviewed had compiled a list of more than a dozen schools. They take expensive SAT prep courses; they make their applications literally bulge with the extracurricular activities that they believe admissions officials are looking for. The news media tell them not to be discouraged (and their parents not to panic) if they don't get into an Ivy League school; there are many second-tier "hidden gems" out there.

Students are persuaded that they must begin this collecting early, as early as junior high school. They must set out to zealously collect the "right" achievements and experiences, those that will coalesce into a package sufficiently attractive to officials at their desired college destinations. The experience consumes them; rarely do journalists talk about life beyond the application process. The value of an experience is measured by how much it can enhance the package so assiduously constructed by parents and students. Journalists suggest that these experiences are all roughly the same, in terms of what they contribute to the student's chances of gaining admission. The meaning of the events, the history behind them, is simply less important.

When I hear these stories, I wonder: Can these kids truly "move on?" How can they, with parents constantly checking up on them, buzzing them on cell phones to monitor every behavior, checking their e-mail accounts for possibly unsavory messages? Checking up on kids is certainly not a new activity for parents; however, technology has emboldened some parents to chip away at the privacy their children should be allowed to earn even incrementally. This hampers a child's move toward independence.

More important for our discussion, sustaining these high-maintenance connections delays, and may even prevent, moving on. Perhaps we have forgotten, or choose not to acknowledge, that it is perfectly acceptable, even wonderful, for relationships to change, evolve, even end—and perhaps begin again someday. Two 1979 Columbia seniors used a pertinent excerpt from the classic Joni Mitchell song "Big Yellow Taxi" as if to emphasize this point. How can you come to this realization if you are constantly connected to the past, if you do not permit absence to do its work and make the heart grow fonder? With all of this in mind, I asked respondents to describe the "memorable characters" from their pick-up game experiences.

THE IMPENETRABLE FORCE

One piece of speculation before we begin this part of our journey: with so many activities on their agendas, it may be that kids have no time to form anything other than seemingly close friendships that revolve around one or more of those many activities. Focus on structured activities does not allow the quirks of a friend's personality to come through, or for the maintenance of relationships like those experienced in the hall around the corner from CHS room A-303.

Reading the recollections shared by respondents, I was struck by their detail and depth, and by the stability and equality seen in some of these temporary relationships. "Everyone was the same. Everyone had their lucky swings and shots," noted a respondent who grew up in the Sunset Park section of Brooklyn. Games were played with the same group of kids, with additions made, sometimes grudgingly, when the requisite age and ability level was achieved. Yet for all of the stability, intimacy was rarely achieved. "We were all a bunch of friends from the neighborhood," noted a respondent who grew up in Staten Island, New York. "A lot of us are still friends now. We hang out, go out together. It's not like were are a bunch of best friends, but when we go to a bar, these are the kids you call," he said.

Some of the younger respondents offered distinctly performance-driven assessments of their friends. Shawn described a friend nicknamed "Hoover" because he was "great at everything he played. Any sport—he could just dominate. He was fast and never ran out of energy." The nickname came from his stellar shortstop play: "he caught everything that was hit to him," Shawn remembered. Another respondent, also in his twenties, was less than complimentary about his skills. "My brother and his friends were always better at war than me and my friends," said the respondent, who grew up outside of Allentown, Pennsylvania. "They always destroyed my fort." Games of flashlight tag revealed "some really BAD players," he said. "We'd hide for what seemed like forever, and they could never find us." These descriptions should not be taken to suggest that younger respondents are any less sentimental than older respondents about friendships forged during pick-up games.

Mark, from Paterson, New Jersey, offered a more detailed account of how he and his friends deployed their skills. "Everyone was a 'specialist' of some sort," he said. "One guy always had the strong passing arm in football. I kind of mastered the way to use a Wiffle Ball and hold it or throw it a certain way for sinkers, screwballs, sliders, etc. I thought that was great stuff." Mark's favorite team during this period in his life was the Baltimore Orioles. Orioles pitcher Stu Miller, said Mark, "was regarded as one of the greatest 'junkball' throwers of all time." Thanks to his own carefully honed repertoire of pitches, Mark said he "felt like I was him with a Wiffle Ball."

Older respondents often remembered their friends' more colorful sides. A forty-six-year-old respondent from Lynbrook, New York, remembered "Chunky," whom he called the "impenetrable force in hockey." Then there was Danny, who exhibited tremendous foot speed, and George, "who stumbled on to the powers of the super curved hockey stick and dominated our games." Finally, there was Steve, "who would call time in a game to go into his house for a second and disappear for a half-hour."

On Staten Island, the games included one respondent, who was nicknamed "Fat Joe," even though he was not overweight. Another player was given the nickname "LL Cool J," because of his admiration for the well-known rapper. "Another kid was called 'Three Balls' because he has three testicles," the respondent recalled. In Shippensburg, Pennsylvania, a kid named Ron, or "Cheeks," as he was called by Bill (a respondent) and his friends, doled out nicknames to the players. "It was he who gave the play-by-play (along with crowd noises) as we competed," Bill recalled. Some strange rituals came out of these games. A respondent who hails from what he called "a deteriorating steel town in western Pennsylvania," recalled that the player who logged the worst performance in the annual "Gravy Bowl" (a Thanksgiving pick-up football game) was required to "wear a toilet seat around their neck for the rest of the day."

Many stories echoed the description by a respondent who grew up in Rockaway, Queens, of his friends: "plenty of characters and good natured ribbing, rare fights, good competition." Folks took charge, he said. One player, nicknamed "Eggy," acted as the ad hoc stickball commissioner. He "always wanted a commitment on when to play again." As a respondent from my hometown noted, "looking back, we were all characters." The anger among players was often short-lived, said a respondent who grew up in New London, Connecticut. "We could fight one day and be best friends the next. No real fights, just arguments." The same fights today might lead to litigation, he said. "Then, you went home and came back the next day. We all got along."

The "core players," as Kevin labeled them, made all the decisions about games that would occur in their neighborhood outside of

Chicago. "Rick was the boss, deciding what we would play and who would be on what teams, mostly because it was his house (and his basketball hoop)." Kevin remembered that he was the "token scrawny kid who was completely uncoordinated, and of course was picked last—rightfully so, as whatever team I was on always lost, except at Wiffle Ball, which I was okay at."

In actuality, he said, none of his friends were all that skilled. "They certainly never played anything at any level higher than fifth grade intramurals," Kevin said. Ironically, "the three guys who were so superior to me physically and athletically are now—in their thirties—grossly overweight and totally out of shape."

The friendships were sometimes very intense. A native of Bayside, New York, recalled "a core group of guys who were my closest friends" whose numbers were bolstered by "some peripheral people." One of his friends, Tommy, was always late for games. "Whatever time you told him to show, he would be an hour late and show up as if he were on time." The solution? "We took to telling him to show an hour before we wanted him. That worked out fine. I think we loved him because of, and not in spite of, his consistent lateness."

Ken, a graduate student from Delaware whose family moved frequently when he was a kid, remembered more democracy in the organization of pick-up soccer games during his family's time in Indianapolis. The games "were played a proper soccer field," but without a coach. "We organized the get-together, from calling other guys to setting field boundaries." This level of structure led Ken to call this "a kind of hybrid pick-up game."

The tardiness of Matt, the good friend of a respondent from northeast Philadelphia, was also tolerated. "He'd show up late for a tee time with me and Sean . . . like he just woke up," the respondent recalled. "He'd have his PJs still on and sometimes sandals." Matt would take just one practice swing before heading to the first tee, then frequently place his ball closest to the pin, much to his friends' amazement. Other family-related factors complicated the organization of pick-up games. The respondent from Bayside, Queens, recalled that the key to a good game was convincing enough members of one family in his neighborhood, with "five brothers ranging in age from about six to eighteen," to play. "Usually if one could play, he'd bring a couple of brothers along," the respondent said. "But the family was pretty religious and fairly strict, so often they'd have to go in early or weren't allowed to come out."

A respondent who grew up in Durham, North Carolina, during the 1960s experienced similar difficulties trying to keep three of her friends—three sisters—outside to keep the games going. Their family ate dinner early, but the sisters ate quickly in order to rejoin the action—too quickly, the respondent recalled. "Almost without fail, we could hear their mother yelling out, 'Laura, come drink your milk.'" Laura's sister played another important role: she had her learner's permit. "She would drive us to the Seven-Eleven to get Icees," the respondent recalled. With only a few exceptions, however, parents were not involved in pick-up games—at least according to the stories told by respondents. One respondent, who grew up "in a small town in New Jersey where everybody pretty much knew each other," said that her dad organized their games of baseball. However, since he was their best player, "we'd make him bat left-handed and tell him he had to run slow."

RECONNECTING

Respondents often expressed the desire to reconnect with these memorable figures from their past. Some have maintained friendships that began while building a fort or playing Wiffle Ball with a bat corked with wet newspaper. Noelle, whom we met in chapter 3, said that she still plays tennis with Megan, but now they play on a court, not against a train trestle. "We play pretty even," Noelle claims. "She wins one, I win one. Plus, we get some amazing rallies going." The improvised games more than a decade ago honed their games. "Perhaps we learned to be better tennis players just by bending the rules a bit," Noelle surmised.

Jennifer, who lives in Delaware, still counts Joanne as her best friend, nearly four decades after spending large amounts of time playing "relivio" and flashlight tag. Another friend's bout with cancer caused Jennifer to "think about, and cherish, my friends." She offered a partial, but sound, explanation for why more situational friendships are not formed these days: "I realized that all the times when our friendship was really being forged were times when no parents were around. The (child) predators, and the media that make us paranoid about them, have robbed kids of something so essential to finding oneself." She concluded, "Kids, left to their own devices, will find the democratic way most of the time." Perhaps more important, allowing them to find their own way every so often will, Jennifer believes, improve their self-esteem.

Not all of the respondents have been as successful at sustaining these ties. A respondent in his early fifties who grew up in England described his best friend: "Martin was so much cooler than everyone else. His mother drove a Jaguar XK and we all wanted to sit in it or get a lift home from school." Like me and the folks from the CHS hallway, Martin and his friend drifted apart—far apart. "The last time I saw

Martin he was a punk, and as I had long hair, we had a wide cultural divide between us," he said.

Cherrell, who grew up in North Philadelphia, ended up trading the friends with whom she played pick-up games for a renewal of ties within her own family. "Back then, I had my friends but my dad didn't live with us. My mom and grandmother raised me, my sister, and my second cousin," she said. "But when my mom, sister, and I moved, my dad moved with us. So now I have my dad but none of the friends I grew up with." Cherrell is sure that at least some of her friends still live in the old neighborhood. "Now it's all about getting in contact with them, because I definitely miss them. But I will always have the memories and I'm also very competitive to this day."

A respondent who grew up in an "oil industry settlement" in Venezuela suggested that the friends with whom pick-up games were played enjoyed the kind of intense adolescent relationship suggested by Berndt (1982). Within "the gang" were "simple and normal kids," from which emerged "natural leaders and those who wanted to be the leader but were not cut out for that." A few of their charges were top-flight players, who to this day brag that they could have made it to the Major Leagues, the respondent said. But of utmost importance, despite the range of abilities, was sustaining their bond. "We have many characters, as would be usual in a group like this, but we would always try to remain together no matter what," the respondent said.

Not all of the leaders who emerged during pick-up games exercised their power in a just fashion. "Some people were very good, but you always had your leaders who could be ruthless sometimes and cared from no one else's disposition but their own," said a respondent who grew up in Atlanta. Balancing out the leaders were the "sideline watchers who kept everyone's best interests at heart.

Somewhere in between were "the people who just got pushed around in the game and always got out because they didn't stand up for themselves more," the respondent said. And in some cases, the mantle of leadership was unexpectedly passed to a respondent. "I was the ringleader most of the time," recalled Kate, who grew up in southern New Jersey. "For some reason, every kid listened to me and would do anything I would tell them. This got me into trouble more than once."

ALL SHAPES AND SIZES

Respondents were, for the most part, quite tolerant of the different skill levels seen among pick-up games players. "Pretty much all of us had an adequate skill level because we played together almost all of the time over the course of about six years," noted one respondent. As another respondent noted, "We were all good in our own minds." But their goal was to create the conditions for a good game. "There were a couple of guys who were more talented or stronger or faster, but in general there was a pretty even balance. We would pick the teams to get the best balance, and if a game was lopsided, we'd just switch a player or two to even it up." For a respondent who grew up in a rural community, the goal was simple: they "just wanted something to do besides sitting in front of the television and watching movies."

It is an open question whether these written sentiments translated into actual behavior, but the willingness of some respondents to accommodate less skilled players is reassuring. Recalling his youth in Indianapolis, one recalled thinking that "kids come in all sizes and shapes; some are slower than others and some are quicker." Ability levels varied, too. "Some have more balance and agility and some have more analytical skills—thinking up stuff rather than using physical abilities," he wrote.

Having played pick-up games with so many kids, the respondent found it impossible to recall a single memorable figure. "I only know that I learned a lot from playing with all of them and each one taught me something I would use later in my life." A respondent from Danbury, Connecticut, put it more plainly: "We were all pretty decent. I don't recall anyone really excelling in one game; we just played to have fun and pass the time."

At least one respondent questioned why some of the talented athletes with whom he played pick-up games never ventured into organized sports. These were "great natural athletes who were really good at pick-up games." His guess? Maybe "they just were interested or their parents didn't (or couldn't afford to) get them involved. As if that's a bad thing."

Or perhaps it was simple kindness or altruism that caused more talented athletes to dial back their skills. "Oddly enough," wrote the respondent from Staten Island, "we did have a lot of good players" in their pick-up games; several played on their high school teams, and a few played collegiate sports. "It was weird because even though some kids were much better, the games on those fields were always even. It seemed as if because we played in the park kids that were not that good became good because they had some abilities that translated into success there."

Nurturing those abilities were friends such as Dave, who helped Bill improve his skills as a football player. Bill, who grew up in Shippensburg, Pennsylvania, in the 1970s, remembers that Dave was the same age as his older brother, but chose to spend a significant time with him, instead. Dave was "quiet, smart, and a fairly good athletic friend," Bill recalled. They spent long stretches of time on Dave's expansive backyard, "honing football skills" and playing games of tag "in the snow mazes" constructed during the winter.

And in at least one neighborhood, kids found ways to include friends with disabilities in their games. Dan, a college professor who suffered from polio in 1955, remembered that he and his friends "found ways to make it work." He served as umpire during baseball games when the teams were fully stocked. When fewer kids were available, he would serve as "steady" pitcher—or "steady" quarterback during football games. Other children with disabilities were stigmatized by being picked last for the team, he noted. However, "I found that if I brought the ball and the bat to the game I was automatically one of the captains who got to choose one of the teams, even if I didn't participate very well."

COMPETITIVE FIRES

As was suggested in a previous chapter, not every pick-up game was a showcase for tolerance and fair play. Kevin, who grew up in a "staunchly Republican" suburb of Chicago, remembered that a kid about five years younger than he and his close friends (then about ten) "loved to play football with us," despite the very obvious difference in size. "We took endless pleasure in brutalizing him on the field," Kevin recalled, but "only once did we ever succeed in making him cry." That kid went on to a stellar high school football career, "so he has us to thank for his athletic conditioning." A number of the stories shared by respondents included detailed descriptions of in-game strategy based on a player's weakness. "From playing together for so many years," wrote a respondent raised in Pennsylvania's Lehigh Valley, "we were able to calculate each other's weaknesses and use that to our advantage."

In at least one case, these machinations became too involved. At first, wrote a respondent from Westmont, New Jersey, he and his friends from the neighborhood were known as the "geeks." However, as their games of Army became more popular, strategies for winning became more complex. "The really fun part was when certain people would become spies, double agents, triple agents—they pretended to be betraying the team they were on, but they were really betraying the team they were pretending to help. It was a blast," the respondent noted happily.

A respondent from Long Island recalled that only those kids with real athletic talent showed up to play pick-up games in his neighborhood. The roster of players depended entirely on the sport; however, once the good players had staked a claim, he said, "the others didn't really show up for that sport." A respondent from a Philadelphia university noted somewhat angrily, "The biggest kids got the best jobs—team captain, quarterback, pitcher. Everyone else pretty much grumbled, quit, or just went along with it." But such treatment quickly provided her a clear goal. "Showing up those kids was always a challenge worth accepting, though, especially since I was a girl." Not that these confrontations always went well: "I played home-run derby with a boy who ended up hitting a record-breaking home run in high school. He demolished me," she recalled.

Appearances did deceive, however. Away from the ice, for example, one of the players "was the klutziest guy I've ever met. [H]e could barely walk straight, but put him with pads on in front of a hockey goal, and he was Kenny Dryden [a Hall of Fame goalie for the Montreal Canadiens in the 1960s and 1970s] or [New York Rangers standout goalie] Eddie Giacomin." But even then, he would annoy the respondent and the other players with a shrill "Screeeeeeeeen" whine.

A twenty-year-old college student from Cheltenham, a Philadelphia suburb, remembered that one player's considerable height was somehow not a positive attribute during games of basketball. "Even though he was way taller than everyone, he was NOT a big man," the respondent noted. "Even the smallest guys could post him up." Instead of camping out under the basket, he was content to launch long-range jumpers.

Tempers often flared during these games. "One of the calmest guys I know would invariably strike out in a big stickball situation and break the bat against the school wall," the respondent from Long Island said. The show of anger was bad enough, but it also typically ended the game, since it was the only bat the players had. When football season rolled around, the respondent would focus his attention on a "really tall guy" who, while "an excellent receiver," was "always a great target for me, the defensive back, to undercut as he went up for the ball." Especially frustrating for a respondent from Allentown were players who "wanted the story to go their way. They would either start crying or just stop playing." She recalled that the other players were typically faced with options. "You either had to let them control everything or find something else to do."

Too much competitiveness highlighted the tenuous nature of some of these relationships. A respondent who grew up in Amish country in Pennsylvania recalled that his closest friendship formed "only because he lived the closest." Their friendship "was sometimes shaky due to the fact that he was a year older and sometimes pushed me around." His aggressiveness carried over into their games. He "always took things too seriously and sometimes too far," the respondent, now in his late thirties, recalled, including acts of theft and vandalism.

John, who teaches in the chemistry department at a major eastern university, said he was "stunned" at how quickly a relationship between two brothers in his circle of friends could be on the one hand violent, and on the other quite close. "Although their fights were frequent and intense, Tommy would go to great lengths to protect Charlie, if the latter were threatened by someone else." John said his surprise probably stems from his own relatively peaceful upbringing as an only child of older parents. Still, as one of "the biggest in the group, my role was often one of arbitrator and peacemaker," skills that John says have come in handy in a leadership role in his academic department.

During football games in South Philadelphia, a respondent recalled that older boys "would try to take advantage of the younger ones, but we were all able to hold our own." He proudly noted, "We never ran home to tell our parents" when the older players were being too rough.

A female respondent from Maracaibo, Venezuela, remembered that her male counterparts on the basketball court did not take it easy on her because she was a girl. After twice intercepting a hard pass from a male player, the respondent ended up with a fractured ring finger. "It was probably a combination of the guy's strength and my long nails (that was a very girly thing to do; I didn't cut my nails before the game)," she recalled. The injury "left this slight, weird curve in my finger. I can't stretch it completely. That was the first and last time I play[ed] with a guy." Not that her female friends were any less aggressive. "My girlfriends were tough, tougher than me," she said.

Competition also drove relationships built on respect between boys and girls. Nicky, who grew up in Ontario, remembered Kellen, with whom she played rousing games based on the 1980s television show *American Gladiators*. In addition to being "one of my smartest friends," Kellen played organized baseball and hockey. "[H]e was pretty athletic, and I always tried to compete with him to see if I could perform as well as he could," she remembered.

REAL HARMONY?

Numerous respondents wrote, some extensively, about the harmony that existed among racial and ethnic groups in their neighborhoods.

David, who wrote affectionately about games of Rolly Polly played in his Massachusetts town, noted emphatically that the game "had no age discrimination. Lebanese, Syrians, Polish, and Italians populated our neighborhood. There was never any ethnic or racial discrimination when it came to Rolly Polly."

Describing his Massachusetts neighborhood known as the "Flats," David explained that while it was "divided geographically into ethnic neighborhoods," this "block by block ethnicity didn't divide neighbors." The "Flats" was home primarily to blue-collar workers, many of whom worked at a local factory that manufactured roofing shingles, and their families. Ken, the doctoral candidate from Delaware, said he believes that soccer, his favorite sport, is a bridge joining divergent groups. "Wherever I have lived since high school, and even when I travel somewhere, pick-up soccer has provided a way to meet people," he said. "I'll just walk right up to a game and ask to play, no matter the age or ethnicity of the players."

A respondent raised in Oak Park, Illinois, offered a more sophisticated assessment of her neighborhood's evolving demographic makeup. "We had a range of ethnicities on the block, the younger kids mostly," she wrote. There were also "a couple of adopted kids (actually three different families had adopted children of other races) and I think that was quite a change from the usual Irish Catholic kids that had grown up there prior."

Mark, whom we met in chapter 3, asserted that he could not remember "a single one of my Italian friends who was racist" as they grew up in the Riverside section of Paterson, New Jersey, in part because they attended integrated schools. They were, he said, "proud to have black friends." His predominantly Italian neighborhood was diverse, but Mark was quick to point out that his recollection was based on an assessment made "in my naïve way." Still, he remembered little racist behavior from his friends until the racial turmoil of the 1960s more clearly drew lines that the racial and ethnic groups in his neighborhood would not cross. Strong bonds formed among members of the same ethnic groups, but gangs, claimed Mark, were "nearly nonexistent." A number of Italian kids formed a group called the "pafia," primarily to play pick-up games of baseball and football. It was not, Mark said, an "intimidation" group. But there was palpable tension among these groups.

In at least one case, a respondent's religious affiliation prevented even nondisclosive friendships from taking root. Friends were hard to come by for a respondent who grew up near Lancaster, Pennsylvania, in the heart of Amish country. "Most of my friends were spread out over a considerable distance," he said. Closer to his home were farms owned by Amish families; however, their children did not play with kids whose families were not Amish. "Also, my mother was divorced and from out of state, so even some of the other children weren't allowed to play with me due to the closed and conservative nature of the area," the respondent noted.

More tension played out between young boys and girls, who were often excluded from play by their young male counterparts. Sometimes the boys would deign to allow the girls to play. According to a respondent who grew up in Ohio during the 1970s, it was rare for her brother to agree to include her and her girlfriends in their activities. He may have had an ulterior motive, she recalled. "Keep in mind that most of our play was divided by gender and the age at which he sometimes played with me and girlfriends was at an age when he and his friends were also interested in girls." Thus, the rare inclusiveness "provided an endless opportunity for endless, educational flirting—even if no one would ever admit it," she said.

One respondent, who grew up on Long Island, made sure that this kind of discrimination didn't happen. "I played mainly with all males, and they NEVER treated me like a female because I was just as good as them, if not better than some," she said. "Everybody was a character, including myself, because I never let anyone get away with treating me like a female." Her strength of character produced a few of the long-standing relationships found in these stories. "To this day, they are still like my older brothers; they constantly look out for me. They shaped me into who I am today—tough."

John, a college professor who teaches in North Carolina, described what he called "a basic tension" in his organized and pick-up basketball experiences. On one side were his recreational league friends, who were often "the sons of cops." Their fathers "would come to games, cheer for us, and offer post-game advice about how to do better next time," John said.

John's other set of pick-up game experiences came with kids from nearby urban neighborhoods in New Brunswick, New Jersey. "These were kids from the ghetto . . . for whom basketball seemed to be a way of life," John hypothesized. "They were not in your classes in high school, though you probably went to the same school." The destination for both groups after school was the same: "the "nabe," or neighborhood youth center. "So those years were spent watching the parents of one set of my teammates planning to arrest the other set of my teammates," he said.

One player sticks out to John to this day, a young man named Michael. "If you were on his team you were going to win and have fun doing it," John recalled. Michael was an accurate shooter with a strong on-court creative flair. "We were good friends across racial lines in the days before, but only just before, the riots in Watts and Detroit," John recalled. Thanks to a violent incident involving his fourth grade teacher, Michael did not attend school. "As a teenager I had no way to investigate that story; all I knew was that he was on the playground nearly every time I was," John said.

But as Mary, who grew up in Clifton, New Jersey, pointed out, playing pick-up games did allow her and her friends to "know each other on several levels—as kids, as competitors, an ultimately as friends." Such a multilayered relationship seemed to bring out the creativity in everyone. "We used the manhole cover in the street as a marker for badminton and tennis. We always had creative uses for the simple things around us. We didn't know what we didn't have," Mary said. "We thought we had it all. We could walk to the store and the park—and not only our grammar school, but our high school, too. Wow. Imagine that."

Still, for every memory of harmonious relationships, there was at least one of tense, sometimes painful interactions with neighborhood kids. Rachel, a college professor now living in Philadelphia, recalled that the Irish girls in her neighborhood "were positively ferocious in my recollection as athletes and as general all around pushy kids." She acknowledged that her assessment might have been tinged by "a general ethnic prejudice that I internalized, but I also remember Irish girls making fun of me and some of the Italian girls in particular for being girly and wimpy."

After a rough stretch in an organized T-ball league, Rachel turned to hockey, played with the boys in her neighborhood in suburban Chicago. "I was a very fast skater and could find some dignity in that," she recalled. She took solace in the games she made up, like Crusaders (described in a previous chapter). "I was the character that people remember! Kids I didn't even know would stop by my house and ask to be included. That only went on for one summer, but boy was that fun!" Rachel said.

A respondent who grew up in Holland, Michigan, remembered a young girl as her adolescent "nemesis." They were quite competitive, tangling "for 'A-square' on the playground and 'best reader' in the classroom." Thinking about this relationship, the respondent still seemed to be competing: "I can't help but feel somewhat smug that I live in Chicago now, am almost finished with my second M.A. and curate art exhibits in the city, whereas Melissa has stayed in Holland pretty much her entire life." But her competitiveness gave way to a more sober assessment of their lives: "Apparently she married one of the richest guys in town, though, so she probably feels smug as well when comparing herself to me!"

The differing ages of the kids in the neighborhood often proved to be an obstacle to pick-up game play—especially for younger kids, as one respondent noted. The unwillingness of older kids to include their younger siblings (and their friends) made those times "when the older kids condescended to play with us for a while" all the more memorable, she said. Particularly memorable for the respondent was the oldest boy from a family in their Ohio neighborhood, one "dominated by small bungalows and plain farmhouse-style two-story homes." David babysat the respondent, played softball, and ice skated with her and her friends. "We all considered it quite an honor just to hold his hand or just be near him when we played Crack-the-Whip or Red Rover," she recalled.

CONCLUSIONS

It is likely that these stories of memorable figures and harmonious communities have been embellished, because of selective or failing memories, or out of wishful thinking. I am certain, for example, that parents played a more significant, if supporting, role in creating the games played by respondents. At the very least, they allowed their children to run around and hang out with their friends, thereby helping to sustain a fertile environment for pick-up games. I am also relatively certain that parents actually played in more of these games than the respondents can or choose to remember. I remember at least a handful of "running bases" contests in which my mom and dad participated. And they kept at least a fairly close eye on us as we cavorted around the neighborhood, often from lawn chairs on the front porch (when it wasn't being used as our "consecrated spot," as discussed in chapter 3).

I'm relatively certain that the descriptions of the key figures in our pick-up game experiences are one-, or at most, two-dimensional, with certain bits of information airbrushed out in order to fortify the stories. It could also be that respondents simply did not have that information, which supports the notion that these friendships were largely situational, much like those I experienced with my colleagues in the hallway outside room A-303.

Still, the major thematic element in these descriptions is the lack of outside supervision—or the perception held by respondents that they were not supervised. Friendships, both casual and lasting, were formed and either nurtured or neglected by the respondents. They scoured the neighborhood for players, set the rules for games both typical and arcane. They negotiated the entry of younger players into the games. As John explained, "If we needed someone to round out a team, we would draft one of the younger brothers or one of the other 'better' younger kids." At least in John's mind, "it was a great honor for one of them to be picked to play with us."

John's comment, like many of those discussed in this chapter, reminds us that not every pick-up game was a site of innocent, purely imagination-driven play. Some of the game strategies and descriptions of weak players offered by respondents are quite Machiavellian. But many of the games were exactly that: spaces where kids were, in their own minds, anyway, and for a short time, on their own. Perhaps more important, there was no plan, other than the plans concocted by the players. External sources of information were few. As Tonia noted, "we never thought about watching TV, about playing video games, [or] having to have the constant, fast stimulation that so many kids have to have today."

This does not mean that players didn't emulate their favorite professional players or, like me, devour sports-related magazines, looking for tips that could be implemented during games. But at least within our crew, we gathered the information. To be fair, the funding for our informational excursions would typically come from our parents—or in my brother's case, be stolen from them. But we were left alone to put that information to use in ways we developed. One respondent's description of plans for pick-up basketball reflects fairly sophisticated planning: "We'd meet at six p.m. and play outdoors in the summers. We'd also travel to other parks to play the locals. Sometimes far away," he recalled.

Playing with kids of differing sizes and ability levels became a classroom of sorts, although we'd never admit it then. A respondent in his late twenties from a Philadelphia suburb did not hold back his praise for the older kids with whom he played: "Man did we learn a lot from them! Not only how to take a face-off against a guy twice your weight, but about girls (how to endear yourself to them), music, movies, and being cooler than we were."

The same respondent also shared a theory, scary if ever proven, about the violence experienced in games then and now. "There were some rivalries and of course adolescent fights, but nothing like what today's kids (and I'm only twenty-four) would have to worry about—just dropping the gloves." Perhaps young people today are so intense that they can't move past the game once it's over. As a respondent from Long Island said about some fiercely fought pick-up basketball games, "After the normal competitive bravado, we usually made friends."

7

It Didn't Take Much

For as long as they owned the house on Kensington Terrace, my parents were unable to grow grass in our back yard. The primary causes of their trouble, aside from their intermittent interest in home maintenance, were three large, overgrown trees—two maple, one oak, I think—whose very visible root systems consumed much of the yard's ground space, and also punctured a section of the adjacent driveway in front of our garage. The tree nearest the house did serve, for a short time, as home plate, a base for running bases, and a treacherous test track for our Matchbox cars, but the danger posed by the roots to our knees and elbows soon forced my brother and me to move our games to the front porch and on to Kensington Terrace.

As I reached adolescence, however, the back yard once again became an important place for me, as discussed in the chapter on "consecrated spots." Rugged and foreboding as it was, I spent much of my after-school time in the spring and summer there, in the role of totally unequipped landscaper. By this point, my parents had given up on trying to grow grass. Wanting to play my imaginary Mets games on adequate grounds, I planted grass seed—probably in the fall as well as the spring—convinced that I would soon produce a verdant parcel of grass that resembled the Shea Stadium outfield.

Of course, I had no idea what I was doing. I laid down too much seed, then too little. I watered the coffee-colored dirt, but not regularly. Yet somehow, on a few occasions, I produced grass—thin, almost balding, patches that popped up all over the yard. Buoyed by my success, I would invite Chris Young, the Taylors (who only had to hop the four-foot high Sears fence that separated our yards), and the other kids from the neighborhood for a rousing game of running bases.

But just as Charlie Brown's carefully selected Christmas tree drooped from the weight of a single shiny red ornament, the weak grass was decimated by our first few tosses and resultant dashes between bases. After several rounds of reseeding, and a misguided attempt to grow corn that produced two foot-high stalks, I embraced a new approach: take care of what was there, in true Buddhist fashion. Instead of wasting my time coaxing grass to grow, I tended to the dirt as if it were the infield at Shea Stadium, where the Mets, my favorite team, played. Before each pitching session, I would head to the garage, get out the rake, and smooth the dirt, using movements learned by watching the Shea grounds crew drag their giant rectangular rakes across the infield after the top of the fifth inning.

I painstakingly removed rocks and stones, and moved raked leaves to a newly formed compost pile behind the tree closest to the imaginary pitcher's mound. Because of the roots, my perfectly manicured infield (as seen from a helicopter) resembled a large gourd—narrow at the top, nearest the house, and wide at the bottom, where I did my pitching. I craned my neck to watch my sneakers and cleats leave imprints on the freshened dirt. I found the perfect brick behind a neighbor's garage, painted it white, and laid it in a rectangular hole I had carefully dug to serve as my pitching rubber.

I typically did my John McCarthy (once Shea's head groundskeeper) impression by myself, which was completely all right with me. I enjoyed the time alone. And frankly, I had grown tired of waiting for my parents to professionally correct the back yard's flaws. At the time, I was socially inept, partially because I was shy, and partially because I was quite heavy. I interacted most often with the circle of friends introduced in this book. And as discussed in the previous chapter, my interests, including my love of baseball, were quite different from theirs. But this wasn't always painful. Thanks to these experiences, and the others I have shared so far, I learned to value independence, and, later, thinking for myself. I prefer to work problems out on my own. I seek help, but only after trying my own approach. My love of independence has found its way into my teaching. I give guidance and provide ample instruction, but I also encourage my students to come up with their own innovative solutions to problems that pop up as they work on their projects—as when a potential source won't return a phone call or is reluctant to talk on the record as the student tries desperately to write a news story.

Let me offer a more concrete example: each fall, I ask my class of freshman communication students to go two days without laboring to stay in constant touch with everyone in their lives. They are to put away the cell phones, disengage from instant messaging, and try to be by themselves, to "clear their heads," as I note in the syllabus. I assure them that it will not violate the conditions of the assignment if a parent makes contact and wants to talk, or if they need to make an emergency call. But I emphasize that I want them to come as close as possible to having what I believe is a quickly disappearing experience: being alone. They write a short paper about the experience, which, I tell them, can include reflections about the nature of the project and about the professor who cooked it up. These are my only instructions.

To say that my students have a difficult time coming up with fulfilling—even unfulfilling—activities on their own would be an understatement. A few revel in the disconnectedness, but most are frustrated by not having something provided for them to do nearly every second of the day. One or two have told me about sitting on their beds and staring into space, unable to think of something to do. They curse the boredom. They curse me—sometimes with shocking ferocity. And they curse their supposed "addiction" to the devices they have been deprived of—and the behavioral patterns they encourage—but are extremely relieved when they are allowed to resume using them.

It probably would not occur to them to manufacture a miniature Major League infield out of roots and dirt in a back yard. But again, this is not a criticism of the activities in which children now engage, or of their parents for nudging their kids to engage in them. John, like me a college professor, recalled bringing up the subject of pick-up games in one or two of his classes. He was uneasy, but not surprised, at their responses. "It often seems to be a case of they have never missed what they never knew," John said. As we have discussed in earlier chapters, young children still find time to play, and play imaginatively, but the potential significance of pick-up games seems to be waning, as parents seek the purported benefits of organized activities for their children. But there are holdouts. Becky, who lives in Massachusetts, reported that in her neighborhood, "two or three nets are always on the side of the road. Kids use roller blades for street hockey." Her neighbors constructed a "goalie" out of plywood. Festooned with a wig and "hybrid hockey/lacrosse gear," it guards one of the nets. "It freaks people out when they drive [by]," Becky noted.

A respondent who grew up in Long Island, and who now works as a financial advisor, contends that this push "doesn't leave much time for the kids to explore other parts of the socialization process. It doesn't seem to leave time to go the library, or hike." While more top-flight athletes may emerge from the focus on structure, "other skills," such as those discussed in this chapter, may be lost or never developed, he argues.

Eric, a graduate student when he shared his pick-up game experiences, was more emphatic about encouraging parents to dial back the pressure: "To me, kids should be able to be kids and they should be able to play pick-up games every day if they want," he said. Let kids decide on the organized activities. "Parents should not worry about building a resume for their kids while they are still in junior high school. Let them be kids; more often than not, they find their way."

Of course, this approach to life has some significant potential pitfalls, as I can attest. I am uncomfortable asking for help. I struggle to develop solutions to unsolvable problems. I sometimes try to solve a problem without considering a sufficient amount of information. Glynn, a wrestling coach from Canada, says he has been similarly affected by his pick-up game experiences. He cites his reluctance to ask for directions, and his unwillingness to follow assembly instructions for toys. "I simply want to put something together by guess and by gosh, as I did things as a kid even though I know it is not the best way," he said. When conducting research, I have a tendency to write first, driven by curiosity and passion, and ask questions and consult existing theory later.

Recounting my ambition to work with the Shea Stadium grounds crew evokes warm smiles from my wife, but it probably would not sit well with the overanxious parents who encourage their children to participate in many organized activities. This leads me back to the paradox mentioned in a previous chapter: many of the individuals who so fondly remember pick-up game experiences forget or perhaps discount the simplicity and independence of those experiences when guiding their children.

According to a 2004 study by the nonprofit group Public Agenda, their kids clearly recognize, or have been educated to recognize, the benefits of organized activity. Nearly 60 percent of the kids surveyed for the study said that they took part every day in an after-school activity or program; nearly four in ten said they participated in an activity at least two days a week (Duffett and Johnson 2004, 9). Most of their time was spent playing sports, participating in school-related clubs and extracurricular activities, and doing volunteer work.

Most of the students—more than eight out of ten—said that the kids who take part in these activities are "better off" than kids who "have a lot of time to themselves after school." An even larger percentage of students agreed with the statement, "Belonging to a club or team and doing things with other kids gives me a good feeling." Roughly the same percentage said that they needed a nudge from their parents when they complained about taking part in activities "that are good for me."

Public Agenda's president, Ruth Wooden, told the Associated Press in 2004 that the report's message was clear: "Most kids are thriving from out-of-school activities, and it's really worth your time—and a little nagging—to get kids involved ("Carefree Play" 2004, A-7).

These same students have become well acquainted with the notion that being bored is a bad thing. To paraphrase the philosopher Bertrand Russell, they have accepted the "great public propaganda" (1996, 1) that asserts we must work, achieve, and strive all the time if we are to be successful. Or, as noted British writer Tom Hodgkinson observes, "It is a sad fact that from early childhood we are tyrannized by the moral myth that it is right, proper, and good to leap out of bed the moment we wake in order to set about some useful work as quickly and cheerfully as possible" (2005, 1).

Many of the students surveyed by Public Agenda said they had difficulty coming up with things to do, and usually had no plan when they decided to hang out with their friends. More than half noted that their peers complain a great deal about having nothing to do; about half contended that their communities could do more to address this problem, in the form of additional activities. Kids make the connection between having nothing to do and getting in trouble. Nearly 80 percent agreed with the statement, "A lot of kids get into trouble when they're bored and have nothing to do." Their parents would not be pleased with some of the less than savory actions undertaken by their friends to beat the boredom, the kids told Public Agenda. Boredom, not lack of parental attention, or knowing right from wrong, is the chief reason kids get in trouble.

But boredom has its defenders. Dr. Bruce Perry (2007), an internationally renowned expert on child brain development, claims that parents should back off, rather than push, when a child tells them he or she is bored. "We jump in too soon and make the mistake of creating the child's activities for him," Perry said. Instead, we must let kids become bored now and then, "because it is through this transient period of under-stimulation that their internal world can come alive." Enabling kids to work through boredom can have additional benefits, he claims. For one thing, perhaps they would rediscover, as Bertrand Russell suggests, the "capacity for light-heartedness and play which has been to some extent inhibited by the cult of efficiency" (11).

So many of the respondents who shared their pick-up game experiences commented favorably, lovingly in some cases, about how much the chance to be on their own—to make their own fun—meant to them. Why does it seem that these experiences have little relevance in the lives of our children? Some answers may come from the responses to my last question. I asked respondents to discuss what they learned from their pick-up game experiences—what they took away from them, what sticks with them today as adults.

While writing this book, I have had to remind myself that learning was not the point of building our street hockey net or fashioning weapons out of sticks for games of *SWAT*. Sitting down to review the responses, I resigned myself to the fact that they would be tinged by conjecture and nostalgia—an exercise in retroactive wishful thinking. It could very well be that we have applied little or nothing derived from these experiences.

But even wishful thinking has value and can be instructive, as we will learn.

WE MADE IT HAPPEN

Perhaps the most relevant finding from the responses to this question is that these individuals practiced a heady brand of self-reliance. "I think what sticks with me the most was how my brother and sister and me were 'ringleaders' and that nothing really happened unless we made it happen," said a respondent who spent her childhood both in rural Ohio and a small city. She and her siblings "were used to being quite active and so we always organized as wide a variety of activities as [the] town kids would support," she said.

As Barry, a retired newspaper reporter from Detroit, noted, "Children didn't expect adults to organize their play," as they often do now. In fact, "adults tended to interfere with the games you liked best," he said. "The kids who seemed to have the most fun, and who were the most creative about it seemed to be the ones who didn't have much parental supervision," said a respondent raised in Columbus, Ohio in the late 1960s.

Growing up in a small city east of Dallas, John recalled that his parents paid little attention to the pick-up games he played—"unless there was property damage." He decried the "select sports mentality, with hyper-organized, hyper-competitive teams for kids as young as five or six." Parents may know that they are pushing their kids, "but if you want your kids to have a chance to play sports in high school, you're almost forced to go along," John argued.

I am not suggesting that today's kids do not enjoy, or benefit from, organized activities. It is important, however, to consider how the absence of unstructured play alters their experiences and, possibly, their worldview. Ken, an instructor at a Philadelphia university, believes that his son enjoyed playing organized sports. However, "the scheduled games often interrupted his morning sleep and interfered in evening homework." As his son got older, Ken said he saw a change in the level of participation by adults: "They organized, drove, cheered, commiserated and were there, always present, as if it were their game somehow, too."

The missing element, discussed in more detail later in the chapter, was fun, at least according to Mike, a retired sociology professor now living in Pennsylvania. "I wish they had been involved in more of these improvised games and less in watching TV or, in my son's case, video and computer games," he said, describing the experiences of his son and daughter. "The sports they were involved in were all formalized and organized . . . and, while they had a lot to offer, I guess, they seemed to lack much of the simple fun that was always a central part of the games we played when I was growing up."

Lest this book be considered an indictment of video and computer games, a respondent, now in her thirties, from Nazareth, Pennsylvania, remembered that she and her friends spent quite a bit of time in front of the television, playing these games, but balanced the play with time spent outside. "What really sits with me is that today, kids stay in and play video games all summer or when they get home from school," she noted. In addition to video games, "we went outside and played until it got dark and we had to come home." Another younger respondent, twenty-three at the time the responses were sent, said that unsupervised games "probably resulted in a better learning experience overall." But he lamented, "I might have been in the last generation that was free from a deluge of organized games."

Jon, who grew up in several southern towns and cities from the late 1940s to the mid-1950s, asserted that much of what we learned during pick-up games came from watching adults. "We learned limits and conventions of deportment," he said. "We learned how to act when we got physically hurt. That was easier than learning how to act when we got disappointed."

Jon continued: "And we learned, most of us, to be gracious. Then too, we learned about selfishness and bullies and how to coexist with all that. What is amazingly different from today . . . is that we did all this by ourselves. That is, we extrapolated from what we knew of the adult world to what we had to manage on our own, but no one told us if we were right or wrong. It either worked or it didn't." Another respondent, this one from a small town in Michigan, stated it more simply: "Rules should not arbitrarily be mandated by one teacher."

Eric shares this view. Playing pick-up games meant a pressure-free environment, he said. "No coaches, no refs, no parents yelling from the sidelines," he said. "It was just a bunch of guys getting together and creating memories that would last a lifetime." More important, perhaps, the games gave Eric and his friends "a chance to be independent, [to] think for themselves, and be decision-makers." When a football play was executed correctly, he said, "you felt like you were on top of the world, because you did everything on your own."

THE OUTSIDE NATURE OF IT ALL

Many of the respondents remarked about the freedom they felt to do their own thing, to borrow a term from the 1960s. "What sticks with me is the outside nature of it all," said Will, who grew up in London, "and how freely, almost anarchically we roamed around without adult supervision. It seems quite healthy, looking back at it, and very physically active." A respondent who grew up near Chicago said she remembered clearly "how free and how much fun it all felt—perfectly healthy and running super fast and laughing and climbing trees and goofing." This seems a far cry from the assessment of where kids now typically play offered by a *USA Today* reporter in July 2005: "Children today tend to get outdoor exercise by appointment" (Cauchon 2005, 1-A).

Much of this was achieved with little parental involvement. "What sticks with me today is hanging outside until dark," said a respondent who grew up in Durham, North Carolina. "Some mothers would ring a bell to bring their kids in; others would just yell," like the Taylors' father, who would bellow from the front porch to let Chris and Steve know that their presence was immediately required for dinner. Richard, whose childhood was divided between Philadelphia and western Pennsylvania, recalled that his parents only wanted to know where they were going to be. "'Mom, I'm going out to play' seemed to be enough," he said. "If we were going farther, we gave a location."

Jon, who spent most of his childhood in Shreveport, Louisiana, recalled copying what he and his friends saw during his father's factory team softball games—but that was the extent of parental involvement in their own softball games. "I don't think I can recall a single time when an adult watched us play our pickup games. And that was fine with us," he emphasized.

FRISBEE HOCKEY

A young (twenty-four) respondent from Drexel Hill, a suburb of Philadelphia, recalled frequent games of "Frisbee hockey" in his neighborhood. Teams of five (plus a goalie) would pass the Frisbee to each other. Players were allowed only three steps with the Frisbee before having to pass again, or shoot at the goalie. "A goal was scored by getting the Frisbee in the net, normally by skipping [it] off the ground—a kind of deflection," the respondent recalled. What sticks out to the respondent is the fierce competitiveness exhibited by him and his friends. He still basks a bit in "the glory of winning, of having the bragging rights."

It turns out their games often drew substantial crowds. This only heightened the experience, he said. It meant a lot to the players that folks would come to see a game "that we created and enjoyed." Another respondent, from nearby Brookhaven, Pennsylvania, also cited the thrill derived from playing in front of even small crowds—one segment of those crowds in particular. "The best part was the girls who would come to watch us play," he said. "Girls love hockey players," he asserted, "and we didn't mind pretending to be them." Said Albert, who played half-ball, "buck-buck," and touch football with his friends in south Philadelphia, "Whenever you're around girls, you have the tendency to show off." Playing enabled him and his friends to "establish their maleness."

The respondent from Brookhaven believes the connections to his hometown, his current favorite professional teams, and his friends matter more than games won or lost. "I still love sports to this day, and I think much of this passion come from a small-scale knowledge of each game we played and what it's like to win, lose, and play without keeping score," he said. The passage of time has not caused his love for his favorite teams to wane. "Such connections go beyond sporting and into the greater community, and they begin with pick-up games," he stressed.

And for one respondent at least, competition changed the complexion of the games. "The game disintegrated if you got too competitive," he said. Britt, twenty-six, who grew up in Saylorsburg, in Pennsylvania's Pocono Mountains, said he believes the competitiveness inspired by pick-up games was constructive. Playing games of Ultimate Frisbee, for example, "elevate[d] people to a level they did not think they could achieve," he said.

MAKING DO

Many respondents expressed amazement at how creative they were in thinking up pick-up games. "We learned how to have fun and create games ourselves," said a respondent who grew up in my hometown, Maplewood, New Jersey, "which entertained us immensely." Hallie, raised in northeast Philadelphia, recalled that she and her friends concocted the rules to games of wire ball and wall ball. "It's neat to think that when given only a ball, so many games developed out of it," she said.

Glynn, who at one time coached Canada's Olympic wrestling team, took a more pragmatic view. "We were entirely unsupervised and forced to learn to negotiate and, yes, argue, while at the same time being resourceful in using available material to devise toys, weapons, equipment and instruments," he noted. A twenty-one-year-old respondent who grew up in Manhattan applies these lessons in the business world. "It was an invaluable experience as far as quick learning to work with others and develop instant chemistry," he said of basketball games, and "anything from tennis, soccer, softball, or football in Central Park."

Respondents often were forced to be resourceful thanks to a lack of funds. "I think I grew to appreciate how to have fun without having a lot of stuff," said a respondent who grew up in a small town in Michigan, and now lives in Kenya. "I didn't grow up with a lot of money, and neither did my friends, but we amused ourselves nonetheless. It's not like we were playing stickball in the Depression or anything, but [we] didn't need the latest technology to enjoy ourselves. Do kids still do that these days?" The recipe for fun was even simpler for a respondent who moved fifteen times during her childhood: "Time and a space to get together were the main ingredients," she said.

Not what sporting goods manufacturers, who thrive on our desire to have the "right" equipment to play our many sports and games, want to hear. Tonia, who lives in New York City, but grew up in a small town in North Carolina, said she made her way to the nation's largest city before figuring this out. "Being outside and making do with the wide open space, the rural safety of a small town was such a wonderful thing," she said.

At times, Tonia wishes she had never been exposed to life outside of her small town, "so that I felt I was missing out." That "bumpkin" feeling has not gone away completely, she says, "but I have also realized that compared to my peers from large cities, I am never as bored or unsatisfied. I understand the sanctity of silence, the outdoors, and doing 'nothing.'"

MASTER NEGOTIATORS

David grew up in a blue-collar Evansville, Indiana, neighborhood in the early 1960s. He has not returned since 1969, but said he finds himself thinking about the games that he and his friends would play. "There was a camaraderie about them that appears to have more or less disappeared," he noted wistfully. "All the kids in my neighborhood lived outside as much as possible, including the days of the brutal Midwestern winters." The wide availability of air conditioning and video games, he argued, has lessened the attraction of playing outside. A respondent from New Jersey echoed this assessment: "Sure we had video games . . . but it was the early Eighties and this was just starting. We watched TV, but not as much as the kids today, and we weren't on the computers as much, as we had no Internet. We were active and outside."

Dana, now in her mid-twenties, offered similar memories: "I remember arguing about calls, laughing about stupid plays, and having fun. These games produced friendships and sometimes even enemies," she noted. Dana was adamant in her belief that pick-up games "instilled more in me than any organized activity or sport I was involved in."

A respondent, now in his late fifties, who grew up in Chester, Pennsylvania, asserts that playing for fun engendered sound relationships between him and his friends. "Whether we won or lost, we respected one another, teammates or not," he said. The high-pressure environment in which many children participate in sports today is not conducive to this dimension in relationships. "That's lost now," he contends. "Too much parental involvement, too much organization. We didn't need all of that. We didn't need a scorebook, uniforms, trophies, or all-star teams. We appreciated the game for what it was—a game. Now, it's a vehicle for parents to live off their children."

A significant byproduct of the independence was the loyalty that developed among pick-up game players, said John, who grew up, and still lives, in Garwood, New Jersey. "In those days, we decided what we wanted to do and we did it. Of course, we had to learn to become master negotiators. Whether it was arguing a close call or four of us trying to convince the other three to play something they didn't want to play, we always had to give and take," John said. Out of this came battle-tested connections. "No matter how much we fought and rode each other we always stayed together," John concluded.

Negotiating skills were also a significant element in pick-up games played by a respondent, nearing fifty, and his friends, in Lynbrook, New York, on the south shore of Long Island. "When there were disputes, you had to negotiate and somehow discover what a win-win solution was so you could get back to playing the game," he said.

Some respondents saw more opportunities for democracy in their games. One respondent, now in his late forties, remembered grasping "truths about what is fair and what harms others." He and his friends were "always looking for everyone to have a good time and for no one to be left out." A respondent who grew up in Wayne, an affluent suburb of Philadelphia, recalled the inclusiveness practiced "despite no formal structure." Players did not have to be reminded "to let everyone play, because one day it might be you who got to the game late," the respondent said.

While adolescents are not typically known for their friendly treatment of peers outside their social circle, John, who teaches at Wake Forest University, believes that pick-up games might just make us more kind to the person "who hangs around the edge of a social setting, waiting to be noticed or asked in." John said his own talent for basketball was not immediately apparent to other players. "Our society often judges by appearance and familiarity, but that is not the way the talent is handed out," he contended. In his classes, he looks for the "stealth scholar"—a student who just needs "direct pointed feedback" in order for his or her abilities to emerge.

While players may have wanted to enhance their skills at a particular sport, many were well aware that this often didn't mesh well with sustaining a game. "I learned to be fair. I learned to be flexible," said a respondent from Bayside, Queens. "I learned to value people being willing to play more than whether they were good. After all, if you didn't have enough people to play, then you couldn't play at all."

Navigating often tumultuous interpersonal relationships is a large part of John's work as a university department chair. Serving as the arbitrator and peacemaker for his group of close friends prepared him for this task, he claims. The exploits of a pair of brothers were particularly helpful. "Although their fights were frequent and intense, Tommy would go to great lengths to protect Charlie," his younger brother, "if the latter were threatened by someone else," John said.

Samantha, who grew up in Pennsylvania's Lehigh Valley, also cited instances where she put her negotiating skills, nurtured during pick-up games, to use. "I learned how to gather people together for a common activity, which has so many levels of importance being an adult in the corporate and academic worlds," she stressed. She feels gratification in organizing events that generate enthusiasm. "The feeling of coming together for a common purpose is what sticks with me."

THE STRONG OFTEN PREVAIL

Not all of the recollections about pick-up games were warm and fuzzy. The college student from the Squirrel Hill neighborhood in Pittsburgh stressed that tackle football games "honed my trash talking skills." In-game disputes often got out of hand, as a respondent from Atlanta recalled. The games played on the respondent's "quiet street" in a neighborhood with a distinct "small town feel" deteriorated without the presence of what the respondent called a "line judge"—a person "whose job is just to focus on determining whether the person is in or out." Without such a person, "personalities and personal conflicts get taken out on the 'court,' even though it's just a game." This didn't prevent another respondent from northern New Jersey from peaceably settling the "many competitive arguments" that broke out. All it took was the "development of lawyers/realtors to advocate/sell their position[s]," the respondent noted.

David asserted that in his neighborhood, "we learned what we needed to live the life of the working class: the weak get chosen last. The strong usually prevail." But now and then, "wit and intelligence bring down the Goliath"—or Paul, the son of a bartender, famous for inflicting bodily injury on the other kids in the neighborhood. For another respondent, who grew up in a predominantly Italian American neighborhood in South Philadelphia, this type of treatment by older kids produced in their younger charges some inner strength. "We were all able to hold our own. We never ran home to tell our parents," he said.

Growing up in South Philadelphia a few decades later, Albert argued that pick-up games "positioned you on that assumed scale of toughness." Toughness was certainly required for games of "hide the belt." A belt, complete with large buckles, would be hidden somewhere. If you found the belt, you were allowed to chase, and then beat, the other players, who tried to hide before the person wielding the belt found them. The game started with everyone far away from "home base," Albert recalled. "God forbid you were the last person." Exhibiting toughness had to be the only reason kids played the game. "Why [else] would you want to do this?" he asked. For one thing, it was a means to achieve acceptance. "You'd rather be known for your physicality in a tough neighborhood," Albert noted. Players eschewed sports they felt were less demanding. "Soccer was like a pussy game," he said emphatically.

Kevin, from a Chicago suburb, keenly felt the rejection that came with a lack of success at pick-up basketball. "There's no way I can overstate the absolute psychological trauma I suffered being friends with sports fanatics," he said. His inability to win even once at one-on-one basketball led to the development of a strong dislike for competition, one still evident today. But it also made Kevin persistent—that is, until he started playing in a football league. "After one year of running laps with full gear on three nights a week, only to sit on the bench every Saturday morning for two hours, I discovered the law of diminishing returns," he said. His experiences led him to conclude, "Sports can bring people together, but probably not in any meaningful way."

The effects of playing heated games of "Cops and Robbers" with boys ten years her senior have not all been positive for Marla, a college student when she sent her responses. "Although I put on a good front to the boys, when I was hiding alone in the dark, I would be so afraid I would almost be in tears," she said. More upsetting were the times she had to "run in the house because I was so nervous I thought I was never going to make it to the bathroom in time." Soon, she overcame her fears, thanks to a new strategy: she hid with a friend. Eventually, the "boys became cootieless," and Marla "began to hide with the boys I had crushes on."

Despite the tumult, and the fact that she still experiences anxiety when she is chased, Marla believes that her "Cops and Robbers" experiences are significant. "I have won two state (high school) championships in lacrosse, but [I] still think my greatest victories are those celebrated with my childhood best friends during a four-hour game of Cops and Robbers," she stressed.

And rather than strive to reach a professional level of competence, respondents were content to just play well enough. "I learned not to be afraid of anything—just apply yourself and try your best and things always turn out for the better," said a respondent who grew up in Indianapolis. While not "the best at anything," he "could always play everything if I tried hard and never gave up." Being able to convince others to allow you to play was as important as ability, claimed another respondent. "If you're good enough, it doesn't matter what sex you are. But to get your foot in the door, you needed to at least talk the talk."

One clear development since that time, argues Frank, the college professor who hails from the suburbs of New York City, is that fewer kids now have the chance to even open the door. In 2003, Frank coached a travel basketball team, where he tried earnestly to ensure that all of his players had fun. But he ran headlong in to an entrenched mindset among officials, other coaches, and parents that rewards ability and performance. As early as elementary school, the players who will go on to play in high school are identified. "The other kids are told, 'you're not good enough for this,' and they lose interest," Frank said. In Frank's current hometown, "which is real sports-heavy, you see not a hundred kids go out for basketball, you see maybe fifteen, because ten of those kids were told that they were good since they were in the fifth grade."

Such early pigeonholing might have devastated Frank and his childhood friends, who enjoyed the competition, but really only wanted to play. "It was just the joy of playing, competing, and winning," he said. "But when you lost, you all went down to the deli together by yourself; no parents were there, trying to soothe your hurt feelings." Frank and his teammates dealt with shoddy play by their teammates in their own, sometimes violent, fashion. When the team's right fielder dropped a fly ball that cost Frank's team a game, several members of the team "apparently took him in the back, and said 'we're going to teach you how to catch a fly ball,' and then beat the hell out of him. But there were the kids, you see; it wasn't the parents."

These experiences have led Frank to adopt a democratic coaching style. "I play all the kids, but we lose [nearly] every game," he said. His youngest son suggested Frank not coach in 2003 so that the team might win one or two games. During the 2002 Little League season, Frank "played everybody at every position." He was the only coach to adopt that strategy, "and we had a terrible season." The team suffered through some injuries, "and it really ate me up, but I didn't change my style," Frank stressed.

The same strategy led to a similar performance by the travel basketball team coached by Frank that winter. Despite the obvious disappointment felt by his players, Frank believes they understood what he was trying to achieve. "My objective is that you're playing because you want play," not just sit on the bench and watch the more talented kids play. Frank also tried desperately to ensure that his players wouldn't suffer the pounding to their bodies that comes from being so "intensely concentrated on one sport."

THE GAME IS PURE

Still, a few respondents took note of the fact that during pick-up games, players are treated more fairly than during organized activities. "Everyone is on the same level and the game is pure," theorized Eric, a respondent now in his early thirties who grew up in a middle-class Lancaster, Pennsylvania neighborhood. "No coaches yell at you if you make a mistake. No pressure from parents to play well because a college coach might be watching." He inserted a space after this section of his response, creating a pause.

"It is just you, some friends, and a game."

A respondent, now in her late twenties, said she was relatively certain she had not learned much through her participation in pick-up games. Her skills were honed during practice for team sports. Again, having fun and playing for the sake of playing were of the utmost importance. "We had no worries, no expectations on winning; we didn't really care who could hit the home run or who could dribble circles around other players," she recalled. "All that we cared about was having a good time and laughing!" Thea, a college student from Cumberland County, New Jersey, said she believes "the games didn't really matter that much." Interacting with members of her family resonates with her today. "The stuff that sticks is how silly we acted," she recalled.

A particularly attractive aspect of pick-up game play for respondents was that it was planned only infrequently. "Sometimes I would just go to the schoolyard with a ball, not knowing who would be there or what I would do and figure it out when I got there," recalled the respondent from Lynbrook, New York. Such a slapdash approach might make parents today a bit uneasy, as would the willingness of parents in previous eras to allow their children to head off to make their own fun. "Fortunately, it was okay to just go to the schoolyard unsupervised," the respondent added.

Games were easy to find, claims a respondent from nearby Rockaway, Queens. "That culture seems to be completely gone," said the respondent, now in his early fifties. "I remember playing all day . . . and being filthy when returning home" after up to eight hours of play. His sons, one his early twenties, and one almost twenty, have had few similar experiences, the respondent noted.

BUSY AND CLOSE

While many of the relationships described by respondents were situational, supporting Eric Eisenberg's ideas about "jamming," a large number of respondents reported sustaining treasured friendships beyond the pick-up game experiences. "We were all good friends with similar talents, so we could always split up and have very close games," said Joshua, a native of the Philadelphia suburb Cheltenham. "Plus at the end, we would go inside, get something to drink, and hang out."

A respondent from the same area still feels "the incredible bond that formed between me and my boys." Games of football played on the street taught him and his friends "how to unconditionally be devoted to a sport, and to a group of people." Diann, raised in Waldwick, New Jersey, believes she learned "you are blessed to have lifelong friends." She remains very close to Julie, with whom she attempted to build so many forts when both were kids. "I talk to her at least twice a week—we were in each other's wedding, and I am her daughter's godmother," Diann said.

After citing some more typical lessons—treating others fairly, getting along with people "in a competitive setting," and believing in oneself—Nicky, who grew up in Canada, said that pick-up games reminded her of a rough stretch with her brother. "The fact that sticks out throughout all of this is that I did all these things with my brother," she noted. "We went through a few years where we weren't all that close, but in the past twelve months, we've grown to be amazing friends."

A respondent from south Philadelphia, now nearly eighty, can attest to the value of these lasting friendships. "These games really helped keep us together," he said. "We still meet once a month to talk about the old days." In fact, as he was compiling his responses, the respondent was set to attend an upcoming reunion of his old friends. Three former pick-up game players, including a respondent from Philadelphia's Juniata Park section, were also planning a reunion in order to compete in a team golf tournament. The games they played, creative variations on baseball, "kept my friends and I [sic] busy and close," the respondent said. "The three of us remain close to this day."

Perhaps of similar value is the ability to make friends, and to sustain "the incredible bond" between friends (in the words of a respondent from a Philadelphia suburb), rather than having them provided for you. A respondent from Indianapolis, whose family moved frequently, recalled that making friends was an important coping mechanism. "Making new friends became something I had to learn in order to fit in and to have someone to play with," said the respondent, now in his late forties.

John, a college professor from North Carolina, continues to build friendships using the skills learned playing pick-up games. "You could drop me on the moon and I'd find some way to make friends," he asserted. Negotiating his way into basketball games taught him "how to work my way into a social situation without being pushy." He offered this advice: "At the playground, half the time there will be an odd number of players and you make the even number and make the game possible." It does not matter, he said, if you are the last player picked to play—"just get picked. You will prove yourself as the game progresses."

The freedom to create these relationships, unaided by parents, has been taken away from children by "micro-managing" parents, claims Jennifer, who lives in Delaware. This point was underscored as a friend, with whom Jennifer and her best friend shared pick-up games, battled cancer. In the midst of treatment, her friend recalled playing a game in a church parking lot. A priest or other important official entered the lot, but Jennifer's friend urged her compatriots to continue playing. She ended up getting into trouble for her act of defiance. "I realized that all the times when our friendship was really being forged were times when no parents were around," she noted. Fear of child predators caused by extensive news media coverage has robbed children "of something so essential to finding yourself."

Yet several respondents emphasized that their pick-up game exploits took place against a backdrop of community cohesiveness. While many of the women in David's Massachusetts neighborhood "were on the surface the stereotypical homemakers of the nineteen-fifties," they also kept an eye on each other's children—they "cooperatively mothered," as my wife eloquently explained. "The door of every home within shouting distance was always open to me," David recalled. "Food was always at the ready. The streets were safe." No over the top stories about lurking child predators or kidnappers, David suggested. "We could play out at night until well after dark without a warning that danger might be lurking just behind the lamppost—the lamppost that held our apple basket basketball hoop."

Laurie, a speech and language teacher who grew up in Wilmington, Delaware, remembered that the relationships with friends were as close as those formed with family. "We played almost daily, fought and made up, shared sleepovers and meals, and attended family parties and functions together," she recalled. One neighbor became a second mother. "She was a stay-at-home mom whereas my mom was a nurse and always worked," Laurie recalled. "If we were ill at school or there was inclement weather," the neighbor, also a close friend of Laurie's mom, "was my mom's backup to pick us up from school."

Laurie also surmised that she and her friends learned a great deal just by hanging out with each other's families. "You learned how other families lived and interacted within the home," she said. Today, children spend more time engaged in activities with friends "rather than on the home turf." Not that everything we observed as kids was positive. Within my families of my closest circle of friends, I can remember observing everything from obvious bigotry to overt sexism to possible alcoholism. But at least it was a realistic picture of family life, one that, if Robert Putnam is right, we don't see—because we visit each other less often. His point was rammed home for me when I accidentally locked my then three-year-old son and myself out of our house after his bus dropped him off from pre-school. Taken in by a kindly neighbor, it dawned on me that we had lived in our home for nearly two years (at that point) and had never engaged her in even semi-deep conversation, much less seen the inside of her home.

GETTING THROUGH THE DAY?

In light of how much we Baby Boomers purportedly learned from playing pick-up games, it seems reasonable to ask: Why aren't parents in larger numbers saving money on lessons and camps, and keeping the minivans and SUVs in their garages so that their kids can more frequently run roughshod through their neighborhoods, concocting new games and negotiating satisfactory settlements to fights?

The simple answer is: they are. Making up games is still a significant activity; it simply has to compete with so many other activities, and with a generation of parents educated to believe that allowing their children to play primarily on their own opens up a clear path to a lifetime of underachievement.

But does the desire to contain play come out of fear, or is it simply an expression of a parent's desire to be efficient? "My own theory is that the loss of neighborhood organization and the subsequent rise of sports teams, and ongoing year-round league play may be a result of the natural desire for American efficiency," offered a respondent from Long Island. The push for structure and focus may also originate in the parents' need to simply get through the day—"to be more efficient with their time [and] to satisfy their own needs at the expense of the children," he said.

Much of the literature supports the idea that parents are simply scared to allow their kids to roam freely. Barry Glassner (1999) would argue that parents don't allow their kids more freedom out of fear they'll be kidnapped or sexually assaulted, even though the news media have exaggerated the actual frequent of these incidents. The evidence typically offered by journalists to support their claims, for example, that children face a heightened risk of being kidnapped is weak and far from conclusive. Parents are inundated with stories about how their children are being exposed to massive amounts of Internet porn, receiving solicitations from online predators, and being enticed by the riches promised by a life spent gambling—it's little wonder that some overreact by making sure that their children don't have time for an unorganized thought. They see media-endorsed figures such as John Walsh, creator of *America's Most Wanted* and used frequently by journalists in stories in child abductions, and figure, as Walsh told a reporter, "It can happen anywhere. These creeps are all over the place. They're mobile" (quoted in Glassner, 63–64).

The news media complete the picture, Glassner suggests, by running numerous stories about children and teenagers who commit violent acts, such as the tragic murders at Virginia Tech and Columbine High School. Most of the stories about children included in a 1997 study published in the *American Journal of Public Health*, he noted, revolved around acts of violence—committed by them or on them (70). The NBC newsmagazine *Dateline* has taken the overemphasis on threats to children to a new level with its *To Catch a Predator* series. Intrepid NBC reporter Chris Hansen claims to have confronted more than two hundred Internet child predators during the segment's three-year run.

A troubling result of the news media's self-indulgent fascination with these stories, says Dr. Stanton Peele, a leading addiction specialist, is that "children's lives are unquestionably more circumscribed than they were in the past." He suggests that many parents would not consider allowing their children "to take a bus into the city or ride a bike into town on their own." Excessive caution by parents destroys "the idea that children can learn and grow from exploration, independence, and even a degree of risk and adventure," Peele contends (250).

But on a lighter note, at least one major league coach, Rich Donnelly of the Los Angeles Dodgers, believes firmly that not engaging in apple fights may actually prevent a player from realizing his (and, someday, her) full potential as a major league pitcher. Donnelly told Murray Chass of the *New York Times* (2007, 6) that he and his friends developed stunning accuracy on their throws by hurling apples at each other now and then while growing up in Steubenville, Ohio. "You'd try to hit somebody, smash them in the head with a green apple," he told Chass.

Because today's pitchers have followed the expected path of participation in sports discussed in an earlier chapter, "their accuracy is awful," Donnelly claims. This translates into difficulty getting the ball over the plate, which lessens their chances of pitching far into games, and of winning them.

Perhaps the connection between apple fights and pitching success at the major league level is, at best, tenuous, but the "*how quaint*" reactions experienced by some of you upon reading about it underscores just how much we, with more than ample help from the news media, have marginalized play and acts of imagination.

8

Leave Those Kids Alone

We can all agree by this point (I hope) that unstructured play is beneficial to children, and that it might not be a bad idea for parents to, once in a while, allow their kids time to stare at the clouds, run around the neighborhood, or try to "make a time machine out of a VCR," as one respondent described a task unsuccessfully undertaken by her and her siblings when they were kids.

If recent news media coverage is accurate, the nation is rediscovering the joys of free play. Corporations are offering support; the Nickelodeon cable television channel in 2006 gave away more than $1 million in grants to schools and communities to enhance their play spaces. The grants are part of the channel's "Let's Just Play" campaign, one that the organization proudly calls "pro-social," and which is designed to promote "healthy and active lifestyles for kids and families" ("Nickelodeon Announces" 2006). Nickelodeon claims that its program, which in 2006 doubled the amount of money distributed in grants a year earlier, is "a much-needed antidote to reports of the rise in childhood obesity, the concerns about reduction of PE (physical education classes) in schools and in after-school programs, and the over-scheduled and sedentary lifestyles of kids today."

Recess now has its champions, including the National Parent-Teacher Association (PTA), and cable television's Cartoon Network, owned by media giant Time Warner. In February 2005, Cartoon Network announced the launch of "Get Animated," a program that, in the organization's words, "inspires and empowers kids to get active, get healthy, and get involved." The National PTA teamed up with Cartoon Network to launch "Rescuing Recess," an effort to convince officials in the four out of ten schools across the country that have eliminated recess to restore it ("Recess is at Risk" 2006).

The American Association for the Child's Right to Play has fallen in line, working to persuade educators and boards of education to restore recess. By March 2006, three states required their schools to include recess in their students' daily schedules. A visit to the organization's Web site (www.ipausa.org) provides parents with a host of play-related resources, including a lengthy, thoroughly referenced report on "How to Plan, Organize, and Implement a Play Day."

And the news media have caught on, offering increased coverage during the last year about the benefits of unstructured play, and giving reporters and columnists space to reminisce about games they played during their childhoods. Former *Sports Illustrated* columnist Steve Rushin explored what he called the "recess recession," taking issue with school districts across the country that have banned tag and other games that revolve around the participants chasing each other. "Trouble is, *life* is a chase game," Rushin wrote in December 2006. His next sentence underscored the fear of injury to children (and possible resultant lawsuits) that motivates school officials to enact such policies: "At my elementary school every recess ended like Round 8 of a prize-fight: with a bell, the mending of cuts, and at least two parties forced to sit in a corner."

The increased attention would seem to be good news; the twin needs to reinstate recess and to allow kids to have more time to play have pushed themselves back onto the public's agenda. Articles (e.g., Atlas 2007, E3) offer reassuring lists of the benefits of free play, and provide tips for setting up the perfect "safe and controlled environment" for your child's activities. More play is just the thing, suggest reporters, to help us combat the childhood obesity epidemic. It is more than a little disquieting that we have to be reintroduced to these concepts, especially given our professed love for the games of our youth, but progress is progress.

Still, some adults have literally made a sport out of co-opting kids' games.

Three recreational sports leagues in the Portland, Oregon, area in 2006 joined forces to form Recess Time Sports Leagues (www.recesstimesports.com). Since their union, the organization's Web site proudly claims, more than four thousand would-be athletes "in their twenties, thirties, forties, and fifties" have "flooded" facilities in the area, "looking to connect with nostalgic social recreational activities."

The Recess Time Web site resembles the sites crafted by professional sports organizations. Photos of championship teams, trophies and beverage cans in hand, appear next to registration instructions for upcoming leagues. More than seventy teams will compete this year in the tenth season of the organization's kickball league. The "top story" on the site described opening day: "It started with a fear of rain but the kickball gods were behind us. The clouds parted and the balls were booted." After the games, the victors were toasted and losers consoled—both with the aid of Budweiser beer, a league sponsor. The story went on to assure those who did not make any of the league's teams that they would be able to play in one of the pick-up games hosted by the league on weekends.

You may recall that dodge ball was the subject of a 2004 feature film, *Dodgeball: A True Underdog Story,* starring Vince Vaughn and Ben Stiller. Dodge ball leagues have popped up all over the country. The International Dodge Ball Federation launched in 1996; the group's initial aim, noted on its Web site, was to make players "feel as though the game was a real sport instead of a schoolyard pastime" (www.dodgeball.com). As of this writing, the National Dodgeball League is set to host its 2007 national championship in August in Las Vegas (www.nationaldodgeball.com). The league encourages teams from across the country to play for a chance to compete for the championship. During a June 2007 stop in Malta, New York, a team called "Erie Beach Trash" bested the heavily favored "Gods of Dodgeball."

Kickball has become just as organized. The World Adult Kickball Association (WAKA) recently marked its tenth anniversary as "the preeminent adult kickball organization and the world authority and governing body of kickball" (www.kickball.com). In September 2007, teams competed in Boston for the league's Founders Cup. Would-be players can find the local league nearest to them and sign up to play.

Even the childhood game Rock-Paper-Scissors now has its own national league (www.usarps.com). Visitors to the U.S. Rock Paper Scissors League's Web site can read about a visit with last year's national champion, read up on the league's upcoming national championship (held in July 2007), and partake of training tips. The 2006 championship was held at the Mandalay Bay resort in Las Vegas, and was nationally televised.

Finally, we have what author Christopher Noxon calls "rejuveniles." These are adults who have rediscovered the joy associated with Saturday morning cartoons and simple childhood games such as marbles and hopscotch—and are keeping all the fun for themselves. Frightened by 9/11 and the uncertain state of the world, they are rejecting more "mature pursuits" ("Rejuvenile" 2007) in favor of kids' games. Their "free-floating anxiety," Noxon writes, "seems uniquely sated by childlike comforts."

Can't we just share our rediscovery with our kids?

FRAME ANALYSIS

Let's take a closer look at the news media coverage of our rediscovery of unstructured play. I conducted a frame analysis of thirty-two newspaper articles and the transcripts of twelve broadcast segments on unstructured play, the value of play, childhood games, childhood pastimes, and the disappearance (or reappearance) of recess that appeared between January 1, 2005, and July 1, 2007. Stories were included in the analysis only if a reporter or television commentator focused (spent most of the time or space in a story or segment) on one of these topics.

An explanation of framing begins with the work of revered sociologist Erving Goffman, who in 1974 explained that a frame is a "principle of organization which governs events—at least social ones—and our subjective involvement in them" (11). Frames enable us to "locate, perceive, identify, and label a seemingly infinite number of concrete occurrences" (21). In short, we create and apply frames in order to make sense of the world around us.

Journalists engage in the same activity as they cobble together the stories we see and read from the information that presents itself to them as a story emerges. Reporters make careful choices about the information, quotes, visuals, and descriptions that go into a story. They highlight some parts of a story, making them seem more significant than other parts. Framing takes place when journalists "select some aspects of a perceived reality and make them more salient in a communicating text" (Entman 1993, 52). By attempting to organize experiences for readers, journalists "highlight some bits of information about an item that is the subject of communication, thereby elevating them in salience" (53).

Journalists create news frames to help them "simplify, prioritize, and structure the narrative flow of events (Norris 1995, 357). Oscar Gandy (2001) explains that frames "are used purposively to direct attention and then to guide the processing of information so that the preferred reading of the facts come to dominate public understanding" (365). Jamieson and Waldman (2002) contend that frames are "the structures underlying the depictions that the public reads, hears, and watches" (xii).

And even though a journalist might not have the time or the space to create an exhaustive report about an event, he or she is obligated to piece together what famed journalist Bob Woodward calls "the best available version of the truth"—a version that is accurate, fair, and balanced, and that does not favor a particular worldview or ideology.

In this section, I will explore the "keywords, stock phrases, stereotyped images, sources of information, and sentences that provide reinforcing clusters of facts or judgments" (Entman, 52) about the rediscovery of unstructured play. I will also examine the range of sources called on by journalists for perspective and expertise. Journalists select sources because they are credible, and believe that even a longstanding frame has value because it contains "a range of viewpoints that is potentially useful" to our understanding of an issue (D'Angelo 2002, 877).

Paul D'Angelo cautions that a frame can limit our understanding of a subject or an issue. He supports Entman's claim that ideas contained in frames can push out, or marginalize, competing interpretations of events. "While framing does not eliminate challenges to the dominant story line, it subverts their influence by diminishing their salience," he argues (21). In his well-known book, *The Whole World is Watching,* Todd Gitlin asserts that frames are "persistent patterns of cognition, organization, and presentation, of selection, emphasis, and exclusion, by which symbol-handlers routinely organize discourse, whether verbal or visual" (7).

In short, frames give shape to what parts of a story are told, what parts are given prominence, which sources are used, what groups are marginalized through their portrayal as deviant or illegitimate, and what words are used to describe the parties to a story.

With these ideas in mind, let's explore the themes that emerge from these stories.

The Movement

Journalists clearly suggest that an organized *movement* has emerged to champion the cause of recess. "So you're saying that parents need to unite and talk to the schools and make this point," *The Today Show's* Ann Curry said to a New York pediatrician brought on to the show to discuss the need to restore recess. Courrege (2006) described efforts by a South Carolina parent who took issue with a local school's ban on playing touch football. One parent sent a letter to the other parents in his son's elementary school class, asking them to sign if they disagreed with the rule. "Seven parents signed and returned the form, and Leto said he would continue fighting for students," Courrege wrote (A1).

"There's a movement," claims an education professor in a *New York Times* article (Williams 2007, 1). The interest in childhood games, writes the *Times* reporter, "is an outgrowth of a broader campaign, spearheaded by a growing number of national and local advocacy and research organizations" who labor to convince parents, educators, and school officials of the value of play, and to find a place for games such as four square and hopscotch on the curriculum. At least some of the adults who have fueled the interest among their peers in kids' games have tried to share their new hobby with kids, suggests the *Times*. More than 150 kids were set to take part in a formerly all-adult kickball league, for example.

These games are easy for kids to pick up, the *Times* writer noted without any irony. "You're going to see a real revolution," said a New Jersey parent, fresh from teaching her kids how to play tag, hopscotch, and how to properly deploy a Hula-Hoop.

A story in the *Birmingham News* discussed growing support to restore recess to schools in Jefferson County, following the lead of McAdory Elementary School. "A movement is underway," wrote *News* reporter Gigi Douban (2006), "in line with national trends, to persuade the county Board of Education to mandate recess at all elementary schools" (1A). Earlier in the article, Douban referred to the American Association for the Child's Right to Play as a "play advocacy group."

Newsweek's Peg Tyre (2006) told the story of Rebecca Lamphere, who after moving into a new home in Virginia, became troubled that her new neighborhood "was quiet—too quiet." Having moved in next door to a local elementary school, she expected to hear children playing, but soon learned that the school had done away with recess. Tyre explains that Lamphere successfully spearheaded an effort to restore recess to the state's schools. "Now parents, physicians, and educators around the country are taking up Lamphere's campaign," Tyre wrote in the *Newsweek* piece.

With more of us concerned about childhood obesity, "activists are demanding that schools bring recess back—providing kids with a minimum of 15 minutes of free play each day." Tyre used the word *activist* several times in her story to describe the actions of concerned parents and teachers. She called one parent from Florida "a pro-recess advocate." The phrase suggests protestors taking to the streets to call attention to their cause.

An article in the *Washington Post* (Angvall 2006, F2), provided parents with instructions for lobbying school districts that plan to do away with purportedly dangerous playground equipment, following the lead of districts "from Portland, Oregon to Broward County, Florida." To maximize their chances for success, and the benefits of play for their children, parents should "be willing to accept some degree of risk for their children," and, more significantly, "fight efforts to remove swings, slides, and climbing equipment from playgrounds." The cause will require advocates to "work with school districts, nursery schools, and parks to increase the number of play areas with natural materials and unfenced areas that allow children to use their imaginations when they play," Angvall wrote.

Using the word *advocate,* or *activist,* suggests that a person has a cause, to which he or she is zealously devoted. The person has decided to try to address what they believe is a problem in an organized fashion. In cases where the cause is unpopular, the news media tend to treat activists as being outside the boundaries of the mainstream. For example, the news media have tended to treat antiwar activist Cindy Sheehan as unpatriotic, despite the loss of her son during the war in Iraq. Media scholar Daniel Hallin would argue that Sheehan, like other folks who advocate for unpopular causes, are kept by the media in the "sphere of deviance." Occupying this space are "those political actors and views which journalists and the political mainstream of society reject as unworthy of being heard" (116–17).

Journalists, through the deployment of particular themes, rhetorically guard the boundary between this zone and the "sphere of legitimate controversy," where public officials are allowed to determine how and when we discuss important issues. Those in the "sphere of deviance" rarely get near the innermost sphere in Hallin's model, the "sphere of consensus," where hallowed ideas and values—Hallin calls it the "region of motherhood and apple pie" (116)—are kept and protected, in part by journalists whose actions suggest that debate on these ideas and values would be pointless.

But when an idea is popular, or at least not controversial—such as the importance of unstructured play—reporters portray activists as having the best interests of children, in this case, at heart. But at the same time, their work suggests that only through more organization, not less, can these interests be served.

Peter Pan

Those who do rediscover the joys of play and of children's games often do so with zeal, to the point that they end up stealing the games for their own. They will go to great lengths to once again experience childhood. Thus, news coverage suggests a *Peter Pan* frame. Journalists sidestep, or flatly diminish, the origin of the games in childhood. Introducing a segment on adults playing table tennis, *CBS Early Show* host Harry Smith (2005) noted that the sport "was once nothing more than a childhood game played in basements across the country." In the story itself, CBS personality Dave Price stressed that table tennis is "a serious sport for serious athletes," going on to note that "ping-pong [was] out of the basement, and a worldwide phenomenon, [with] over 300 million people playing around the globe." Weinstein (2007) trumpeted the benefits to the body of using a Hula-Hoop. "It's all in the wiggle. The latest craze to hit the streets of Manhattan is hooping. Drop the hula" (42). Later, Weinstein asserted that the activity "has risen to a new level of dance movement and exercise."

In the spate of publicity for the rise of the Rock-Paper-Scissors League, journalists similarly tried to downplay the origins of the game. "Money talks in Las Vegas, which helps explain how a simple childhood game was elevated to a championship contest with tens of thousands of prize money at stake," said NBC's Lester Holt (2007) in an introduction to a story on the league. League commissioner Matti Leshem stated proudly that the game "has been played . . . before recorded history" but was now legitimate, thanks to the fact that it "is now finally codified here in America with a league."

CBS reporter John Blackstone (Osgood 2006a) took viewers to a California winery where Rock-Paper-Scissors is played, most notably by an individual who calls himself "Master Roshambola," after the French count Rochambeau, for whom the game is named in some parts of the world. "The enthusiastic crowd" seen at the winery in the story, Blackstone noted, "seems evidence Rock, Paper, Scissors [*sic*] is no longer just child's play." Charles Osgood introduced the story by noting that a federal judge in Orlando, Florida, had ordered lawyers in a civil lawsuit to settle their differences by playing Rock-Paper-Scissors on the courthouse steps (Houck 2006, 1). "Since no law school teaches that childhood game, attorneys everywhere might want to get a refresher course" at the winery, Osgood noted. Doug Walker, the author of a strategy guide for the game, told Blackstone that many of us "stop playing this game in grade school, dismissing it as a game of chance." But only adults can seen the hidden challenge to the game, using "adult psychology, game theory—those kind of things." Wrote the *Tampa Tribune*'s Jeff Houck in the lead to a June 2006 story, "Who knew a simple childhood game could still be so popular?"

The Peter Pan frame is evident in print coverage of play. Journalists cast doubt on the previous iterations of the games. Writing about the national Rock-Paper-Scissors competition, Steve Friess of the *Boston Globe* (2007, C1) asked, "Wait—there's a national title for that? And money? For that innocuous childhood game and conflict resolution method most often used to decide who gets the last Creamsicle?"

A reporter for the *New York Daily News* (Connor 2006, 12) began a story about a Manhattan kickball league for young professionals by letting readers know that the game had clearly changed: "Maybe it's the girls sipping margaritas on the bench or the FBI guy at third base, but something says this isn't the same kind of kickball you played in grammar school." Games of Capture the Flag played by "restless twentysomethings and Generation X'ers" are similar to the older version, "but there are adult twists to this child's play." Players "use cell phones to communicate and city buses to zip across the grid [of city streets] while uninitiated pedestrians gawk at the chaos," the reporter wrote. Such an approach diminishes the significance of these games for children, both present and past. They are only to be played seriously. They should have been played seriously in the past, reporters suggest.

Disconnect

The *disconnect* with older forms of play experienced by parents is a second frame that emerges from news coverage of play. Discussing the benefits of unstructured play, Charles Osgood of CBS noted that it "can help children become more creative, discover their own passion, relate to each other, and have fun. Yes, fun! Remember that?" (2006b). Helaine Olen (2006, B5), writing in the *Washington Post*, discussed her decision to end formal lessons for her son. "I've decided we don't need to pay to play. I'm going to let my children play—on their own," she wrote. "I'm sure they'll learn to sing and tumble without professional help. After all, my mother swears I did just that."

Journalists, and some of the parents interviewed for their stories, act surprised that their children do not have the time to play. Like their activist counterparts discussed in an earlier section, the parents who decide to cut activities from their kids' schedules or who encourage them to embrace boredom, are treated like rebels. In the second paragraph of her story on play, Deam (2006, F4) quoted a woman from Denver as saying, "I think a little boredom is healthy." Deam noted that the woman uses "the dreaded b-word" in conversations with her children "without apology."

Going against the legions of parents who "feel duty-bound to fill their children's every waking moment" with activities, she did the "unthinkable" and "jumped off the hamster wheel of kids activities."

Deem concluded hers was a "revolutionary notion" (F4). One columnist (Weber 2006) created the impression that unstructured play is an anomaly by beginning an April 2006 column this way:

Sitting on my porch the other day, I had an unrestricted view of a rare athletic event that I thought had gone the way of the Hula Hoop and penny candy at the corner store. A group of kids, drawn by nothing more than the irresistible lure of a sweet spring day, began congregating on the grass field behind the middle school across the street.

Weber then described "a brief though spirited discussion of who would play on what team" after which the kids began to play baseball, complete with "pieces of cardboard for bases." It was, wrote Weber, "a masterpiece of spontaneous youthful design you don't see much anymore," especially since no adults or parents were involved. The column leaves the reader with the impression that kids have completely forsaken the "unsupervised, untutored, unregulated, and largely unstructured brand" of play described with fondness by Weber and other journalists. This is, of course, not true. They still just play, but perhaps not as often. And their parents sometimes miss the value of this play when it does happen—a note of irony, given their fond memories.

Parents are often portrayed as having completely forgotten what it was like to be a kid. "The disconnect is so deep," wrote *Newark Star-Ledger* family issues reporter Peggy O'Crowley (2006), "the parenting magazines include tips on how to play backyard games like 'red light, green light.'" Many articles feature parents—and journalists—pining for the days when play was simpler. "When I was a kid, the mantra was 'go outside and get some sun,'" an Arizona woman told a *Christian Science Monitor* reporter (Gardner 2006, 13). "We played outside all day, riding bikes, exploring the neighborhood." She almost laments the lack of independence experienced by her kids. "It's more like me telling them what we're doing," she said.

Many of the stories included inaccurate memories of childhood shared by journalists and by the individuals quoted in their stories. "Until quite recently, children everywhere went out to play," wrote a London reporter (Palmer 2006, 11). The reporter's assessment is inaccurate, and is based on the prevailing wisdom that suggests children rarely have the time or inclination to engage in unstructured play. Ironically, parents interviewed by journalists preface their comments about the difficulty of keeping their children busy with fond recollections of their own more uncomplicated childhood activities.

One woman interviewed by Gardner (2006, 13) recalled "lying on our backs finding shapes in the clouds." Rather than explore what could be gained from this activity, Gardner then reacquaints readers with the amount of organization purportedly required to provide play opportunities for kids. "Every get-together has to be scheduled and planned," said a mother from Illinois. "Who will drive? How long will you be gone? What should you bring? Will a parent be there?" The hectic nature of play is a far cry from her childhood, "when I would just yell in the door, 'Hey, Mom! I'm going to Sara's."

Reporters gird this frame by suggesting that children today are stunned at the freedom enjoyed by their parents. Gardner (2006, 13) interviewed Neil Gussman, a Massachusetts native who rode his bicycle into Boston from his suburban hometown when he was eight years old. "They could not conceive of doing something like that," said Gussman about telling that story to his kids. "I think they suspected my mother of neglect." Said Gussman, who sends all of his children to camp: "My kids and I grew up on different planets."

Productivity

The *productivity* frame assures readers that if kids are allowed to play, escaping their desks and classrooms for the freedom of recess, they will still achieve. Play is seen as a means to an end, another potential catalyst for success, rather than something for children to enjoy, journalists suggest. The American Academy of Pediatrics report discussed at various points during this chapter "says so-called unstructured free play time helps kids develop a whole set of skills and has the added benefit of actually being fun," said NBC anchor Brian Williams (2006). Without unstructured play, noted a South Carolina journalist (Courrege 2006, A1), kids "miss the chance to put into practice what they learn in the classrooms." The professor emphasized, "we're taking away the opportunity for them to practice social skills."

A first grade teacher interviewed by Douban (2006), for example, suggested that her students are more productive after coming back from recess. "Our afternoons are a lot more focused. We get a lot more accomplished," she told Douban (1A). A child interviewed for the same article assured the reporter "his head would be clear of daydreams about playing outside" thanks to the availability of recess. "It takes your mind off it some because you done did it," the student said. Short breaks, noted Peg Tyre of *Newsweek* (2006), "makes kids more focused, less fidgety, and less disruptive."

Parents claim to be concerned about the lack of recess, yet three of the four people interviewed by *The Today Show*'s Ann Curry (2006) focused on what could be achieved thanks to more free time. "It's the time when they get to really burn up the energy from the day," said one. "It gives them an important break so that it gets some of their excess energy so that they can then focus on school for the rest of the day," said another. "They can learn more and learn better when they've had some time to run around and get the wigglies out," said a third.

In an interview with Katie Couric (2006), anchor of the *CBS Evening News*, Dr. Kenneth Ginsburg, author of the American Academy of Pediatrics' report highlighting the need for more play opportunities, emphasized that play or taking part in recess "allows kids to reboot. And as they reboot, you're going to absorb all of the rest of life's lessons more effectively."

And, journalists suggest, they will be in better physical condition. John Berman of *ABC News* in April 2006 interviewed several kids working out in a facility specially designed for children battling obesity. Dr. Madeleine Weiser, the pediatrician who founded Youth Movement Fitness told Berman (Vargas 2006), that her generation was far more active than the kids she works with, largely because they were able to spend much of their time outside. "You ran out first thing in the morning, and you didn't come back until, you know, your mother yelled for dinner," Weiser said. An expert from Yale University expressed disappointment that the problem had become so severe as to necessitate the opening of "kids-only" health clubs. "The saddest fact of all is that we have to have these gyms in the first place," said Kelly Brownell. "We've completely engineered physical activity out of the day-to-day lives of our children."

Comments from the children could have just as easily come from adults in the midst of a morning workout. "I wouldn't like to have high cholesterol because that usually leads to a heart attack or stroke," said a seven-year-old boy. A loss of six pounds since the previous fall fueled another boy's desire to achieve: "It makes me feel good," he told Berman. "It also makes me try and set my goals higher." Couric deflected Ginsburg's assertion that too many activities were causing children to suffer "the manifestations of stress," to the point that when they reach college, "there seems to be increasing levels of anxiety and depression."

Parents, Couric said, "fear slowing the pace means not keeping up with the Joneses—or the Joneses' kids." Even when parents attempt to lessen their children's load, they appear to be micromanaging. Responding to Couric's question about the perils of overscheduling, a woman said "we actually had to make a conscious decision to unschedule them and to make more family time because we realized we were raising kids we didn't even see." A second parent used similarly formal language to describe the steps taken: "we tried to really underprogram, as opposed to overprogram."

Even groups that advocate for more free play opportunities strengthen this frame through their comments. Responding to questions from an ABC News journalist (Sreenivasan 2006), Mark Ginsberg, executive director of the National Association for the Education of Young Children, stressed that when children "don't have an opportunity to engage in unstructured free time, when they don't have a break, when they don't have a time to release some of the stress of the classroom in the day in school . . . it can . . . interfere with the child's ability to attend, that is to listen and learn and the child's ability to perform as they go through the school day." Earlier in the interview, Ginsburg told the reporter, "Recess is actually in the service of learning, not the other way around."

An article by Linda Tarr of the *Olympian* newspaper in Washington suggests that parents can use the promise of play to hide their true intention—ensuring their kids learn. "This summer, your kids can explore caves, climb mountains—or a giant strangler fig—and have jungle adventures all in the same spot," Tarr wrote, drawing on the *containment* frame. "Oh, and by the way," Tarr wrote, almost with a wink and a nudge, "through all this play, they'll gain an education in nature."

Containment

The *containment* frame seen in coverage of play reinforces the idea that children need unstructured play, but only in carefully managed settings. Allowing kids to simply get out and run around is not a valid option for parents, note journalists. A parent of one of the boys interviewed by ABC's Berman (Vargas 2006) commented, "Getting the fresh air and running around would definitely be better. But that's just not realistic." Journalists often noted the difficulty faced by parents in fitting play into their schedules.

"Parents are very busy, and outside play takes a lot of supervision," said an associate professor of education interviewed by a reporter (Gardner 2006, 13). "You don't dare say to your child at age 8 or 10, 'just go out and play and I'll see you at dinnertime,' Jim Butler, executive director of Pop Warner Football told a CNN reporter (Hilgers 2006). Butler's quote caused the reporter to note, "As unstructured play has gone by the wayside, competitive league sports have filled the vacuum."

In a guest column written for the *Pittsburgh Post-Gazette* in January 2006, Dr. Scott Shalaway described in detail his pick-up game experiences. "From the time I was 7 or 8 years old, I spent most of my free time outdoors," he wrote. "If there were other kids around, we played baseball or football from dawn until dusk. In the fall, we'd rake leaves in the end zone to jump into after a long touchdown."

Later, Shalaway (2006, C14) recounted for readers a key reason for the decline of play: "Few parents let their children out of sight for more than a few minutes in the backyard, much less all day." Parents who had the temerity to do so would "probably be reported for neglecting their children." Shalaway failed to offer any support from law enforcement officials for this pronouncement, or his later assertion that "stalkers, child molesters, serial rapists, murders, and garden variety perverts make even suburban back yards a seemingly dangerous place."

The solution suggested by Shalaway is to reintroduce the children "who know more about tropical rain forests and African savannas than the plants and animals in their own back yard" to the joys of nature, at least as those joys are described in a recently released book by Richard Louv (2006). Parents must read the book—not simply let their children play—"to learn how go get our children back to nature." It might be more accurate to say that the parents interviewed by reporters have a difficult time giving up containing their kids' activities. "There is more pressure for today's parent to create activities and schedules," said the mother of two teenage sons. Even informal activities have to be arranged, journalists suggest. "It's important for kids to just sit outside and read a book, or for a preschooler to watch a bug crawl from here to there without having to rush off to somewhere else," the president of the Families and Work Institute told Gardner (2006, 13).

Parents are cautioned not to allow their children too much freedom. The creativity and inventiveness exhibited by kids "does not mean parents should drop the reins completely," Deam wrote (F4). It is still a dangerous world, journalists suggest. "Safety issues prevent most kids today from simply running out the back door for hours on end without a parent in sight," Deam concludes. Here, Deam follows the lead of other reporters in exaggerating the dangers in society to children, as Glassner contends.

Journalists add to the urgency by citing the safety-related concerns of school officials. "I have the responsibility of keeping 750 kids safe. I just want it to be a safe environment," said the principal of the South Carolina school district, which allows schools to ban sports like touch football during recess, told a reporter (Courrege 2006, A1). Kickball is still allowed in the district featured by the journalist, but only when adults play. The PTA president "supports the rules because parents don't want calls about their children getting hurt at school, and the kids still get to play," wrote the reporter.

One way for parents to eliminate the potential for accidents is to avail themselves of the latest play equipment. Having failed to find an arts and crafts class for their daughter, a California couple interviewed by Cho (2006, C1) opened "Tinker," a play space parents rent by the hour for their kids. It is "an open space with big tables and small chairs; shelves lined with scissors, glue, and stamps; jars full of sequins, bottle caps, and beads; and tubs overflowing with fabric, plastic bottles, and yarn," Cho wrote. Classes run throughout the week, but "the key to Tinker is its come anytime, do anything philosophy." So long as you do it inside the facility, and not in your backyard. The couple also sells "Tinker to go" kits to parents so they can complete "small projects at home." This presumes that parents lack the ability to come up with simple games to pass the time with their kids.

ORGANIZATION

Perhaps the most compelling frame detected in the news coverage of play suggests that only through *organization* can parents provide for their children the full benefits of play, and avoid the pitfalls of "over-programming our kids," as Ann Curry (2006) noted in an interview with Dr. Melvin Oatis of New York University's Child Study Center. Parents need detailed instructions to include play, and maximize its impact, in their still full daily schedules, journalists suggest. Reporters suggest scaling back involvement in other activities.

Stories typically include lists of the steps parents can take: "Setting up time to have play dates; giving them a chance to run and get onto the playground and actually expend that free energy," Oatis told Curry. "Finding time for them to be creative, to do things that they want to do, that self-directed learning, allows you to learn what's important to your child and what sorts of things they are going to be able to do in their future." Rather than treat play as something kids engage in strictly for enjoyment, its mastery is portrayed by journalists as another skill, another ability to be honed.

Turn watching television from into an interactive experience, suggested an *Austin American-Statesman* editorial ("Give Kids" 2006, A18). "Rather than just plopping children in front of the TV, parents should watch TV with them and engage them in discussion about what they're watching," the editorial notes. "Watch their reactions. Ask them questions. Laugh with them," says a University of Texas professor quoted by the newspaper. The same professor acknowledges that some children will be able to create fun on their own, "but many will benefit from adult guidance on things to do—such as educational games, or artwork or building blocks—that encourage creative expression" (C18).

Or parents can follow the advice of PBS, whose experts suggest "laying out materials such as clay, wire, wood, and paper for them to develop their own ideas on what to make with them." Parents should then discuss with their children the ideas they come up with as they play. They can engage in unstructured play—so long as the activities and playthings are selected for them, and parents are involved, suggest journalists.

Parents should determine if their employer is, or is planning, to offer "summer friendly" work hours (Gardner 2006) as part of which employees are paid 80 percent of their salary all year but are allowed to take significant time off during the summer to hang out with their children.

Deam (2006, F4) instructs parents to "nurture inventiveness" by encouraging kids to come up with their own games. "Often it is surprisingly creative, such as bowling with pop cans or elaborate games of hide-and-go-seek," she writes. An expert quoted by Deam asserts, "One of the greatest things a parent can give a kid is an appliance box." Children raised on constant activity might balk at the change in tempo, but experts urge parents to keep trying—"even if you have to pencil it on your calendar," one told Deam.

Gayle White of the *Atlanta Journal-Constitution* (2006, 1A) offered uneasy parents "a primer on play," which included pieces of advice including "[O]veruse of 'passive entertainment' such as television and computer games should be avoided," and, "[S]pending time together talking and listening rather than loading kids up with extracurricular activities can help parents serve as role models and prepare children for success." While preparing their children for success through play, however, they should not suggest "that every child needs to excel in many areas to be a success," White noted.

EXPERTS

Finally, coverage by journalists of the issues surrounding the rediscovery of unstructured play suggests that only with the help of *experts* on play will children, their parents, teachers, and others be able to properly reintroduce unstructured play into their lives. Readers turn to a journalist, for example, to reacquaint themselves with the rules and nuances of hopscotch (Ellinor 2006, 8). "A simple game of hopscotch is good for strength, balance, and cardiovascular fitness," the *Tampa Tribune's* Amy Ellinor writes. "It's also just plain fun!"

Experts cited by journalists have told parents that their kids should play outside more often, make up their own games, and that watching TV or playing video games for hours on end isn't necessarily good for them. Yet it is another cadre of experts (with some overlap) who now suggest creating unstructured play opportunities with more than a little structure. Williams (2007, 1) writes about Michael Cohill, a toy designer who spends his time teaching marbles seminars to "thousands of children at schools, parks, and scout meetings." He claims that children today "have the exact same experience kids did with marbles a hundred years ago"—without the need to attend a seminar to learn how to play, I would think.

Cohill and others, writes Williams, are driving newfound interest in childhood games by "attending play conferences, teaching courses on how to play, and starting leagues for the kinds of activities that didn't used to need leagues" (1). Books such as those authored by Louv, Noxon, and Conn Iggulden (author of the best-selling *The Dangerous Book for Boys*) are the touchpoints for this new movement.

These experts have told parents that their kids should get out more, that watching TV or playing video games for hours on end isn't necessarily good for them. Now, instead of informally teaching their kids these games, as once happened, or allowing their kids to figure the games out for themselves, parents have in some cases enthusiastically embraced the expert's role, and now teach their children with organizational élan. Most of the children in a New Jersey woman's neighborhood require her help when they first try to grasp tag or hopscotch, a *New York Times* reporter noted. Once they master the basics of these games, "they can immediately adapt and get into it," she told the reporter (Williams 2007, 1). Perhaps their enthusiasm indirectly comes from being told for so long that they are "incapable" of teaching their children how to play, and that they should leave it to the experts at children's play companies such as Gymboree and My Gym (Olen 2007).

But the well-documented reliance by journalists on a narrow range of experts on a variety of subjects, including play, supports the contention of sociologist Anthony Giddens (1991) that we no longer can look to experts to completely erase doubt. Journalists have contributed to what Giddens calls "an indefinite pluralism of expertise." The purpose of the experts, he might argue, is not to eliminate the doubt a parent might feel about scaling back or cutting organized play from a child's schedule. "Modes of expertise are fuelled by the very principle of doubt," Giddens wrote. Parents come away from our encounters with experts, such as those cited by these journalists, with only prolonged skepticism, even stronger doubt about how to proceed.

CONCLUSIONS

The frames discussed in this chapter paint a picture of parents who will support the idea of play by making purchases, opening businesses, keeping their kids occupied by building them state of the art play spaces, mounting movements to restore recess, by becoming experts on games that lend themselves more readily to unstructured play—anything but leaving their kids alone to play. The sources cited by journalists who advocate increased independence for kids believe they can best achieve this independence by introducing a little more organization into their lives. Few voices come out in favor of just letting kids go off and do their own thing, and none advocate allowing kids to do their own thing unsupervised.

The stories analyzed in this chapter suggest that we have embraced play, advocated for play—everything but just permitted play to happen. We have, suggest journalists, co-opted children's games, sucked the very soul right out of them, all in the name of competition and national beer company sponsorships. The stories give us approval for pulling our Peter Pan number. You kids do the organized unorganized games; we'll play kickball and kick the can for money.

These stories convey the impression that kids should be allowed to play, but only if they still can achieve—become better players. The message that "if their children are not stimulated by and exposed to as many activities as possible they will fall behind" (Deam 2006, F4) is still resonating with parents. Kids can play, but only if they do so in clearly defined spaces, with still clearly defined schedules. We still need to protect them, after all, from the real and imagined (mostly imagined) threats that plague our nation.

As adults, however, we need no such protection when we head out to the field to play kickball. We take away tag and touch football and cut back on recess to keep the lawsuit potential down, but we can go out, ignore our creaky bodies, and wrack up injuries playing their games. It doesn't seem fair. Leave it to Baby Boomers to overschedule and micromanage freedom.

9

They Call It "Tennockey"

The base of my left thumb throbs a lot these days. Why? Advancing age, for one thing. But the primary reason came in the spring of 2006, right around Easter, when I played a game of catch in my in-laws' back yard in New Jersey with my bright, funny, and, I hadn't noticed until that point, strapping nephew, Brian, a sophomore at a major Eastern university.

As I have mentioned at various points in the book, I periodically long for the chance to play catch, with anyone—students, colleagues, strangers. I keep two mitts and a baseball in the back of my car, in case the mood to throw strikes someone at the same time it does me. Perhaps I only wish that I longed to play. At various times during my classes, I suggest to my students without the slightest measure of subtlety that a game of catch is a great way to clear one's head and address the problems of the day.

But there we were—a beautiful, warm spring day, my nephew and I standing about thirty feet apart, tossing a baseball back and forth. He had borrowed a Rawlings mitt from me; I was using my black Mizuno glove, purchased for me by my wonderful wife. Of all the baseball gloves I have owned in my travels, it has the most perfectly formed pocket.

And black looks cool.

I impressed myself, fleetingly anyway, with the velocity of my throws. I proudly determined that my arm hadn't required its usual twenty minutes of soft tossing warm-ups. I even told myself not to hold back. Don't take it easy on him. He's a big guy; he can take it. But the velocity of my throws did not appreciably increase after I made this bold decision. Meanwhile, my nephew's were coming in with sometimes startling speed. Years of practice, through organized and unorganized play, had left my nephew with a powerful throwing arm. I threw some barely breaking curve balls; he answered with throws that whizzed at my body and crashed loudly into my black Mizuno mitt.

We had swapped roles. Where years earlier I had to take it easy during backyard games of catch on him and his equally bright, equally funny sister, my nephew—at my begrudging request, I must admit—was now diminishing his velocity in order to lessen the risk of injury to his aging, more nearsighted than ever uncle.

While he kindly complied with my request, my thumb did not reap the benefits of my quick thinking. One of his last ten or so throws smacked ferociously into my mitt, most of its impact delivered to the padding allegedly protecting my left thumb. I felt as though I had been stabbed in the hand. But I gamely—stupidly—continued to throw and catch, the pain in my hand increasing even as my nephew slowed down his throws.

Fortunately for my hand, my family was soon ready to head out for Easter dinner. In true dumb macho stereotype fashion, I didn't let on to Brian, or to Sheila (until later) just how much my hand hurt. I'm certainly not the only person in their mid-forties with a love for catch to so abruptly experience a frailty of age. But thinking about my experience—and once again flexing my thumb—caused me to consider the pitfalls in making a sweeping conclusion that unstructured play is fading from the scene.

Let's look at what we do know: first, kids, especially those with affluent, and even nearly affluent parents, are taking part in a sometimes mind-boggling array of activities. Second, some parents do respond to the purported threats to their children by not allowing them to spend unregulated stretches of time wandering around their neighborhoods. Their response at least in part is driven by the cottage fear-mongering industry populated by safety experts, school officials, and the news media.

Third, kids do spend a great deal of their time watching television and playing video and computer games. Few, if any, are addicted to either, despite the ominous warnings sounded by physicians, psychiatrists, and journalists.

But despite these factors, kids still play. It may not take the shape of the pick-up games so fondly remembered by the respondents, but they play. They flex their imaginations. And they do it with no particular goal in mind, as painful as that might be for some parents to hear. It also turns out that some of their experiences are not all that different from those we had as kids, as we will see later.

Sheila now and then has to remind me that the fact that an experience happened during my childhood does not automatically make it simpler or more positive than the experiences of "kids today." Like the respondents who have so generously shared their pick-up game experiences, I am fairly selective when it comes to my pick-up game memories. They make for a compelling, coherent narrative, but it's not one that accurately depicts reality. Narratives never do. We must keep reminding ourselves, fellow Boomers, that we have not cornered the market on inventive solutions for a lack of equipment or not enough players.

Anne, a college professor, shared a story that provokes some additional discussion of our unstructured play narrative. In the summer of 2003, she recalled, a few local fathers decided to organize Saturday morning pick-up baseball games. "Yep—'organized' pick-up games. How paradoxical is that?" Anne asked in her response. The games were the product, she asserted, of "parents who felt their kids were missing out on the pick-up game experiences they had had themselves."

The result? Indifference. The games took place, but the kids wanted no part of their parents' less than transparent attempt to co-opt their play. "The parents hung out while the kids played baseball like we did as kids—unimpeded by adult intervention." The kids played while the parents consumed coffee. "As it turned out, the kids were far less excited by it than the parents and couldn't have cared less on rainy Saturdays," Anne said, adding somewhat wistfully, "you just can't go home again!"

While the irony of parents trying to organize what should be unorganized play makes me wince, Anne's comments support this broader narrative, the one where kids try desperately to navigate their bulging schedules, without any time to play. As we discussed in chapter 8, the news media have contributed to the narrative's resonance by suggesting that kids should engage in unstructured play, but only so that they can realize the myriad benefits promoted by play experts, doctors, and educators. They should play, but only if their play is organized, like Anne's pick-up baseball games, and only if the play is enhanced by the proper equipment. Even when we want kids to play, it's not enough to just let them play. They have to play the way we played—with better stuff, of course, and on schedule. Trouble is, as comforting as our memories are, we never played the way we think we played, as a close friend of mine pointed out.

But as mentioned earlier, this narrative, like most narratives, is inaccurate. We find solace in the inaccuracy. It hangs together nicely, gives us the chance to revisit our childhoods, and has clearly identifiable heroes, but they're not who you would think: the heroes are our younger selves, who climbed the fences, built the forts, and invented the games. In short, we want to play like we did then—but we can't. Kids can—and do.

OF MANHUNT AND LEMONADE STANDS

Through the kindness of two fellow teachers, I was lucky enough to explore the pick-up game experiences of a fairly large group of middle school–aged kids. In May 2007, I conducted interviews with four students at a middle school located in Havertown, a Philadelphia suburb. A month later, I received 109 responses to my pick-up games flyer from students at a middle school in a suburban, predominantly white, north central New Jersey community. Their teacher, the father of one of my current students, was kind enough to encourage his students to respond to my flyer. A comment from him in the note attached to the kids' responses brilliantly sums up the gap between the narrative of play we've explored and the reality of his students' experiences: "Kids are kids are kids . . . and are creative when there is nothing," he wrote.

A few key findings, right up front: kids are still making up games. They still find the time to play, and have both close and strong situational relationships with their friends. Having fun seems to be the goal. Khrystoffer, a sixth-grader from Pennsylvania, said he and his friends play with "no goals in mind." Bobby, twelve, agreed, citing the enjoyment—and the exercise—he and his friends derived from hanging out. Elizabeth, a sixth grader from Pennsylvania, said that unstructured play "makes me happy." She also cited the closeness she feels to her neighbors, which so many experts believe is waning. "Everyone is always comfortable" in her neighborhood, she said.

Parents hang out, and keep tabs on their kids. "I know everyone on my street. My old school is next to me," she said. Close friends live down the street. It doesn't take a lot of cajoling by Elizabeth to get her friends to set up a lemonade stand at various times during the summer on a nearby street corner. They create signs, grab a table and chairs, and set up the stand "whenever we feel like it," charging twenty-five cents per cup. A recent spring election in the neighborhood helped the group rake in a record profit of seventeen dollars.

Games of wall ball, dodge ball, basketball, and hockey frequently take place, along with slightly more esoteric games such as "Ghost in the Graveyard" and "Spit, Spit, You're It." Elizabeth said she and the sister of J. T., a top pick-up games player in the neighborhood, are in charge of organizing these games. "I give them options," she said, even if that means laying on the ground and looking up at the clouds. As the two oldest kids, "she and I are like the boss," Elizabeth noted. J. T. uses old-fashioned persistence to convince Elizabeth to play. "He likes to play with me," she said. "He bugs me to play until I give in." Elizabeth added that she often takes it upon herself to sustain the conversation within the group through the use of humor. "I always smile when they smile—even if [the joke] isn't funny," she said.

Like her friends, Elizabeth can't just head off to another part of the neighborhood to play. Parents must first be consulted. "I have to respect that," she said, noting that failure to consult means she would "get in a lot of trouble." Khrystoffer learned this firsthand. His family lives across the street from the Merion Golf Club—one of the nation's top golf courses, as Khrystoffer noted. On a couple of occasions, he journeyed to a nearby park without permission. Now, he receives a call on his cell phone when it's time to come home. Bobby said telling his parents where he is headed is enough, so long as he stays in the neighborhood.

"It would be better if we had more time," said Bobby, also twelve, "so that we could hang out more." Bobby and his friends use pick-up games as a testing ground for skills honed by participating in organized sports. More games would give them the chance "to see how we've improved," he said.

Street hockey is the dominant game in Chelsea's neighborhood. Games are played "practically every day" on her street, located near a large shopping center. "We go out whenever we want," she said. Teams are created democratically. Captains for games of basketball, football, and baseball change for each game, said Khrystoffer. One of Chelsea's friends has developed the ability to make equipment simply appear. He "always finds sticks in the trash," she said. Like Bobby, Chelsea has taken part in organized sports for some time. But pick-up games "are more fun," she said. You "can play whenever you want." Games happen every day, and there are no reminders about when to be at practice, she said. Even Chelsea's dad plays hockey with her and her friends—and he's pretty good.

Nor is resourcefulness in short supply—a fear of many play advocates. The kids interviewed for the book own, and use, a wide range of manufactured equipment in their games, but they still make a lot of their own stuff. Bobby and his friends place a trashcan at the end of a driveway, or a section of fence, to establish the boundary for their hockey surface. Khrystoffer explained that a broomstick is used for games of stickball, along with a spongy rubber ball. Empty baskets and trashcans become basketball equipment, he said. Chelsea and her friends invented a game they call "tennockey." A person stands in the middle of the street and tries to slam a ball into the hockey net, now placed in someone's yard, using a tennis racket.

Bobby explained that he often faces a shortage of players, a problem also dealt with by Khrystoffer, who said spring and summer, when folks head off on vacation, can be dry periods for play. Only eight kids live in Bobby's neighborhood, so full teams are out. Deploying steady batters is a partial solution, he said; the problem worsens during football season. Scheduled activities also interrupt play, he said. One friend has Hebrew School on Wednesday and sometimes on Monday, so games are played on Friday so that he can be included. Lack of space also frustrates the players, he said. Their activities sometimes arouse the ire of neighbors, who "come out and yell," Bobby said. This is typically followed by warnings to quiet down and steer clear of property, and then, in a few cases, threats. The chance to hang out with friends is worth the risk, he suggested.

The simplest solution to the space problem would be to move the games to a nearby school that has "nicer fields," but it is located on the other side of a heavily used street. Parents are reluctant to grant Bobby and his friends permission to cross "because it's too busy."

Memorable characters populate their stories. Chelsea talked about Luke, "an amazing goalie," who, despite his aggressive playing style, exemplified by dives on the concrete, "never gets hurt." Khrystoffer cited Neil and Ross as the friends with the longest track record; they have been hanging out since second grade. They have since been joined by Daniel, who lives in the house directly behind Khrystoffer's, James, and Tommy, who also live close by. They manage to carve out time for games despite Khrystoffer's busy schedule of organized activities, which take up "three days of my week, and all of my weekend." James and Daniel specialize in basketball, said Khrystoffer, who was wearing an Andre Iguodala (a star player for the Philadelphia 76ers of the NBA) jersey during our interview, while Khrystoffer is the lacrosse expert.

Elizabeth noted proudly how she and John, who is four years her junior, "dominate" neighborhood dodgeball games. Mike, Justin, and Eddie typically join Bobby for games in his neighborhood. Justin can hit a baseball "really, really far," while Mike is "really funny," Bobby said. Before his family moved to their current home, Bobby played on a street that ran perpendicular to a well-traveled road in that community. His friend, Dan, was so strong that he could reach the intersection with a blow from his bat. When Dan and Jack, another friend, moved away, Bobby "didn't play as much." As time passed, however, he found himself getting out to play "a lot more," a practice that continues in his new neighborhood.

Many of the kids from the New Jersey school sent along long lists of games; here's one from a young girl: soccer, basketball, hockey (street hockey), Wiffle Ball, kickball, tag, manhunt, swimming, spud, football, baseball, lacrosse, volleyball, racing, foursquare, jackpot, water gun fight, water balloons, red rover, obstacle courses, capture the flag, rock climbing, tennis, golf, biking, rafting.

What is striking is how much their descriptions of these games resemble those provided by the older respondents, a point we'll consider later in more detail. The old favorites—kickball, capture the flag, running bases, manhunt, red rover—are still played, with gusto. And new games are made up with regularity. A young boy and his friends concocted a game called "Dodge It." His description of the game is missing (I think) a key step, but I'll let him explain: "We get as many dodgeballs, beachballs, and basketballs as we can get and put them on my trampoline. Then we take our shoes off and put them on the trampoline, too." The game consists of three rounds. I'll speculate that someone jumps on the trampoline, causing the balls and shoes to fly off in different directions.

In the first round, which lasts ten minutes, other players have to stand still—near, not on, the trampoline. If you are struck by something, you have to sit down for a count of five. The second round allows for more movement by the players. The goal, said the young boy, is to not sit a lot. You win if you've sat for the shortest cumulative time.

Some of the made-up games don't require a lot of explanation. Filling a snowy yard with footprints is a favorite pastime of one young student and her friends. Making piles of leaves and then jumping headlong into them is still around. A young girl and her friends play "pogo stick tag." As the name suggests, one person jumps up and down using the pogo stick—that person is "it." The others are not allowed to run; they must walk to avoid the person on the stick—and they can show no fear, the young girl said. Another game, "night scare," requires only darkness and a bunch of friends. "Until it's pitch black outside, we run around the house and scare each other." Even simpler is the game "chase the cats." Said the young girl, "The title says it all." A young boy was similarly brief in his description of "Dart War": "What does it sound like? Dart guns, Velcro vests, ammo. You get the point."

"Statues," played by a respondent and his friends, involves trying to catch a fellow player moving. "The statues can't be seen moving or they're out," he explained.

A classmate created a game called "Skate," which is a variation on the popular game "Horse." After assembling ramps out of wood and plastic, the first player attempts to land a trick. If he or she is successful, the next rider has to "land the trick you nailed." If the rider fails to land the trick, he or she receives an "S," and later a "K," and so on.

Then there's "Head Punting," which requires only a large ball and the heads of its participants, according to a young girl from the school. A person throws the ball in the air. The others have to keep the ball in the air, using only their heads. "You keep going until the ball drops," she noted.

A young girl described a bicycle-based game that she and a friend imagined was set in the 1940s. Pretending their bikes were horses, they would ride around the area. A nearby farm became much older in their minds; another house was transformed into a market. "We would pretend we were being chased by the mean farmer," the respondent said.

"The Powers," as described a twelve-year--old boy from the school, involves finding items from around the house and pretending that they have magical powers. The newly charged items are then used in fictional fights. A young girl described "Stand or Freeze," where participants stand on the ice and try not to fall. The last player standing wins the game. She and her friends also play "Fortunes." Questions about the direction life will take in the future are asked. A basketball is tossed toward a hoop; if the shot goes in, "the answer is yes; if not, it's no," she wrote.

"Turbobooster" requires only a swimming pool, said another young female student. "You had to push off the side of the pool and whoever went the farthest wins," she said. Another young girl wrote that she and her friends head to the park to see "who can face the windy snow the longest." That person gets to decide "what to do next," which, during the winter, usually means heading "to my house to have hot cocoa!"

Finally, there's "Gerbil Hockey," made up by a young respondent and her friend. "It is a fun creative game," she said. Players man scooters and pretend that they are playing hockey. "I like it because it is imaginative and fun. You only need a friend, a scooter, and your imagination," the respondent said.

Friends of another young girl have formed a swimming club for the summer; its meetings, which include the deployment of water balloons, will take place at her family's pool. The person who manages the fastest trip down the adjoining water slide will be able to determine what everyone will play, she said. A moderate amount of danger is part of another pool-based game, this one made up by a young boy. After positioning a raft containing his friend in front of and below the diving board, the respondent jumped into the unoccupied side of the raft. The goal? "To see how high he would go" upon impact, the respondent said.

Variations on existing games abound. A young girl and her friends play "basketball" by throwing rocks at a large enough hole in a tree. "Once we made it in," she said, "we would take a step back. Once we missed, we would stick a stick in the ground and let the next person go." The person who completes a toss from the longest distance wins, she said.

Marla, from the original group of respondents, described herself as "the epitome of a tomboy." Now in her early twenties, she claims to have been selected first for most pick-up games, "and I never backed down to the boys." Summer evenings, she said, "were completely dedicated to cops and robbers, kick the can, capture the flag, and kickball." The rules for cops and robbers, she recalled, "were simple and the game was invigorating." Her next-door neighbor, an older boy, typically invited his friends from high school to play. "They always picked me to be on their team because I was so small and fast," Marla noted. Two teams were formed—"the girls separated of course"—and players would hide throughout the cul-de-sac located in the Philadelphia suburb.

Players could not go into the woods, leave the cul-de-sac at all, or hide in houses. If a player was found, he or she had to run "as fast as you could" away from the "cop." If you were caught, you received a stint in jail—her next-door neighbor's porch. The sentence ended only when a teammate came back to the jail and tagged out the inmate.

Marla came to have a special role in the game: "designated getaway girl." The boys required her to "hide in the bushes in front of the jail and tag out our teammates when they were captured," they recalled. "I still have scars up and down my arm from getting caught on the bushes."

Jessica, another respondent from the first group, said her experiences growing up near Charlottesville, Virginia, were more "peaceful." She and her friends played in the woods on her parents' six-acre parcel of land. "We would imagine that each area was a different house, or even community," said Jessica, now in her twenties and co-founder of a recently launched public relations firm. "Visits" to these areas were accomplished by walking through an adjacent stream, or via rope swing.

"We would also 'discover' new areas/communities, by walking through the woods to places we hadn't been to before," she recalled. Conquering these new venues was not their goal. "We would just discover them, and maybe meet the people that lived there." Jessica was hard-pressed to determine what she and her friends took away from these visits. "Unlike sports, we didn't have to worry about not being good at it, or losing. We just played and it was always fun," she concluded.

Enjoyment, even revelry, is clearly evident in the responses from the New Jersey students. One respondent described games of baseball, softball, and kickball in the neighborhood, which is "full of kids." Friends who have moved away have left behind younger kids, however. They ride bikes and "might even go to the park." The respondent finds opportunities to play in a variety of places. "Even when I'm on my boat I play with my friends," the respondent wrote. "Water war" is a favorite game. Players use their boats as bases. "Next, we shoot water guns and try to attack the other boat's base," the respondent said. "It's a lot of fun!"

Parents are involved in many of the games described by the students. "My dad and I throw a tennis ball on to the roof," wrote a young girl. "As soon as you throw it, you have to run around the made up bases before the person catches it." They call their game "roofball."

Another young girl and her friends play more aggressively during sleepovers. The game revolves around "bombarding the other team," usually with clothes, stuffed animals, and pillows seized from siblings. "When they were least expecting it, we would attack them with the stuffed animals," she recalled. "This would go on until one team had nothing left."

Like many of the games played by the older respondents, and on Kensington Terrace, these games often depend on improvised—scrounged—equipment. Games of kickball played by a young boy and six other people (he was very firm about the number) require a ball and the use of "our surroundings." The same group plays cops and robbers. "One team has to get a ball or small rock to one place while the other team tries to stop them," the young boy wrote. For a "neighborhood game" of kickball proudly organized by a young boy, "we use a kickball, a rock for first [base], a tree for second, another rock for third, and a cone for home."

The lack of a trampoline did not stop a young respondent and her friend from playing a game that involved a lot of jumping. "We asked her dad and he said that he had a bunch of big [what I assume are plastic or rubber] tubes that he had from when he was growing up." The tubes thus acquired, she and her friend would "jump from one to the other. It was like a real trampoline. It was a lot of fun," she said.

A young female student and her friends "assign trees and spots of grass as bases" for games of Wiffle Ball. Even the pecking orders discussed in earlier chapters are still around. Younger players, the young girl noted, serve as goalposts for games of soccer, and hold the flag at the finish line of their bike races.

Sticks and leaves are used to demarcate the kickball field used by another young girl and her friends. When she plays field hockey by herself in the spring, she uses "the space under my cars as the goal." Cars also come in handy as safe "bases" during games of tag played in the summer. Her inventiveness carries over to summer camp, which is not equipped with basketball hoops. "We use string and sticks to make a hoop," she noted.

At least one young respondent said that the overall quality of the non-improvised equipment is what sets today's play apart from our games of *SWAT* played with sticks for rifles. "Kids do get together and play," she said, but "just not in the way that they used to because they have the proper equipment." She then listed nineteen games in which she engages, all but one of which is at least enhanced by having store-bought equipment.

Imaginations continue to be nourished by unstructured play, even when store-bought items are involved. Lindsey, now in her early twenties, recalled how much she loved receiving and playing with dolls from the well-known American Girl series. While the dolls came with outfits specific to a particular era, and with "extensive stories," Lindsey and her sister made up their own stories, which were "advanced" by these items.

"I used to love to play when I had 'props,'" she recalled. She would convert the wooden bunk beds that came with the dolls into cars, boats, and trains. "I loved when I could create things like that," she said. "I remember liking the process over the product."

Out of this imaginative play came thoughts of a career. Lindsey recently began her first job as teacher of children with special needs. "Playing with these dolls so much I really became a stereotypical girl," she recalled. "I always LOVED my dolls, especially the baby dolls." Lindsey would ensure that they were properly clothed and fed, and had enough exercise, all before putting them to bed. "From a child development standpoint, I was just completely mimicking what my mother did every day," she said.

Her love of children intensified, and as she got older, so did her desire to be a mother. Lindsey recalled that a Christmas video "truly defines how gender roles are formed." In it, she is eighteen months old, playing with her first doll. "I show it to my mother, who then cradles the baby and models how to rock and hold a baby," Lindsey said. She takes the doll back and copies what she has just seen. "I told my mom when I was five I wanted to teach 'little kids,' but looking back my love of kids probably started way earlier than five," she noted.

THERE'S ALWAYS TIME

Will these kids soon find themselves with less time for games of Gerbil Hockey, The Powers, Turbobooster, and Tennockey? Will they soon be weighed down with activities, as in the case of Shawn's sister? While in high school, she was "up to all hours of the night doing homework." In addition, she plays in several softball leagues and on her school's team. In the winter, her attention turns to basketball. "It seems like my parents are carting her around all the time," Shawn said. "But as a youngster, she definitely had more time for herself." Age does bring more responsibility, and less free time, but not to the extent feared by those convinced play is disappearing.

Now in his mid-twenties, Shawn, who at the time he shared his story worked as assistant director of media relations for a university in the northeastern United States, noted that that pick-up games in which he takes part are fairly organized. "We have set time (eight a.m. on Tuesdays and Thursdays) and the teams are pretty much the same," he said. "Is that still considered a pick-up game?"

It works for me.

As has been suggested at various points during our journey, pick-up games still happen. Kids still find the time, despite what seem to be busy lives, to play. I think it's worth pausing there for a moment to consider just how busy we Boomers were when we were kids. This is reflected in descriptions from older respondents of having to navigate around catechism classes, Hebrew School, and piano lessons in order to hatch a decent game of baseball or running bases—or *SWAT*, for that matter. Back on Kensington Terrace, Joe Kuhl had young nieces and nephews to look after, as well as a burgeoning interest in cars. I loved to play the drums and watch pretty much any sport on TV; I also spent a lot of my time on the road, especially as a teenager, working with my father, the pipe organ builder. Chris Young soon solved the problem of not having enough time for each other: he took a job with my father, too, as did both Taylor brothers when we were teenagers. And we mustn't forget homework; we may not have had as much as today's students do—as I write this, they're probably just getting to their lengthy summer reading lists—but it had to be completed, on time, and sometimes not.

Many parents earnestly try to afford their kids this kind of freedom. Paul, who works at a university in Philadelphia, described his insistence that his two sons set aside, and enjoy, "a completely down day with nothing to do." He and his sons quickly created a basement hockey league—"their rules, their equipment," Paul said. The league soon disbanded after Paul's older son tired of his younger sibling's penchant for excessive rulemaking. Paul later bought the boys a football; they played for two hours. "Instead of saying, 'this is how you play,'" Paul said, they tried without the rules—"do whatever." He wanted to convey the idea to his sons that they have "the rest of life to be ordered around."

In the end, then, it's about freedom—not in the Mel Gibson/William Wallace shout until your lungs burst sense, but just having some time for yourself. Paul wondered if by denying kids enough time to wander, wonder, and clear their heads, we are actually "inhibiting their ability to compete and succeed in the world." This is not the view we are used to hearing in a culture that purportedly worships the drive and focus of Tiger Woods. While our obsession with success is troubling, I am sure—I want to be sure—that many parents share Paul's view, even though the prevailing wisdom dictates that organized, commodified, packaged to reward even minimum effort experiences make clear the path to success. "Maybe we're all wrong," he said.

Not likely, but it is worth asking—with everyone from President Barack Obama (Kantor 2007) to former president Bill Clinton, to Hillary Clinton, to famed director Rob Reiner, to even TV meteorologist Al Roker (Cohen 2001) trumpeting the joys of the simple games played during childhoods shaped by more than ample amounts of freedom—why we don't dip into this reservoir of memories with a little more regularity. Why do we wait until we're ancient? Why don't we highlight these experiences in conversations with our children, instead of yammering on about the benefits of perseverance and hard work? Have we convinced ourselves that lessons learned, if any, playing *Emergency* have no value? Or are we just operating under the illusion that an experience has no impact if it isn't a teachable moment?

Why aren't these our dominant narratives?

The fondness, the love, the enduring friendships, the more tenuous, situational connections—even the anger, the competitiveness, the macho posturing, the sneakiness, the pettiness—shaped us. For me, it comes back to the comment by Frank, the college professor who grew up in Long Island; these games enabled us to create a "world of our own." It's great to rediscover "the gift of imagination and the wonder of childhood," as Steven Cohen wrote in the introduction to his book, *The Games We Played,* which features pick-up game stories from a host of famous people, but we shouldn't bludgeon our kids with our rediscovery. The last thing I want is for our love of pick-up games to find its way onto those corny motivational posters sold in mall kiosks and advertised in airline magazines. It's hard enough to get my mind around the concept of a national kickball league.

One last story before we conclude: my son is 7 years old. He suffers from cystic fibrosis, and has significant developmental delays, including low muscle tone (hypotonia). He hasn't yet learned to walk on his own, although he deftly pilots his walker through the halls of his school and the more cramped confines of our first floor. He communicates using a limited range of signs, including his favorite, "all done," (think of an abbreviated "safe" call by an umpire), usually deployed when he's had enough to eat.

I would be lying if I said I have never thought about all of the typical, and even atypical, "father and son" activities we aren't able to participate in because of his disabilities. In my selfish moments, I feel cheated. He and I will likely never fan out in the back yard for a game of catch. I may never be able to replay the climactic scene in *Field of Dreams*, where Kevin Costner (as Ray Kinsella) reconnects with the spirit of his father by playing catch on the baseball diamond constructed in his Iowa cornfield.

Since I have only modest success at putting my needs and wants aside, it took me a while to give catch a try with my son. Then, about two years ago, I started gently nudging him to hold a tennis ball, then a street hockey ball, and, eventually, a baseball. At first, his hypotonia prevented him from holding even the lightest of the balls in his small hand. Then he held them tentatively. He then struggled bravely to raise them above his head. He was at first able only to drop the ball into my first baseman's mitt.

I have no idea why, other than the increased strength in his hands, that he persisted; not once have I seen the "all done" sign. But one morning during the early weeks of the 2006 baseball season, I stood next to the wheelchair, ready to receive the ball. But Neil reared back and threw the ball; it deflected off of my stomach and plopped into the glove. My only words during the next five minutes were "way to go, buddy!"

Today, I stand ten or fifteen feet from the wheelchair. His throws typically bounce a couple of times, but they reach me. I walk back, congratulate him on every throw, kiss his head, and place the ball back in his hand. Now and then, he reaches me on the fly. Now and then, he throws the ball into my toolbox, a nearby empty joint compound bucket, the wheelbarrow, and the peppermint plant in our herb garden, located directly outside the entrance to the garage—and then laughs heartily at the sounds he makes.

If I never play catch with anyone else, I'm happy.

I'm not sure that he gains anything from playing catch. It may have helped to strengthen his arms and hands, but that's not the point. He likes it. I like it. We do it together, then move on with our days. We may play the next day, or I might let him help me sweep the magnolia leaves from in front of the garage. No drive to achieve. No attempt to keep score. It makes him laugh, and almost always makes me cry.

Which brings me back, finally, to the last question asked of my respondents: What did you take away from your pick-up game experiences? If you take anything away from this book, let it be this: pass the joy of play on to your kids; don't keep it to yourselves. It may take some effort, since the narrative we tell each other about the wonders of organized activities is so entrenched. Don't make play an organized affair designed to help them achieve. Don't become part of movements that advocate for play. Cancel the play dates, keep them home from camp, let them run around in the back yard, make forts out of boxes, and stare at the clouds—and whatever you do, don't ever write the words "play time" on your calendar or Blackberry.

Let them play—no, really, just let them play. The way *they* want to.

APPENDIX

Participation Flyer

DID YOU PLAY PICK-UP GAMES WHEN YOU WERE A KID?

I fondly remember the pick-up games that my friends and I would play when we were kids. We made our own regulation-sized hockey net out of scrap pieces of pine. We got the bright idea to nail pieces of sheet metal to a wooden frame. What we didn't plan on was that it would make the net so heavy that it took four of us to carry it.

Today, with kids participating in so many activities, I wonder if they have any time to get some friends together and just play. **I'm writing a book** that explores the cultural importance of pick-up games and what we can learn by revisiting these experiences.

I hope you'll consider sharing your pick-up game experiences with me. I'd like to learn about:

your hometown (location-size-population-rural/urban/suburban)
your neighborhood
the games you would play
the equipment you used
your friends and what you gained from these experiences

The story can be as long as you like. The only personal information I need from you is whether you're *male or female*, your *age* and your *zip code*. You can get your story to me:

By email: rcbsam@comcast.net (write "pick up games" in the subject line)
By mail: Dr. Ronald Bishop, 569 Hemingway Drive, Hockessin, DE 19707

Or by taking my online survey at:
chnm.gmu.edu/tools/surveys/form/343

Please let me know if you'd be willing to sit down for an in-person interview about your experiences or to take me on a tour of where you played pick-up games. If you'd like to set up an interview or a tour, please make sure to include your name, phone number, and email address as part of your story. ***Thanks for your help!***

References

Aaron, H., and L. Wheeler. 1991. *If I had a hammer*. New York: HarperCollins.

Akers, M., and G. Lewis. 2000. *The game and the glory*. Grand Rapids: Zondervan.

Allan, G. 1996. *Kinship and friendship in modern Britain*. Oxford: Oxford University Press.

Ang, I. 1985. Watching 'Dallas': Soap opera and the melodramatic imagination. London: Methuen.

Angvall, E. 2006, June 6. Unsafe for play? *Washington Post*, F2.

Aronowitz, S. 1979. Foreword. In C. Goodman, *Choosing sides: Playground and street life on the Lower East Side*. New York: Schocken, x.

Atlas, J. 2007, June 12. Kids need time to pretend and explore. *Wilmington News-Journal*, E-3.

Bahktin, M., M. Holquist, V. Liapunov, and K. Brostrom. 1982. *The dialogic imagination: Four essays*. Austin: University of Texas Press.

Battiata, M. 2004, January 11. A walk on the wild side. *Washington Post*, W8.

Bellah, R. N., R. Madsen, W. M. Sullivan, A. Swidler, and S. M. Tipton. 1985; 1996. *Habits of the heart. Individualism and commitment in American life*, 2nd ed. Berkeley: University of California Press.

Berdayes, L. C., and V. Berdayes. 1998. The information highway in contemporary magazine narrative. *Journal of Communication* 48, no. 2: 109–24.

Berger, J. 2006, July 9. Sidewalk proposal turns into a street fight. *New York Times*, 14-WC.

Berndt, T. 1982. The features and effects of friendship in early adolescence. *Child Development* 53: 1447–60.

Bigelow, B., T. Moroney, and L. Hall. 2001. *Just let the kids play*. Deerfield Beach. FL: Health Communications.

Bird, S. E. 1992. *For enquiring minds: A cultural study of supermarket tabloids*. Knoxville: University of Tennessee Press.

Bogues, T., and D. Levine. 1994. *In the land of giants*. New York: Little, Brown.

Burdette, H., and R. Whitaker. 2005, January. Resurrecting free play in young children. *Archives of Pediatric Adolescent Medicine* 149: 46–50.

Carefree play time after day of classes is oh, so preschool. 2004, November 16. *Wilmington News Journal*, A-7.

Carmichael, A. 2006, July 20. Much of the neighborhood is in step against sidewalks. *Sacramento Bee*, G1.

Cauchon, D. 2005, July 12. Childhood pastimes are increasingly moving indoors. *USA Today*, 1-A.

Chass, M. 2007, April 1. Of rocks and apples and the disappearance of 20-game winners. *New York Times*, 8-A, 6.

Chick, G. 1998, February. What is play for? Sexual selection and the evolution of play. Keynote address presented at the annual meeting of The Association for the Study of Play, St. Petersburg, Florida.

Cho, C. 2006, July 12. Mother of invention inspires studio for kids. *Los Angeles Times*, C1.

Cohen, S. 2001. *The games we played*. New York: Simon and Schuster.

Connor, T. 2005, July 30. Adults getting their kicks, too. *New York Daily News*, 12.

Couric, K. (Host). 2006, October 9. American Academy of Pediatrics releases study advising children need unstructured play time. *CBS Evening News* [Television broadcast]. New York: Columbia Broadcasting System.

Courrege, D. 2006, March 16. Playing it too safe? *Charleston Post and Courier*, A1.

Curry, A. (Host). 2006, November 24. Schools are scaling back recess despite related concerns. *The Today Show* [Television broadcast]. New York: National Broadcasting Company.

D'Angelo, P. 2002. News-framing as a multiparadigmatic research: A response to Entman. *Journal of Communication* 52: 870–88.

Deam, J. 2006, July 31. To de-stress your kids, give them a play break. *Denver Post*, F4.

Debord, G. 1994. *The society of the spectacle*. New York: Zone Books.

Douban, G. 2006, March 15. Recess! Jeffco schools may bring it back. *Birmingham News*, 1A.

Dowell. W., T. Drummond, J. Grace, M. Harrington, S. Monroe, and E. Shannon. 1999, July 12. Inside the crazy culture of kids sports: How competitive athletics can help keep children happy and out of trouble—but takes over some families' lives. *Time*. Retrieved October 29, 2002, from http://infotrac.galegroup.com.

Doyle, M. E., and M. K. Smith. 2002. Friendship: theory and experience. *The encyclopedia of informal education*. Retrieved April 18, 2007, from www.infed.org.

Duany, A., E. Plater-Zyberk, and J. Speck. 2000. *Suburban nation: The rise of sprawl and the decline of the American dream*. New York: North Point Press.

Duffett, A., and J. Johnson. 2004. *All work and no play?: Listening to what kids and parents really want from out-of-school time*. Report prepared for Public Agenda, Washington, DC.

Eig, J. 2005. *Luckiest man: The life and death of Lou Gehrig*. New York: Simon and Schuster.

Elkind, D. 1981. *The hurried child*. Reading, MA: Addison-Wesley.

Engh, F. 2002. *Why Johnny hates sports*. Garden City Park, NY: Square One.

Entman, R. M. 1993. Framing: Toward clarification of a fractured paradigm. *Journal of Communication* 43: 51–58.

Fisher, W. 1987. *Human communication as narration: Toward a philosophy of reason, value, and action*. Columbia: University of South Carolina Press.

Flanagan, K. 1985. Liturgy, ambiguity, and silence: The ritual management of real absence. *British Journal of Sociology* 36: 193–223.

Foss, S. 1996. *Rhetorical criticism: Exploration and practice*. Prospect Heights, IL: Waveland Press.

Friess, S. 2007, May 12. A show of hands—leagues, titles, cash prizes? *Boston Globe*, C1.

Gadamer, H. G. 1988. *Truth and method*. New York: Crossroads.

Gandy, O. 2001. Epilogue. In *Framing public life*, ed. S. Reese, O. H. Gandy Jr., and A. Grant, 365. Mahwah, NJ: Lawrence Erlbaum.

Gardner, M. 2006, June 29. For more children, less time for outdoor play. *Christian Science Monitor*, 13.

Giddens, A. 1991. *Modernity and self-identity: Self and society in the late modern age*. Palo Alto: Stanford University Press. Retrieved September 27, 2006, from www2.pfeiffer.edu/~lridener/courses/GIDDENS.HTML.

Gitlin, T. 1980. *The whole world is watching*. Berkeley: University of California Press.

Give kids a little unstructured time, and turn off the tube. 2006, July 15. *Austin American-Statesman*, A18.

Glassner, B. 1999. *The culture of fear: Why Americans are afraid of the wrong things*. New York: Perseus.

Goodman, C. 1979. *Choosing sides: Playground and street life on the Lower East Side*. New York: Schocken.

Goffman, E. 1974. *Frame analysis*. Boston: Northeastern University Press.

Guttmann, A. 1988. *A whole new ball game*. Chapel Hill: University of North Carolina Press.

Hall, S. 1975. Introduction. In *Paper voices: The popular press and social change, 1935–1965*, ed. A. C. H. Smith, 11–24. London: Chatto and Windus.

Hallin, D. 1986. *The uncensored war.* New York: Oxford University Press.

Hartley, R., L. Frank, and R. Goldenson. 1957. *Understanding children's play*. New York: Columbia University Press.

Heinzmann, G. 2002. Parental violence in youth sports: Facts, myths, and videotape. *Youth Sports Research Council*, Rutgers University, New Brunswick. NJ. Retrieved July 21, 2006, from http://youthsports.rutgers.edu/.

Hilgers, L. 2006, July 3. Youth sports drawing more than ever. CNN.com. Retrieved August 31, 2006, from www.lexis-nexis.com.

Hill, L., and P. McCarthy. 1999. Hume, Smith, and Ferguson: Friendship in commercial society. *Critical Review of International Social and Political Philosophy* 2, no. 4.

Hirsh-Pasek, K., and R. Mishnick-Golinkoff. 2003. *Einstein never used flash cards*. Emmaus, PA: Rodale Press.

Hodgkinson, T. 2005. *How to be idle*. New York: HarperCollins.

Holt, L. (Host). 2007, May 19. Rock, paper, scissors championship in Las Vegas. *NBC Nightly News* [Television broadcast]. New York: National Broadcasting Company.

Houck, J. 2006, June 30. Smash, cover, cut. *Tampa Tribune*, 1.

Hurlbert, A. 2006, July 16. Confidant crisis. *New York Times Magazine*, 15–16.

Jackson, K. M. 2001, Spring. From control to adaptation: America's toy story. *Journal of American and Comparative Culture* 24, no. 1–2: 139–45.

Jamieson, K., and P. Waldman. 2003. *The press effect: Politicians, journalists, and the stories that shaped the political world.* New York: Oxford University Press.

Kantor, J. 2007, June 1. One place where Obama goes elbow to elbow. *New York Times*. Retrieved June 4, 2007, from www.nytimes.com.

Kieff, J. 2001. The silencing of recess bells. *Childhood Education*, Annual Theme: 319–20.

Kraft, R. 2006, May 26. Emmaus sidewalk law is "unreasonable," woman says in lawsuit. *Allentown Morning Call*, B4.

Leavy, J. 2003. *Sandy Koufax: A lefty's legacy*. New York: HarperCollins.

Louv, R. 2006. *Last child in the woods*. Chapel Hill: Algonquin Books.

Low, S. 2001. The edge and the center: Gated communities and the discourse of urban fear. *American Anthropologist* 103: 45–58.

Lule, J. 1989. Victimage in *Times* coverage of the KAL Flight 007 shooting. *Journalism Quarterly* 66: 615–20, 778.

———. 1995. The rape of Mike Tyson: Race, the press and symbolic types. *Critical Studies in Mass Communication* 12: 176–95.

Lynott, P., and B. Logue. 1993, September. The 'hurried child': The myth of lost childhood in contemporary American society. *Sociological Forum* 8, no. 3: 471–91.

McCarthy, M. 2006, August 9. Fantasy leagues can use baseball stats. *USA Today*. Retrieved August 28, 2006, from www.usatoday.com.

McGinn, D. 2006, October 2. The benefits of busy. *Newsweek*, 43.

Marano, H. E. 1999, July-August. The power of play. *Psychology Today*. Retrieved November 29, 2006, from www.psychologytoday.com.

Masterman, L. 1985. *Teaching the media*. New York: Routledge.

Murphy, D. 2005, May 8. Stressed out. *San Francisco Chronicle*. Retrieved October 14, 2005, from http://sfgate.com/cgi-bin/article.cgi?f=/c/a/2005/05/08/MNG44CLV1V1.DTL.

Myerhoff, B. 1975. Organization and ecstasy. In *Symbol and practice in communal ideology*, ed. S. Moore and B. Myerhoff, 33–67. Ithaca: Cornell University Press.

Nickelodeon announces 'Let's Just Play Giveaway' winners. 2006, May 8. *PR Newswire*. Retrieved August 31, 2006, from www.lexis-nexis.com.

Norris, P. 1995. The restless search: Network news framing of the post–Cold War world. *Political Communication* 12: 357–70.

O'Crowley, P. 2006, March 30. The inside story: Remember when kids went out to play? *Newhouse News Service*. Retrieved August 31, 2006, from www.lexis-nexis.com.

Olen, H. 2006, April 30. Meet you at the sandbox—after class. *Washington Post*, B5.

Osgood, C. 2006a, July 30. Hand to hand. *Sunday Morning* [Television broadcast]. New York: Columbia Broadcasting System.
———. 2006b, October 9. Kids need unstructured play. *The Osgood File* [Radio broadcast]. New York: Columbia Broadcasting System.
Pahl, R. 2000. *On friendship*. Cambridge: Polity.
Palmer, S. 2006, July 1. The play's the thing. *The Daily Telegraph*, 11.
Pellegrini, A. D. 2001. Outdoor recess: Is it really necessary? *Principal* 70, no. 5: 40.
Perry. B. 2007. The importance of pleasure in play. *Scholastic*. Retrieved June 25, 2007, from http://teacher.scholastic.com.
Postman, N. 1982. *The disappearance of childhood*. New York: Vantage.
Putnam, R. 2000. *Bowling alone: The collapse and revival of the American community*. New York: Simon and Schuster.
Recess is at risk, new campaign comes to the rescue. 2006, March 13. *PR Newswire*. Retrieved August 31, 2006, from www.lexis-nexis.com.
Rejuvenile: Why adults are attracted to kid stuff. 2006, July 11. *Talk of the Nation* [Radio broadcast]. Washington, DC: National Public Radio. Retrieved July 9, 2007, from http://www.npr.org/templates/story/story.php?storyId=5549381.
Reston, M. 2005, September 10. Santorum criticizes Weather Service. *Pittsburgh Post-Gazette*. Retrieved August 28, 2006 from www.post-gazette.com/pg/pp/05253/569133.stm.
Ritzer, G., and T. Stillman. 2001. The modern Las Vegas casino-hotel: The paradigmatic new means of consumption. *Management* 4, no. 3: 83–99.
Rosenfeld, A., N. Wise, and R. Coles. 2001. *The overscheduled child: Avoiding the hyper-parenting trap*. New York: St. Martin's-Griffin.
Roy, A. 1996. Marion Barry's road to redemption: A textual analysis of ABC's news story aired on 14 September 1994. *Howard Journal of Communication* 7: 315–27.
Rushin, S. 2006, December 4. Give the kids a break. *Sports Illustrated*, 17.
Russell, B. 1996. *In praise of idleness*. London: Routledge.
Saar. M. 2002. Genealogy and subjectivity. *European Journal of Philosophy* 10: 231–45.
Schor, J. 1998. *The overspent American*. New York: Harper Perennial.
Sennett, R. 1974. *The fall of public man*. New York: Norton.
Shalaway, S. 2006, January 1. Children need to learn about nature. *Pittsburgh Post-Gazette*, C14.

Sheff, D. 2006, June 20. For 7th grade jocks, is there ever an off-season? *New York Times*, E-1.

Skiba, R. 2000, August. *Zero tolerance, zero evidence: An analysis of school disciplinary practice*. Indiana Education Policy Center, Policy Research Report #SRS2.

Smith, A. 1759. *The theory of sentiments*. Retrieved April 18, 2007, from www.marxists.org/reference/archive/smith-adam/works/moral/index.htm.

———. 1776. *The wealth of nations*. Retrieved April 18, 2007, from www.marxists.org/reference/archive/smith-adam/works/wealth-of-nations/index.htm.

Smith, H. (Host). 2005, June 28. Young brothers are table tennis champs. *CBS Early Show* [Television broadcast]. New York: Columbia Broadcasting System.

Sports injury statistics. 2006. *Children's Hospital of Boston*. Available: http://www.childrenshospital.org/az/Site1112/mainpageS1112P0.html. Retrieved July 21, 2006.

Sreenivasan, H. (Host). 2006, June 1. Recess rebuff. *ABC News Now* [Television broadcast]. New York: American Broadcasting Company.

Stern-Gillett, S. 1995. *Aristotle's philosophy of friendship*. Albany: State University of New York Press.

The Strength of Internet Ties. 2006. Pew Internet and American Life Project. Washington, DC.

Sullivan, H. S. 1953. *The interpersonal theory of psychiatry*. New York: Norton.

Sutton-Smith, B. 1997. The ambiguity of play. Cambridge: Harvard University Press.

T-Ball coach trial. 2006, September 25. *Sports Illustrated*, 26.

Tyre, M. 2006. Is jump-rope the answer to the obesity epidemic? *Newsweek*. Retrieved August 31, 2006, from www.msnbc.msn.com.

Vargas, E. (Host). 2006, April 12. Children at play. *World News Tonight* [Television broadcast]. New York: American Broadcasting Company.

Waite-Stupiansky, S. 2001, Fall. The fourth R: Recess and its link to learning. *The Educational Forum* 66: 16–25.

Weber, T. 2006, April 20. Kids need time alone to play ball. *Bangor Daily News*. Retrieved August 31, 2006, from www.lexis-nexis.com.

Weinstein, F. 2007, May 24. Hoops! They did it again. *New York Post*, 42.

White, G. 2006, October 9. Prescription for kids: play. *Atlanta Journal-Constitution*, 1A.

Whoriskey, P. 2002, February 18. Games played in the street out of bounds in Fairfax City. *Washington Post,* B1.

Wieberg, S. 2004, October 5. Millions of dollars pour into high school football. *USA Today*. Retrieved July 21, 2006, from www.usa today.com.

Williams, A. 2007, May 20. Putting the skinned knees back into playtime. *New York Times*, Sect. 9, 1.

Williams, B. (Host). 2006, October 9. American Academy of Pediatrics tells parents to let kids play. *NBC Nightly News* [Television broadcast]. New York: National Broadcasting Company.

Index